A PASSION
FOR PRINT

A PASSION FOR PRINT

Promoting Reading and Books to Teens

Kristine Mahood

Libraries Unlimited Professional Guides for Young Adult Librarians Series
C. Allen Nichols and Mary Anne Nichols, Series Editors

LIBRARIES
UNLIMITED
A Member of the Greenwood Publishing Group

Westport, Connecticut • London

Library of Congress Cataloging-in-Publication Data

Mahood, Kristine.
  A passion for print : promoting reading and books to teens / by Kristine Mahood.
    p. cm.—(Libraries Unlimited professional guides for young adult librarians series)
  Includes bibliographical references and index.
  ISBN 1-59158-146-X (pbk. : alk. paper)
    1. Libraries and teenagers—United States. 2. Young adults' libraries—Activity
programs—United States. 3. Young adults' libraries—Collection development—United
States. 4. Teenagers—Books and reading—United States. 5. Reading promotion—United
States. I. Title. II. Series: Libraries Unlimited professional guides for young adult
librarians.
Z718.5M34 2006
027.62'6—dc22   2006003716

British Library Cataloguing in Publication Data is available.

Library of Congress Catalog Card Number: 2006003716
ISBN: 1-59158-146-X
ISSN: 1532-5571

First published in 2006

Libraries Unlimited, 88 Post Road West, Westport, CT 06881
A Member of the Greenwood Publishing Group, Inc.
www.lu.com

Printed in the United States of America

The paper used in this book complies with the
Permanent Paper Standard issued by the National
Information Standards Organization (Z39.48–1984).

10 9 8 7 6 5 4 3 2 1

CONTENTS

SERIES FOREWORD

We firmly believe in young adult library services and advocate for teens whenever we can. We are proud of our association with Libraries Unlimited and Greenwood Publishing Group and grateful for their acknowledgment of the need for additional resources for teen-serving librarians. We intend for this series to fill those needs, providing useful and practical handbooks for library staff. Readers will find some theory and philosophical musings, but for the most part, this series will focus on real-life library issues with answers and suggestions for frontline librarians.

Our passion for young adult librarian services continues to reach new peaks. As we travel to present workshops on the various facets of working with teens in public libraries, we are encouraged by the desire of librarians everywhere to learn what they can do in their libraries to make teens welcome. This is a positive sign since too often libraries choose to ignore this underserved group of patrons. We hope you find this series to be a useful tool in fostering your own enthusiasm for teens.

C. Allen Nichols
Mary Anne Nichols
Series Editors

ACKNOWLEDGMENTS

The author gratefully acknowledges Timberland Regional Library for its support of library collections, services, and programs for teens; for its support of staff training in teen services; and for its permission to use the photographs included in this book.

I would like to thank my editors, Barbara Ittner at Libraries Unlimited, and Mary Anne Nichols, series editor, for editorial suggestions and encouragement, and C. Allen Nichols, for asking me if I'd be interested in writing a book about promoting reading and books to teens.

Special thanks goes to Sheila B. Anderson, for friendship, collaboration on writing projects and conference programs, and ongoing discussions of all things YA.

I also want to thank Susan Henderson, good friend and fellow young adult librarian. Her great advice helped me to start booktalking—and I haven't stopped.

And always, Jim Mahood, husband and best friend. Thank you for everything!

INTRODUCTION

Teens read books.

Fifty-seven percent of teens who participated in a Teenage Research Unlimited (TRU) study reported reading books for pleasure sometime in the past seven days (Zollo 2004, 258). How many hours per week did these teens read for pleasure? According to the study, 3.32 hours (12- to 15-year-olds), 3.01 hours (16- to 17-year-olds), and 3.48 hours (18- to 19-year-olds) (Zollo 2004, 266). An average of 3.27 hours per week doesn't sound like much. But TRU also asked teen participants about the hours they spent per week on forty different activities, excluding eating, sleeping, and going to school. At 3.27 average hours, reading books for pleasure compares favorably with such highly publicized teen activities as going to the mall (3.82 average hours), instant messaging (4.64 average hours), and playing sports (3.77 average hours).

Teens read for many reasons.

They read to relax, to be entertained, to find out about things, and to experience intense emotions and situations. They read to find out about themselves, other people, and the world. They're reading books recommended by friends and assigned at school. They're reading books they bought in bookstores. And they're reading books they checked out at the public library.

A Passion for Print is intended to give you ideas, examples, and strategies for putting books into teens' hands. The premise of this book is that everything in your library—from the physical space and signage to the collection, publicity, and programs—provides you with opportunities to promote reading and books. In Chapter 1 you'll learn about teens' reading abilities and experiences, and how they affect their assumptions about reading, books, and libraries. In Chapter 2 you'll discover how consumer products and services are marketed to teens, and learn how to apply marketing principles to promoting books.

Chapters 3 through 7 show you how to create library environments and materials that make books available and attractive to teens. Chapters address collections, teen spaces, displays, print promotions, and teen web sites.

Finally, you'll find some interactive and experiential methods for promoting reading and books. Chapters 8 through 10 explore readers' advisory, booktalking, and book-centered activities and events.

By promoting reading and books to teens, you also promote curiosity, fun, and proactive thinking. The young adult fantasy novel that asks, "What if...?" can encourage teens to look around and ask the same question about their own world. The young adult realistic novel that depicts teens meeting life's challenges with courage, humor, and resilience can reassure teens that their problems and joys are normal. Nonfiction books about real life, personal interests, making things, and the future can inspire teens with self-reliance and hope.

One of the most important things librarians and educators can do to promote reading and books to teens is to read young adult books. Your enthusiasm and love for young adult literature will shine through in your creation of welcoming reading spaces, eclectic collections, imaginative displays, thought-provoking booklists, and eye-popping web sites. These qualities also suffuse friendly readers' advisory conversations, compelling booktalks, and lively book discussion groups and other activities. And by creating the conditions for teens to tell other teens about good books, you will make it possible for that enthusiasm and love to radiate ever outward.

It is our privilege, as young adult librarians and educators, to work with teens. Teens are in the process of becoming themselves. It is a process that never ends—if we have the courage to keep growing and to keep learning from one another, whatever our age.

REFERENCES AND SUGGESTED READING

Zollo, Peter. 2004. *Getting Wiser to Teens: More Insights into Marketing to Teenagers.* Ithaca, NY: New Strategist Publications.

1

UNDERSTANDING TEEN ASSUMPTIONS ABOUT READING, BOOKS, AND LIBRARIES

Teens like to read. Teens don't like to read. Teens read, but their reading skills are limited. Teens read and discuss thoughtful, complex fiction and nonfiction. Teens would read more if they had more time. Teens read magazines, chat messages, IMs, and web sites, but not "books."

Young adult librarians working in public libraries are bombarded with statistics, studies, anecdotes, and advice about teens, reading, and books. And they've observed a variety of teen responses to reading and books in their own libraries. There are days when not even one teen disturbs the perfect order of books on the shelves in the teen space. There are days when the shelving trucks are loaded with young adult books. "My son hates to read!" announces one parent, hoping you can come up with books that her son will read. While creating a list of titles, you see a teen boy lope across the library to the circulation desk, toting a 700-page fantasy novel.

How can you better promote reading and books to teens? How can you better promote the experiences—entertainment, information, and enlightenment—that open to teens through reading? Book displays, book-lists and bookmarks, web sites, booktalking in schools, readers' advisory, book-related events—there are many ways to reach teens, whether they are committed, occasional, or resistant readers. Advertisers promoting products and services to teens study not only teen spending habits, but also the life experiences that form their assumptions, attitudes, and desires. They know that teens do not spend their money in a vacuum, but rather, in the context of their experiences, as both individuals and social beings.

Similarly, as a young adult librarian, you can benefit from studying not only teen reading habits, but also the reading experiences that have formed their assumptions, attitudes, and desires about reading and books. Their reading experiences include the following: learning to read, types of reading, reasons why they do and don't read, reading skills, reading in school, and reading on their own. Teens walk into stores with assumptions about products and services based on their prior experiences and word of mouth. Likewise, teens walk into libraries with assumptions about reading and books. These experiences influence how readily they will respond to library promotions that are designed to appeal to their likes and to overcome their dislikes.

This chapter reviews a sampling of reading studies. Some studies involved many thousands of teens; others, under 2,000 teens. Some studies were based on random samples, others on self-selected responses. No one study tells the entire story of teens and reading, but all tell part of the story, and sometimes their results overlap. Each area of research has its own application to the promotion of reading and books to teens. By learning how we learn to read, types of reading, and types of nonreaders, librarians can better understand teens' relationship with reading. By knowing why teens read (or not), librarians can better showcase books that will appeal to the positive feelings about books held by reading teens and overcome the negative feelings about books held by nonreading teens. By reviewing national and state reading skills statistics, librarians can get a general idea of the reading ability of teens. And by finding out about teen reading experiences in schools, public librarians can gain insight into how reading skills are formed and fostered, and what attitudes about reading such experiences may inculcate.

These studies identify patterns and trends among teens and reading that can lead to corrective or compensating action in schools and public libraries. They also give you methods for gauging the reading experiences of and assumptions about reading and books of teens using your library. Methods can be as simple as asking teens what they're reading, or as elaborate as distributing reading interest surveys via English teachers in middle and high schools. The point is, these studies offer you many ways to get the scoop on teens, reading, and books.

THE EXPERIENCE OF READING

Put yourself in a teen's shoes. You've only been reading for between seven and twelve years. Much of that reading has been assigned and tested. Because, after all, you're expected to learn something from what you've read and to re-create it for a test, discussion, or term paper.

Think of the latest issue of *VOYA, Library Journal,* or *American Libraries* as a social studies textbook. You read the funny columns and the two-page article about teen book groups, but you skipped that article with all the graphs, tables, pie charts, and other numerical representations. You're planning to get around to reading it later, but why rush? It's not like there's going to be a test on it.

See what I mean?

Imagine what it would be like if you knew that you would be tested on your comprehension of the contents of professional journal articles. Imagine what it would be like if you were assigned books to read that you had to "discuss" with your colleagues, and your supervisor posed a question, glanced around the silent room, and put *you* on the spot to answer it. Imagine what it would be like to have to write book reports again. Imagine what it would be like to be assigned books to read for the specific purpose of improving your reading ability—as measured by some standardized test.

Why am I going on and on about this? Because I want you to re-experience what the relationship between teens and reading can be like. And despite the dire reading experiences cited above, I'm not suggesting that reading is difficult, unpleasant, and anxiety-provoking for all teens. I just want to remind you that the experience of reading is not the same for teens as it is for adults. For teens, not every book is of their own choosing, and generally, there's going to be a test.

LEARNING TO READ

The nature of teens' relationship with reading is influenced by how well they have learned to read.

In *Stages of Reading Development,* Jeanne Chall (1983, 40–58) proposes that people learn to read over the course of about twenty years, which she divides into six stages. She acknowledges the similarity of reading stages to levels of cognitive and language development, and is aware of the influence upon the reader of home, school, community, and society. Chall's stages of reading ability development reflect the reader's ability not only to understand more complex language structures, but also to bring a broader and deeper experience of the world to reading. Chall acknowledges that no one conforms exactly to her guidelines, and that stages overlap. Her stages do, however, provide young adult librarians with a model of where teens have been, where they are, and where they could go as readers.

In Stage Zero (preschool), children learn the basics of language, what books are, and what books are used for. Reading aloud to children before they enter school facilitates this stage. Reading and books thus attain a reality before they are associated with school, tests, and classification.

In Stage One (kindergarten and grade one), children learn to turn written symbols into sounds, words, and meaning, focusing their reading skills on the words on the page. Presumably, children who have had positive preschool experiences with reading and books will enjoy getting the key that opens them. Chall refers to this skill as "decoding."

In Stage Two (grades two and three), children pick up speed and accuracy in reading. Readers begin to match what they read on the page with their developing language skills and their growing knowledge of the world. The more a child reads—solidifying the gains of Stages One and Two—the better prepared he is for Stage Three, and the more positive an experience reading becomes. Chall refers to this skill as "fluency."

In Stage Three, children in grades four through eight focus on increasingly complex reading tasks. They are now ready to take in and retain new information through reading: their knowledge is no longer dependent on direct experience. They gain vocabulary, and read different types of writing, such as poetry, fiction, essays, and textbooks. They learn to read for different reasons, such as finding facts, understanding tasks, outlining a subject, or analyzing an argument. With its multiple viewpoints and presentation of emotion and drama, fiction begins to be appreciated. Chall refers to this skill as the first step in "reading for learning the new."

In Stage Four, teens in grades nine through twelve learn to examine what they've read in order to weigh evidence, evaluate arguments, and make judgments. High school textbooks and assigned reading present more layers of facts and ideas than elementary or middle school books. Reading more challenging fiction—young adult, adult, and classic—also builds teens' ability to understand more than one point of view. Chall refers to this stage as "reading for multiple viewpoints."

In Stage Five, college-age young adults must bring increased cognitive abilities, knowledge, and self-direction to the texts they read. Chall differentiates Stage Five from Stage Four by emphasizing the need for readers to synthesize what they have read. It is no longer sufficient to analyze discrete texts; readers must make connections and from this synthesizing process create new knowledge.

Readers may reach a stage of reading development and not progress further. Also, they may attain different stages for different types of text. For example, the literary scholar's Stage Five reading of literary theory may drop back to Stage Three when it comes to reading an advanced biology textbook.

TYPES OF READING

In *The Reader, the Text, and the Poem*, Louise Rosenblatt (1978, 22–47) identifies two types of reading experience: efferent and aesthetic. Efferent reading is reading with a stated purpose: to get the information needed to pass a test, solve a problem, or master a skill. Derived from the Latin verb *efferre*, meaning "to carry away," efferent reading is a means to an end. Examples of materials read in this manner include school textbooks, driver's license handbooks, how-to nonfiction books, and electronic equipment manuals. These reading choices are dictated by the reader's needs. There are always exceptions, but usually these materials are not read for fun—for entertainment or to satisfy intellectual curiosity—they do not offer any type of emotional experience, and they are not much discussed with other readers.

Aesthetic reading is reading for enjoyment, when the writing sets off within the reader associations, emotions, and ideas that commingle with the text. Readers can derive enjoyment from the free exploration of facts and ideas—without having to worry about passing a test, solving a problem, or mastering a skill. Examples of material that is read in this manner include fiction and popular nonfiction such as biography, history, science, true adventure, travel, religion, psychology, and philosophy. These reading choices are inspired by the reader's interests. They are usually read for fun, and can arouse passionate discussions among readers. The reader's primary purpose for reading is what happens in the mind while reading.

A judicious mix of efferent and aesthetic reading materials can help readers progress through the stages of reading development. And access to different types of reading materials can influence what teens think about reading. Teens who enjoy reading fiction and find plenty of it may, in turn, say they like to read. Teens who enjoy reading nonfiction and don't find very much of it may say they don't like to read—when what they really mean is they don't like to read fiction.

WHY TEENS READ

Remember that teen boy who was lugging a 700-page fantasy novel? Or those shelving trucks crammed with young adult fiction titles? Maybe you were booktalking at a school and at the end of your presentation you asked teens if they had any good books to recommend, and they sang out dozens of titles.

Teens are reading. Why? Because they like it.

"I like to read because you are in a world of you [sic]. With movies you don't get to live in a world of you [sic]" (Carroll and Gregg 2003, 60).

"I think reading is great. It lets you explore your imagination and no two people reading the same book will be imagining the same thing" (SmartGirl 2003).

Mary Kay Chelton and James Rosinia explained the appeal of young adult fiction by linking it to adolescent development. "[Young adult novels] re-create psychologically the reality of the young adult's 'personal fable' with all its exaggerated sense of feeling unique. A personal fable is a realistic fantasy in which a young protagonist solves personal problems without adult help or interference, as if this were the first and only time that anyone had faced these particular problems" (1993, 12–13).

As such, reading is another means by which teens can expand their world and keep looking for an answer to the question, "Who am I?" Personal fables in fiction offer teens role models, demonstrations of relationships and problem solving, and depictions of the intensity of teen lives. Nonfiction and magazines feed teens' need to find out about themselves, each other, and the world.

WHY TEENS DON'T READ

Not all teens are reading. Why not?

"I think that reading is *extremely* boring and it gives me stress! The only thing I will willingly read is a magazine" (SmartGirl 1999).

"I think that reading takes up a lot of time that I don't have, and I enjoy reading when it's a good book that I'm interested in, but I don't have time for books like that since the reading that I have to do is for school, and I don't like the books they choose for me" (SmartGirl 1999).

Dr. G. Kyleen Beers differentiates among three types of nonreaders. Readers who are "dormant" like to read but only under certain circumstances, usually when they feel they have the time. Readers who are "uncommitted" are confident that when they need to read something, they'll do it. Unlike dormant readers, uncommitted readers don't enjoy reading and think of it as a skill rather than as a pleasant activity. Readers who are "unmotivated" declare that they won't read, ever, because reading is boring and useless. One teen explained that the reason she found reading to be boring was that she could not visualize the scenes described in a book: she could decode the words but could not enjoy the story (1996, 33).

Reviewing research, studies, and interviews with educators, Patrick Clinton (2002, L5) suggests that the time and money spent on early childhood education is paying off. Children are learning to decode written symbols into sounds, words, and meaning, and they are also gaining the speed and accuracy necessary to achieve a fourth-grade reading level. But the pace of improvement begins to slow for some readers, and they lag behind in the acquisition of vocabulary, the understanding of more complex sentence structures, and the ability to adapt reading skills to handle different types of text. Clinton suggests that older kids and teens are expected just to "get it" without the same level of structure and support that was devoted to their achieving reading skills in early grades. If they don't get it, the act of reading itself becomes a struggle, and every difficult encounter with a book reinforces a sense of inadequacy and failure. If you were lousy at baseball, computer games, or playing a musical instrument, would you seek out opportunities to feel bad?

Baseball, computer games, and playing musical instruments are optional activities. However, in a society increasingly dependent upon escalating levels of information literacy—in jobs, health care, finance, and politics, to name only a few arenas—basic reading and communication skills are no longer sufficient for success. The bar has been raised.

TEEN READING SKILLS

The National Assessment of Educational Progress (NAEP), of the U.S. Department of Education, studies the academic achievement of U.S. kids and teens periodically, issuing its findings in the *Nation's Report Card*. Among the academic skills the NAEP tests is reading. (Details and results of reading assessment surveys for several years are available at the NAEP web site, located at http://nces.ed.gov/nationsreportcard/.) While the studied population varies in number and location from year to year, the design of the reading assessment test remains constant. Students in fourth, eighth, and twelfth grades are given three reading samples, each intended to measure their ability to read for literary experience, to read for information, and to read in order to perform a task (eighth and twelfth grades only).

Questions based on the reading samples are of two types. Multiple-choice questions gauge students' understanding of individual reading samples and their ability to put together concepts from all three samples. Constructed-response questions elicit written responses from students based on their understanding of the samples. Both types of questions are designed to measure students' ability to do the following: form a general understanding of the reading sample and develop an interpretation, make reader/text connections, and examine the content and structure of the reading sample itself.

Students' reading achievement levels are characterized as follows:

- *below basic*, defined as below partial mastery of knowledge and skills necessary for proficient work at grade level;
- *basic*, defined as partial mastery of knowledge and skills necessary for proficient work at grade level;

Table 1.1.
Reading Achievement Levels, 2002–2003 (NAEP)

Grade 4

Below Basic		At or Above Basic		At or Above Proficient		Advanced	
2002	2003	2002	2003	2002	2003	2002	2003
38%	38%	62%	62%	30%	30%	6%	7%

Grade 8

Below Basic		At or Above Basic		At or Above Proficient		Advanced	
2002	2003	2002	2003	2002	2003	2002	2003
26%	28%	74%	72%	31%	30%	2%	3%

Grade 12*

Below Basic	At or Above Basic	At or Above Proficient	Advanced
2002	2002	2002	2002
26%	74%	36%	5%

*Results not available for 2003.

- *proficient*, defined as solid grasp of subject matter, including subject knowledge, application of knowledge, and analytical skills; and
- *advanced*, defined as superior academic performance.

Even taking into consideration that the reading samples were not of the students' choosing and may have held less interest than chosen reading—thus reducing reader involvement with the text—these results suggest that while most American students master reading at basic levels, the trajectory of their reading ability flattens. It's possible that only a third of the teens who visit your library would ever consider picking up a book to read for entertainment or to satisfy their curiosity.

Concern over gender disparities in these and other reading skills scores, as well as the preponderance of boys in remedial reading classes, has drawn attention to boys and reading (Smith 2002, 1–4). Boys are reading magazines; computer game manuals; and adventure, fantasy, and science fiction. But these are seldom the types of texts used in assigned school reading, classroom discussion, or standardized tests (Aronson 2001, 101). Like the participant in the SmartGirl Survey who reads magazines but describes reading as "*extremely* boring," a teen boy who declares that he doesn't like to read may be thinking of "reading" as assigned school reading, rather than the types of materials he reads on his own. He may not have enjoyed reading an assigned book and all of the classroom activities designed to foster and measure reading skill: vocabulary tests, plot summaries, and class discussions. Such negative associations can cast a pall over reading itself.

TEEN READING EXPERIENCES
Assigned Reading

Teens have to read textbooks. Even if the subject is interesting and the presentation is appealing, reading a textbook is *work*—shadowed by an upcoming test. Doing work on which you will be tested and judged may lead to some anxiety, even distaste, for reading. However, it's also important to remember that the teen years see a growth spurt in cognitive development (Strauch 2003, 15–21). Teen brains are growing, and they are hungry. They are capable of gobbling up facts as disparate as Revolutionary War battle dates and chemical formulae. Intellectual curiosity is real, and the pop culture stereotype of a teen rolling his eyes at the thought of reading a textbook is only *a* fact, not *the* fact, of teen life at school.

Let's take a closer look at textbooks. Typical textbook design is such that sustained, linear reading is constantly interrupted by sidebars, highlighted sections, graphs, and captioned illustrations. This is not to say that teens are unable to pick up the information they read by reading pied pages. And textbook layout is a good preparation for efferent reading encountered later in life, such as driver's handbooks.

Eliza T. Dresang (1998, 19) asserts that "digital age children" are able to engage in both efferent and aesthetic reading of text presented in non-linear and nonsequential formats. Today's children and teens are not the first to be presented with content in pictures, designs, and nonlinear texts: youth and adults reading medieval illuminated texts, the Torah and its commentary, Gothic stained glass windows, the Aztec calendar, and the patchwork layouts of nineteenth-century newspapers come to mind. While few people ever even saw a book in medieval times, much later, many read newspapers. Today, kids, teens, and adults live in a print and electronic world of multiple points of access and nonsequential information. Recognizing words on a page or a screen does not, however, guarantee the ability to visualize a scene in a novel or to follow the development of an idea. This type of reading is dependent on the ability to comprehend linear writing. As Chall and others have pointed out, reading is not a skill that is fully developed by fourth grade, when children have succeeded in decoding words and stringing them together with fluency and accuracy. In order for students' reading ability to continue to develop, they need to absorb the complexity of content in written form. They need to do more than recognize signage.

Accelerated Reader

Accelerated Reader (AR) is a reading program purchased by many schools in order to help struggling readers. The first product in the AR package is the Standardized Test for Assessment of Reading (STAR). STAR is a computer test designed to assess a student's reading level—without the aid of oral reading comprehension or reader observation, as critics have noted (Biggers 2001, 72). Once students have been labeled with a reading level, they are encouraged to choose books at their reading level from a list of titles for which their school has purchased the second product, AR tests on CD-ROM. Each book in AR's pool of 50,000 titles is rated for reading level and points. The reading level is based on the Flesch-Kincaid index. The point level is calculated from the reading level and the page length. Content and reading appeal are not factored into the calculation. After reading books, students take computerized tests made up of between five and twenty objective, multiple-choice questions. For each of these literal-recall questions, there is only one correct answer.

Teachers, school media specialists, and parents have found that for some children and teens, AR is the program that has spurred them to read and to keep reading (Greer 2003, 32). Which is wonderful. And then there's that time you're booktalking in a school. Teens are hanging on every word, and you know they want to read the book when . . .

"Is that an AR book?" a teen asks.

Excitement, hope, and anxiety are packed into that question. That teen (and possibly others) is excited about reading that book. She's hoping it's on the AR list. She's a little anxious that it isn't. And so if your answer is "yes," there's relief. If your answer is "no," there's disappointment. Dormant or uncommitted readers might like the sound of the book, but if they have been assigned reading from their school's AR list, they may not think they have time to read a book that isn't on the list, no matter how much they want to read it. The good news is that some schools permit students to choose books for which they have not purchased tests, and the schools themselves create their own tests.

Sustained Silent Reading

Sustained Silent Reading (SSR) is a school reading program that's so simple, it's brilliant. Every day, there is a time period during which students read. In some schools, everybody reads: students, teachers, administrators, and staff. The purpose of SSR is to foster reading for pleasure (Anderson 2000, 258). Therefore, SSR is not the time to catch up on reading textbooks or other assigned materials. The rules of SSR model how to read outside of the classroom:

- Find a place where you'll be comfortable and load up on a good selection of books and magazines, which means you can always find something you want to read.
- Drink water, visit the restroom, and take care of your needs before you start to read.
- Sit where you can't touch another human being.
- Don't be distracted by random sights or sound and don't distract others by talking, whispering, giggling, and the like. Just read.

By banning textbooks and assigned reading from SSR, schools show teens that reading is not just for school. By promoting reading in the classroom, schools show teens that everybody reads: their friends, their foes, people they know, people they don't know, teachers—everybody. And by devoting class time to reading, schools show their support of reading as the foundation of learning.

Freely Chosen Reading

One of the best ways to find out about teens and reading is to ask them what they like to read. Educators Pamela Sissi Carroll and Gail P. Gregg distributed a reading survey to middle schools. Their purpose was to find ways to foster freely chosen reading and, at the same time, to support the improvement of reading skills. In all, 2,076 sixth, seventh, and eighth grade teens responded, from schools in Arizona, Connecticut, Florida, Illinois, Kentucky, North Dakota, Ohio, Oregon, Washington, and Wisconsin.

Most of the survey's questions focused on freely chosen reading. One question, however, asked teens if they enjoyed books assigned in their English or language arts classes. One teen wrote, "I like the books but most of the time hate the activities that go along with them, which take away from my enjoyment of the books" (Carroll and Gregg 2003, 62). His sentiment is echoed in an article by educator Peggy Silva, who quotes a question that one of her students asked her at the start of every day: "Can we read today, or do we hafta do English?" (2003, 29). Teachers are working hard to measure the reading skills of their students and so have devised various methods, including plot summaries, character lists, comprehension tests, and the like. They are trying to ensure that students understand what they are reading and that they continue to receive instruction and support that will keep their reading skills—and interest in reading—from flattening or nose-diving. Unfortunately, there isn't always enough time for teachers to sit down with each one of their students in order to discuss books. "The activities" elicit necessary information that helps teachers to continue to build their students' reading skills—yet for some students, the activities detract from the aesthetic experience of reading. Any adult with memories of the parsing of great literature in high school or college can relate to teen distaste for the activities, however ultimately enlightening.

The survey also asked, "What is your favorite book?" and "Why?" The hands-down favorites among all teens were the Harry Potter books by J. K. Rowling. Why?

"All kids dream about having powers and all the creativity in the magical world makes it interesting."

"It has so many twists and turns and it's not just a one topic book. It has all topics, like horror, romance, fantasy, adventure, excitement" (Carroll and Gregg 2003, 61).

Complexly plotted novels buoyed by humor and haunted by tragedy, the Harry Potter books appeal to two of teens' strongest reading interests—fantasy and problem solving—as they address many of their concerns: family, friends, school, being an individual while fitting in, and finding one's place in the world. Emerging from childhood, teens are facing dilemmas and choices, and they can relate to Harry's struggles and his striving to do the right thing. The popularity and availability of the Harry Potter books make their selection as favorite books likely.

The similarity of their underlying themes to those of other books named by teens who responded to this survey suggests that Harry's popularity is an expression of widespread reading interests. Other books named as favorites include the following: J.R.R. Tolkien's tales of Middle Earth, fantasy fiction featuring female protagonists, realistic adventure novels, Holocaust fiction, and nonfiction titles such as *Chicken Soup for the Teenage Soul* (Canfield 1997+). Like Harry Potter, the heroes and heroines of these books are confronted by dangers both physical and psychological. And yet through courage, patience, perseverance, and help from friends, these protagonists emerge with new strength and wisdom. They grow up.

SmartGirl Surveys

The Young Adult Library Services Association (YALSA), the teen services division of the American Library Association, has promoted teen reading for decades through such initiatives as annual "best books" lists, awards, workshops, and conference programs. Since 1999, YALSA has sponsored Teen Read Week, a celebration of teens and reading during the third week of October. Public and school libraries, bookstores, educational organizations, and corporate partners and sponsors have joined YALSA in promoting reading and books to teens, and in educating the general public about teens and reading.

One of the participants in Teen Read Week has been the SmartGirl web site, which posts online reading surveys. The purpose of the SmartGirl Surveys has been to elicit teen reading experiences, interests, and opinions about reading. Respondents are self-selected and do not answer every question. The survey itself does not claim to be scientific. Still, librarians can find out what teens think about reading from teens who care enough about books to spend the time to take the survey.

In 2003, of the 3,677 teens who answered the survey's question about their gender, 60.5 percent were female and 39.5 percent were male (SmartGirl 2003). The median age was 12, with 13 a close second. Of the 3,496 teens who answered the question about their location, 40.7 percent lived in towns, 30.7 percent lived in suburbs, 11.7 percent lived in big cities, 10.6 percent lived in rural areas, and 6.3 percent lived in villages.

Out of 3,681 respondents, teens who said they liked reading "a lot" accounted for 48.2 percent, while 38 percent said they liked reading "a little," and 13.8 percent said they did not enjoy reading at all.

3,633 teens responded to the statement "I don't like to read because it isn't cool." 51.1 percent strongly disagreed, 28.5 percent disagreed, 12.7 percent were neutral, 2.8 percent agreed, and 5 percent strongly agreed.

3,647 teens responded to the statement "I always read about things I am passionate about." 22.3 percent strongly agreed, 34.1 percent agreed, 28.2 percent were neutral, 8.2 percent disagreed, and 7.2 percent strongly disagreed.

Yet another way to gauge teen reading is from the response of 3,645 teens to the statement "I don't have much time to read for pleasure, but I like to when I get the chance." 17.5 percent strongly agreed, 32.5 percent agreed, 20.8 percent were neutral, 15.2 percent disagreed, and 14 percent strongly disagreed. Additional questions asked teens about favorite reading materials, the frequency of their reading of specific materials, and school and parental influences on reading.

The SmartGirl and other reading surveys give librarians information about what is working, that is, what teens are reading and what they think about reading and books. The surveys' value is not limited to their results. Librarians can get ideas for questions they can ask teens in their own surveys and during reader advisory interviews, school visits, and book group meetings. Talking with teens about reading and books builds up the culture of reading (Silva 2003, 29) that exists beyond school walls, beyond library walls, and into their own lives.

Many teens say they'd read more if they had more time. And so let's take a look at how they spend some of their free time. Before striving to make the culture of reading more attractive to teens, let's review the attractions of another culture—one that depends for its survival on its ability to promote products, services, and experiences to teens. It is pervasive, it is successful, and it offers models for promoting reading and books to teens. It is the culture of jeans, pizza, MTV, and cell phones.

REFERENCES AND SUGGESTED READINGS

Anderson, Cynthia. 2000. "Sustained Silent Reading: Try It, You'll Like It!" *The Reading Teacher*. (November): 258–259.

Aronson, Marc. 2001. *Exploding the Myths: The Truth about Teens and Reading*. Lanham, MD: Scarecrow Press.

Beers, G. Kyleen. 1996. "No Time, No Interest, No Way! The 3 Voices of Aliteracy, Part One." *School Library Journal*. (February): 30–33.

Biggers, Deborah. 2001. "The Argument against Accelerated Reader." *Journal of Adolescent and Adult Literacy*. (September): 72–75.

Canfield, Jack. 1997+. *Chicken Soup for the Teenage Soul*. Deerfield Beach, FL: Health Communications.

Carroll, Pamela Sissi, and Gail P. Gregg. 2003. "Literature-Based Instruction for Middle School Readers: Harry Potter and More." *ALAN Review*. (Spring/Summer): 60–64.

Chall, Jeanne. 1983. *Stages of Reading Development*. New York: McGraw-Hill.

Chelton, Mary Kay, and James Rosinia. 1993. *Bare Bones: Young Adult Service Tips for Public Library Generalists*. Chicago: American Library Association.

Clinton, Patrick. 2002. "The Crisis You Don't Know About, Part One." *Book*. (September/October): L4–L9.

Dresang, Eliza T. 1998. *Radical Change: Books for Youth in a Digital Age*. New York: H. W. Wilson.

Greer, JaKay. 2003. "Point: A Positive Experience with Accelerated Reader." *Teacher Librarian*. (April): 32.

National Assessment of Educational Progress. 2002. *Nation's Report Card: Reading*. URL: http://nces.ed.gov/nationsreportcard/reading/results2002/nat achieve-g12.asp (accessed November 10, 2003).

National Assessment of Educational Progress. 2003. *Nation's Report Card: Reading*. URL: http://nces.ed.gov/nationsreportcard/reading/results2003/district achieve.asp (accessed March 11, 2005).

Rosenblatt, Louise M. 1978. *The Reader, the Text, the Poem: The Transactional Theory of Literary Work*. Carbondale and Edwardsville: Southern Illinois University Press.

Silva, Peggy. 2003. "Can We Read Today, or Do We Hafta Do English?" *English Journal*. (September): 29–32.

SmartGirl. *SmartGirl Survey*. 1999. URL: http://www.smartgirl.org/speakout/archives/trw1999/trwsummary.html (accessed April 1, 2005).

SmartGirl. *SmartGirl Survey*. 2003. URL: http://www.smartgirl.org/reports/2734196.html (accessed March 11, 2005).

Smith, Michael W., and Jeffrey D. Wilhelm. 2002. *"Reading Don't Fix No Chevys": Literacy in the Lives of Young Men*. Portsmouth, NH: Heinemann.

Strauch, Barbara. 2003. *The Primal Teen: What the New Discoveries about the Teenage Brain Tell Us about Our Kids*. New York: Doubleday.

2

⬦⬦⬦ ⬦⬦⬦ ⬦⬦⬦

SO ... WHERE DID YOU GET THOSE JEANS?

Just as young adult librarians are bombarded with information about teens, reading, and books, so also are they bombarded with statistics, surveys, studies, generalizations, anecdotes, advice, and mass media images about teens and their consumption of teen pop culture. Sometimes these resources agree, sometimes they do not. Mass media images assure teens that "everybody" is wearing this cool pair of jeans, listening to that hot CD, keeping in touch via this multipurpose cell phone, and chowing down at those hip eateries (Sheridan 2003, 35).

Teens in your library may concur. Or they may dismiss brand mania as phony, while enjoying country and classical music, contenting themselves with e-mail or the telephone, and boycotting teen fashion dictates. Mass media hype aside, some teens reject the brands that make them look like walking magazine ads, preferring to shop for value at discount stores (Young 2003, 38S) or to sleuth out quirky styles at thrift stores (Doyle 2002, C.1). What these contradictions confirm is that, as in other aspects of life, there is no one immutable truth about all teens. As people, readers, and consumers, teens are individuals. Some of their choices may be influenced by what "everybody" is doing. Other choices are influenced by parents or friends. And then there are those product and service choices that spring up out of the seeming blue, that is, that place of individuality.

Companies spend millions on consultants, focus groups, and advertisers to craft that triple appeal: to crowd, friends, and self. Teens today see and hear more information about more products, more services, and more experiences than any previous generation (Lee 2003, 2). In fact, before an American child enters first grade, he or she will have been exposed to 30,000 advertisements (Lempert 2002, 70). Companies know that success comes not from one magic-bullet marketing tool. Instead, it comes from understanding customer needs and then using *all* possible appeals to satisfy them (119).

Without spending millions, young adult librarians can do the same by studying the advertising and other merchandising tools employed by companies to sell their products and services.

In Chapter 1, we examined the reading experiences of teens that form their assumptions, attitudes, and desires about reading and books. We studied teens and their experiences of both assigned and freely chosen reading.

In this chapter, we'll look at the commercial world that is competing for teens' attention and dollars. We'll start by studying teens as independent consumers of products and services. By independent, I mean the consumer decisions that teens are making with their own money—an independence mirrored by the reading decisions that teens are making with their own library cards. Mom and Dad used to buy their clothes, decide where and what to eat in restaurants, and check out their library materials. It's different now. Next, we'll pick up some teen magazines to mine for ideas that we'll use in subsequent chapters on displays, print promotions, and web sites. We'll go to the mall and walk around some stores, picking up ideas for promoting collections and services. And then we'll walk through the library as though it were a store, finding ways to apply the ideas we picked up at the mall.

TEENS AS CONSUMERS

Why should you care about jeans, pizza, MTV, and cell phones? Because as a young adult librarian, you can learn a lot about promoting reading and books to teens from the methods by which popular and alternative cultures are sold to teens. Manipulation of teen consumers is at an all-time high (Quart 2003, 5). Not only are companies bombarding teens with print, web, radio, and TV advertising, but they are also trading on teens' desire for their voices to be heard by using them as unpaid participants in product focus groups (18) and as unpaid sales reps pushing products to peers (19).

This chapter is not going to be a treatise about how public libraries could be so much more attractive to teens if they modeled themselves on successful retail outlets. The mission and purpose of the public library remain different from those of commercial enterprises. Moreover, there is a downside to trying to re-create teen consumer culture in library services. Not all teens are interested in the personalities peddled by teen magazines and web sites, nor can all teens afford the products advertised by these venues. Many teens laugh or cringe at the concept of cool defined by teen consumer culture.

The reason to study the commercial world is not to copy *Teen People* magazine and Hot Topic stores for the next five years. Or six months. *Teen People* is just one magazine and Hot Topic is just one store, and the crowd may have moved on by the time you read this sentence. The reason is to get into the habit of periodically looking outside the library world for successful examples of promotions to teens. Marketers are aware of what young adult librarians have long known: a 13-year-old teen is not the same person as a 17-year-old teen, and no one "teen" approach will fit all teens (Meyer 2001, 14). As young teens, girls are experimenting with clothes and makeup. As middle teens, their bodies are changing dramatically: self-consciousness rises and self-esteem drops. As older teens, these girls are now solidifying their knowledge of who they are as human beings, what they want, and where they're going in life. Boys also undergo physical and intellectual changes. On average, teen boys grow 12 to 18 inches and can gain up to 100 pounds. Their interests expand from video games and skateboarding to more hobbies and sports, entertainment, dating, and where they're going in life.

Advertisers play to the stages of teen development, pitching "young" advertisements to younger teens and more sophisticated advertisements to older teens. So also can young adult librarians ask themselves, when putting together a book display, a booklist, or a booktalk program, how do these products and services meet what's going on in teens' lives?

WHAT DO TEENS BUY?

Like adult spending, teen spending reflects and expresses their needs and desires. Unlike adults, however, teens' spending is almost entirely discretionary. As dependents, they're usually not making house payments, or paying for rent, utilities, groceries, insurance, and so on. Older teens may have car-related expenses—car payments, insurance, gas, repairs—but for the most part, teen dollars are going for clothing and personal care, food, music, and electronics. A 2002 study by U.S. Bancorp Piper Jaffrey found that high school girls spent roughly 59 percent of their disposable income on clothes, accessories, personal care, and shoes. High school boys spent 34 percent of their disposable income on these items, as well as 28 percent on electronics and 25 percent on food (*Chain Store Age* 2002, 35).

How does knowing that help you promote reading and books to teens?

First, the nature of teens' spending is less about meeting basic survival needs than it is about meeting psychological and social needs: developing and expressing identity, and connecting with others. Fashion and music express individuality, while shared meals, personal electronics, and shopping with friends foster connections. What are two of the major themes of adolescent life development—and young adult fiction? Developing and expressing identity, and connecting with others.

Second, incorporating teen-appeal merchandise as design elements in library promotions—that is, print promotions and the teen web site— identifies them as teen oriented. Here are some examples:

Merchandise: Clothing.

Promotion: Create a poster using a giant shopping bag—complete with semicircle handles—as the background for information about a teen event.

Merchandise: Food.

Promotion: This is a tricky one, because if you use graphics or a border featuring teen-appeal food, teens may expect to find them at the event. Pizza is a perennial favorite. Look around your local pizza places for inspiration, and design posters or booklists to look like menus.

Merchandise: Music.

Promotion: Public libraries have adapted the universally recognized $4\frac{3}{4}$" square of CD jewel cases and liner notes as booklists, brochures, fliers, and postcards. The more the graphics look like CD cover art, the better.

Merchandise: Personal electronics.

Promotion: Teens have traditionally been identified with communication technology, from talking on telephones to chatting via

IMs. Fill up a poster with a big graphic of a PDA and put the title of a teen event, date, and time on the screen, using Verdana, an instantly readable font that was developed expressly for the Internet. Add the brushed-metal sheen of cell phones and other personal electronics to the color palette of printed materials and web pages.

MAGAZINES AND WEB SITES

This book is about promoting reading and books to teens, so why look at magazines and web sites? Because teens read them.

In many libraries, if there's one type of reading material that's lying around in the teen space, it's teen magazines. Walk by a row of computers, and teens are using e-mail or chat, or visiting web sites. Magazine and web formats are designed to catch teen eyes, their contents are written to engage teen minds, and their advertisements are created to grab teen dollars. By staying aware of the content and adapting the design elements of teen magazines and web sites, your collections, displays, print materials, and web sites will be more likely to seem part of the mass communication universe with which teens are already familiar. Familiarity leads to credibility.

By poring over magazine and web site content, you can learn about teen interests and concerns, which translate into the nonfiction subjects and fiction themes we'll examine in Chapter 3. Magazine and web site page layouts, colors, graphics, fonts, and language give you ideas for library displays, print promotions, and web sites. These will be discussed in Chapters 5, 6, and 7.

However, you don't have time to look at a stack of teen magazines right now, or visit web sites 'til your eyes burn. Your bus just pulled up. You're going to the mall!

LET'S GO TO THE MALL

Its educational mission aside, in many respects the public library resembles a retail outlet more than it does a school. The public library, unlike school, is a place where teens choose to be. Some are told by their parents to go to the public library after school. Some would go to the library regardless. But attendance is not required. Retail outlets, movie theaters, parks, and restaurants, like public libraries, are public places where teens make their own decisions about products and services. Teens go shopping in four types of retail outlets:

- Teen-appeal specialty stores, such as Alloy, Citizens of Humanity, Hot Topic, Old Navy, Abercrombie & Fitch, American Eagle, Gadzooks, and Forever 21.
- Teen boutiques and brands inside department stores, such as Macy's, Dillard's, JCPenney, and the like.
- Discount stores, such as Target, Wal-Mart, KMart, and Ross.
- Thrift stores, such as Goodwill Industries, Salvation Army, and Value Village.

One weekend afternoon, I visited ten retail outlets. One outlet was a stand-alone store facing a big parking lot, another was a teen boutique in a department store, and the rest were small teen-appeal specialty stores. I looked at store entrances, floor plans, fixtures, merchandise displays, non-shopping areas, cash register areas, print promotions, and exits. Here's what I saw, together with some promotion ideas for libraries.

Entrance

Two huge, identical signs were plastered in the front windows of the stand-alone clothing store, each declaring "WINTER CLEARANCE 50%–80%" in a harmonious color palette of blue background and pale blue, yellow, and white text. The message was easy to see and read. Shoebox-shaped specialty stores squeezed side by side in the mall tried the same ploy but were less successful because in a crowded mall sight lines are blocked, and the approach to individual stores—unlike the walk from a parking lot or a bus stop—is less protracted.

Promotion idea: Signs on the front windows of the library or at the entrance to the teen space work best if they are big, clear, and visible from a distance.

Floor Plan

Virtually every store I visited forced shoppers to stop within a few feet of the entrance, and then navigate around merchandise displays. This is understandable: in a small store, just as in a small public library, every square foot must do its duty. However, once inside the store, shoppers simultaneously begin thinking about what they need to buy, and start adjusting to simply being inside, registering light, heat, noise level, people, and the basic floor plan. Retail consultant Paco Underhill (1999, 46) calls this area of a retail outlet the transition zone between the outside world and the inside world of the store. Shoppers need time and a bit of space to adjust to their new environment before they are ready to shop. A few of the stores I visited balanced their need to attract shoppers' attention with shoppers' need for a transition zone by placing merchandise displays at a 45 degree angle on either side of the entrance, leaving the way open to the rest of the store. These displays caught the attention of shoppers without creating an obstacle.

Promotion idea: Set up teen book displays just past your library's entrance, at a 45 degree angle from the entrance.

In one store, merchandise lined the walls and display racks on wheels dotted the floor, with lots of space in between. The open space made it easy to see all the displays and actually to find merchandise. The exact opposite floor plan prevailed in a teen boutique in a department store. So much merchandise was crowded into display racks that it was difficult to see any of it, it all looked the same, the atmosphere was oppressive, and I couldn't wait to get out of there.

Promotion idea: Take a look at your teen space. Can you see the collections? Or is the space so crammed with display fixtures and collections—like those dusty spinners stuffed with yellowing paperbacks—that you can't see anything? Weeding collections and cleaning display fixtures will help to strike a balance between having enough library materials to meet teen needs and desires, and being able to see them.

Fixtures

The predominant shelving style I found in stores was industrial: metal shelving, vertical metal bookshelf strips and shelves, and stainless steel or black-painted wire grids to hook up merchandise. Décor varied. Some stores featured a goth color scheme (black, black, and black), some went for the warehouse look (cement or faux cement floors), and others went for high-gloss traditional (hardwood floors and pale painted paneled walls). At the department store, the four-armed directional signs hanging above intersections made it easy to find the teen boutique. Signs inside boutiques or specialty stores reflected the types of merchandise and teen identities being sold to teen consumers. One store included its initials on every sign, ensuring that consumers stayed aware of its brand. Black print on silver/metallic gray sold video games to heavy metal rockers, shocking pink or turquoise print on white sold fashion to fashionistas, and lime green or orange soda sold sports and beach wear to skateboarders and surfers.

Promotion idea: Shelving, floors, and walls tend to be standardized throughout most public libraries. Inside the teen space, try using color schemes appealing to teens. Include your library's initials/logo on everything teen so that teens stay aware of your brand.

Merchandise

Store merchandise is what's featured in advertisements in teen magazines and web sites.

Promotion idea: As described in the previous section—What Do Teens Buy?—include teen-appeal merchandise as design elements in print and electronic promotions.

Non-Shopping Area

All the way to the back of one store, two comfortable chairs flanked a sofa around a rug, facing a flat TV showing soft-focus ads for the store's clothing. Teens sat around drinking sodas, chatting with friends while waiting for other friends who were trying on clothes in the fitting rooms.

Promotion idea: What can I say? This non-shopping area looked exactly like a teen space.

Cash Register Area

Cash register areas are where teens wait to pay for merchandise, and so many stores give them something to look at: advertisements for products, promotions for sales, brochures for gift cards, and impulse buys. Several stores' gift card brochures sported the actual plastic cards on the front, giving the card a reality that a photograph in a printed brochure cannot match. Plus, the plastic was shiny and caught my eye from across the store. All of these items give teens reasons to come back to the store.

Promotion idea: Give teens reasons to come back to the library by stocking teen event fliers, teen bookmarks, and other print promotions at service desks. Fasten actual library cards to posters promoting library card applications.

Print Promotions

In addition to placing print promotions in the cash register area, many stores scatter them in display holders throughout the store. This makes it easy for teens to find out about the store without going up to the cash register and asking questions. Making print promotions more readily available also takes advantage of a gender difference. While female shoppers tend to prefer to get information about products by asking a sales person, male shoppers tend to prefer to get information about products by reading about them first, and then asking a sales person (Underhill 1999, 105).

Promotion idea: Display library card applications and other print promotions in the teen space, computer area, service desks, and other areas where teens might find them.

Exit

On the way out of the stand-alone clothing store, a poster asked if I'd like to be added to the store's e-mail mailing list in order to be notified about sales and other special events. Tear-off forms asked only for my e-mail address—no name, street address, or phone number—with boxes to check for specific clothing interests.

Promotion idea: Establish an e-mail group address, such as teens@your library, and print up a pad of tear-off forms asking teens if they'd like to be notified about upcoming teen events and additions to the collection. Ask for teens' name and address as well as e-mail address. Some studies show that approximately 80 percent of teens have access to e-mail (Sheridan 2003, 36), which means that approximately 20 percent of teens do not have access. Few things are as hurtful as blatant exclusion, so make sure your mailing list is open to *all* teens.

Buy Local

Ask teens in your library what they are into and where they get it. Depending on where you live, local retail outlets can include skateboard shops, snowboard shops, comics and graphic novels stores, coffeehouses (both chain and indie), secondhand clothing stores, and music shops that carry indie labels as well as the mass market labels carried by big-box stores. Visit, look around, and pick up sales brochures to study for promotion ideas.

LET'S GO SHOPPING—AT THE LIBRARY

Much of the rest of this chapter will imagine what teens think, imagine, and experience as they journey through your library.

As a teen, you're finding that it's still fun to go shopping with Mom or Dad, and it's definitely cool to have a car trunk to stow stuff in. But it's cool to go places on your own. So you and your friends have hopped the bus to go downtown, or to the mall. You're going to talk, shop, and stop to refuel at that coffeehouse or fast fooderie. And then maybe shop some more. There are a few things you absolutely must have, but it's also fun to find things that you didn't know you needed until you saw them. Your decisions are based on your needs and desires, and influenced by those outlets' space planning, advertising, merchandising, and customer service. And your decisions are also influenced by your friends—whom you trust, because they know you well.

So let's replicate a typical teen trip to the public library. Then we'll review our trip from a retail perspective, and find ways to apply retail promotion techniques to library promotions.

Load up a backpack or a book bag with textbooks (a few clay-surface books will do the job), an apple, a water bottle, and a wallet or purse. Walk out of the library and find the bus or subway stop closest to your library. Turn around. Walk toward your library. Do you have to cross the street? Is there a stoplight, or do you have to wait for a break in the traffic? Walking up to the library, what do you see? A sidewalk, some landscaping, okay, here's the library. Do you walk right in at street level, or are there steps? If the latter, is there a wheelchair access ramp? Is anybody standing around out front? Smokers, maybe, or skateboarders, or moms pushing strollers back and forth?

You weave through the crowd and open the front door. There might be some kind of poster near the door. But if you're like most people, you don't notice it, because the point of going through a door is to get inside.

Once inside, you start thinking about what you need, whether it's resources for a school project or just a place to study. You walk by a rack of library brochures. You breeze by a whiteboard with a few words scrawled on it. A library staff member walking by asks if you need help.

"No, thanks," you mutter, rolling your eyes. You just got here: how do you know if you need help yet? Brochures, whiteboard, and greeter are just obstacles in your path. Until you nail down those resources or stake out that study spot, you don't see anything and you're for sure not ready to talk to any library staff member.

Once past the transition zone, however, although your mission remains uppermost in your mind, you start to slow down enough to see more of what the library has to offer. You may notice that you're walking to the right, a "natural" orientation learned from years of walking down school hallways. Many public libraries (and retail outlets) display eye-catching materials just past the transition zone, such as new books, readers' advisory resources, and baskets for carrying library materials. Just past the transition zone is also a good place for the information desk. In fact, you register a desk as you walk by. A library staff member sitting there smiles at you as you go by but doesn't ask you if you need help or anything, which is fine. You now know where to go and whom to ask if you decide that you do need some assistance.

Continuing to walk through the library, you spot a table. Stowing your backpack underneath, you go over to one of the catalog terminals and find a couple of books for your project, then bring up some magazine articles from a database. The printer . . . Oh, yeah, it's around the corner, on the other side. Waiting for your pages to print, you see a poster advertising a poetry-writing workshop. It's tomorrow afternoon. Didn't your English teacher say something about giving extra credit to students who went to this? You check your calendar. Tomorrow afternoon is clear. The pages print out. Heading back to your table, you spot some of your friends sitting around in the teen space. The research can wait a few minutes. After all, you've found the resources you came in for, you can afford to spend a little time hanging out, so you head into the teen space.

You join your friends, snickering over something in the latest issue of *Teen People*. A couple of guys are playing chess at one of the tables. Another guy is kicking back in a comfortable chair, looking at *Transworld Skateboarding*. Some lady with glasses—a librarian, you figure—is telling a couple of teen girls about a book. It sounds pretty intense, something about a girl being harassed by a creepy clique at school. The librarian sees you, smiles to include you in her spiel, but doesn't get pushy by waving you forward. You take a peek at the cover of the book so you can find it in case those girls don't want it. Meanwhile, you'd probably better get back to your project.

Sometime later, you've accomplished your goal of extracting information from the books and highlighting stuff in the magazine articles. Your friends are packing up to catch the bus home, and so are you. Wait a sec . . . that book. You go back to the teen space. The book is still there: those girls left it on a table. You pick it up, scan the back cover; yes, it looks good. You go to the checkout desk, and standing in line you see that poetry-writing workshop poster again. When you check out the book, the library staff member slips a bookmark inside, smiles, and says something nice. You join your friends hanging out in the lobby and head out the door. Extra credit—good idea!

Now let's go back over your visit to the library, looking for retail outlet parallels and library promotion ideas.

> Retail outlet parallel: You arrived by public transportation, bike, or on foot.

> Promotion idea: Work with your local public transportation company to promote library use by teens with library ads on buses or subways, and bus pass or subway token prize drawings.

> Retail outlet parallel: You had particular resources/merchandise you needed to find, and walked past library brochures/sales catalogs.

> Promotion idea: Use your library's transition zone for big posters about teen events, splashed with eye-catching graphics and just a few words.

> Retail outlet parallel: You veered to the right and found an information desk/sales desk where you could get help if you need it.

> Promotion idea: Position your information desk just past the transition zone. Because teens may need to ask for assistance there, set up a display of pathfinder reference brochures and booklists for them to look at if they have to wait.

> Retail outlet parallel: Waiting for your magazine printouts/merchandise to emerge from the printer, you had the time to read a poster advertising an upcoming library event/sale.

> Promotion idea: Computer terminals and printers are places where teens are stationary, and make great locations for posters, fliers, pathfinders, and booklists.

> Retail outlet parallel: Once you found the resources/merchandise you needed, the pressure was off, and you had time to relax with your friends.

Promotion idea: Make sure your teen space is easy to find. A neon sign helps.

Retail outlet parallel: You noticed a librarian/salesperson showing a book/merchandise to a couple of other teens. The cool thing was, she acknowledged your presence and possible interest with a smile and made sure that you could hear her spiel, but she didn't wave you over and ask you "come join us" as though you were a little kid. If neither of those teens check out/purchase that book, maybe you will.

Promotion idea: Handselling, as it's known in the bookselling trade, is one of the very best ways to promote reading and books. The librarian was handselling directly to the two teen girls. She was handselling indirectly to you. Moreover, she was showing everyone in the teen space that reading, books, and talking about books is what the library is all about, as surely as a cosmetic salesperson's demonstration at the cosmetics counter fosters an atmosphere of shared interest in beauty. The librarian was taking the time to tell the teens about good books, and to judge from her warm and enthusiastic manner, she wasn't just mouthing empty "reading is good for you" boilerplate. Instead, she sounded like she'd actually read the book and really enjoyed it—a powerful endorsement in itself. Customers are hungry for knowledgeable, caring employees (Underhill 1999, 240), and handselling is one of the most powerful demonstrations of a librarian's knowledge and thoughtfulness—as we'll see in more detail in Chapter 8.

Retail outlet parallel: You finished using the library/shopping, and you and your friends were ready to go home. You went back to the teen space/boutique to see if that book/merchandise was still there, grabbed it, and took it to the circulation desk/cash register.

Promotion idea: After handselling books to teens, put them directly into their hands. Touching the merchandise brings the customer one step closer to buying it (Underhill 1999, 167). If teens decide not to take the books and ask, "Where should I put these?" just smile and say, "On one of the tables is fine." Leave the books on tables, in plain sight for teens who might pick them up later. Don't reshelve books you've described to teens: chances are, they will not be able to find them again. Ask your shelvers to leave books lying around until the end of the day. That's when you can add any books you've handsold to a face-out display so that they remain visible. Who knows, those same teens might come back in a day or two: it would be nice if they could easily find the books you told them about.

Retail outlet parallel: Up at the circulation desk/cash register area, you saw that poster again, advertising the poetry-writing workshop. The circulation staff member/cashier put a bookmark/sales advertisement in with your books/merchandise, and was really friendly. They're always so nice at this library/store, you thought, rejoining your friends. You're definitely coming back for that poetry-writing workshop!

Promotion idea: Circulation is the last stop before the exit, so give teens something to look at while they're waiting, and reasons to come back to the library. The reason to come back could be a teen event. It could be a bookmark listing ten new teen books. And it could very well be a friendly staff member.

Teens go to the public library to do homework, get resources for school projects, check their e-mail, look at magazines, meet up with friends, check out books and other library materials, and be in a place between school and home. As we've seen, they may come to the library to look for one kind of merchandise—resources for school—but may also serendipitously find other items, that is, books. The next chapter will discuss how to build up your inventory.

REFERENCES AND SUGGESTED READINGS

Chain Store Age. 2002. "Teens Spending More." (May): 35.

Doyle, Mhari. 2002. "Teen Thrift Shopping: Some Youths Counter Mainstream Fashions." *Columbian.* (November 19): C.1.

Lee, Georgia. 2003. "Personal Touch Is Best Approach to Millennials." *WWD.* (August 13): 2.

Lempert, Phil. 2002. *Being the Shopper: Understanding the Buyer's Choice.* New York: John Wiley & Sons.

Meyer, Patrick. 2001. "Brands Need to Understand the Mindset of Echoboomers in Order to Survive." *Kids Marketing Report.* (January): 14.

Quart, Melissa. 2003. *Branded: The Buying and Selling of American Teenagers.* Cambridge, MA: Perseus Publishing.

Sheridan, Margaret. 2003. "Mad Cool: Appeal to 21st Century Teens Begins by Understanding Their World." *Restaurants and Institutions.* (June 15): 35–38.

Underhill, Paco. 1999. *Why We Buy: The Science of Shopping.* New York: Simon & Schuster.

Young, Kristen. 2003. "Youth Quake: Changes in the Junior and Contemporary Markets Are Forcing the Industry to Take a Hard Look at the Future of the Business." *WWD.* (October 16): 38S.

3

BUILDING TEEN COLLECTIONS

In the previous two chapters, we explored teens' relationship with reading, and some of the promotional principles and practices of retail marketing. Now we're going to focus on what you want to promote to teens.

Reading.

By "reading" I mean reading books that teens themselves choose to read. Textbooks and educational nonfiction can appeal to teens' hunger for facts, but they are not usually read voluntarily. Similarly, while reading improves a person's reading and writing abilities (King 2000, 117), teens, like adults, do not usually read in order to improve their literacy. Rather than assuaging a "need to read," teens read to relax, have fun, be entertained, experience emotions, gain personal insight, learn life skills, explore personal interests—and to find out what is so good about that book their friends are raving about.

These are needs that can be satisfied by realistic fiction, popular fiction, graphic novels, popular nonfiction, and classics. By understanding the appeal of these books, you will be better able to promote them, by creating book displays, bookmarks, booklists, newsletters, and teen web pages, and by offering readers' advisory service, booktalks, and book-centered activities and events. The high quality of many young adult books makes them a pleasure to read—and to promote. As you saw in

Chapter 2, during your visit to the library, the librarian's enthusiastic handselling of a book was in response to both teens' reading interests and her own genuine enjoyment of the book itself.

This chapter serves as a resource for subsequent chapters on promotion methods, and will explain how to build collections: by evaluating your collection; understanding the reading appeal of fiction and nonfiction books; gathering input from teens, library staff, and the community; and using print and online resources to develop your collection.

EVALUATING YOUR COLLECTION

It's 3 p.m. Do you know where your young adult books are?

The first step in promoting books to teens is to get to know the books on your shelves. While you are reading reviews, buying books, adding more books from core collection and awards lists, and reading, what you need to know is what's on your shelves *now*.

Here's a way to find out. Take a little time each day (say, 15 to 30 minutes) to stroll over to the young adult shelves. We'll start with fiction. Starting at "A" authors, take down half a shelf of books, sit down at a table, and look them over. Skim the inside flaps and back covers. Think about how the books would appeal to teens, and the kinds of reader advisory questions the books might answer. Moving to nonfiction, start at "000" and look through some books. Read the table of contents, look at the pictures, and read the captions, sidebars, and some of the text. Think about the reading appeal of each book, that is, not only the topic but also the format: layout, graphics, fonts, text blocks, and colors. Think about the kinds of reference questions each might answer, and about books on similar topics.

You will not remember every detail about every book you've read or looked at. But if you do this steadily, over time your brain will store up titles for displays, print promotions, web sites, readers' advisory, book-talking, and book-centered activities and events. Except for books that are in shreds, resist the urge to weed. Your purpose in these brief forays is to get acquainted with your books. Wait until you've looked through the entire collection before you weed. To meet the reading needs and interests of your teen community, it's best to offer a broad selection of many types of fiction and nonfiction. And while the focus of this book is on print books, additional reading media also give teens the opportunity to read: magazines, zines, graphic novels, web sites, e-books, and more. These reading media are discussed in detail in *Thinking Outside the Book: Alternatives for Today's Teen Collections* (Nichols, 2004). By looking through your collections, you will learn what is available to teens at your library. You will also learn what is less available, or missing. This is the wall of books that teens see when they walk into the teen space, the wall of book spines. Open up the wall. Know what's inside it.

REALISTIC YOUNG ADULT FICTION

As we saw in Chapter 1, teens read for many reasons. They read to laugh, to cry, to see into the heart of things, to learn the why of things, to satisfy curiosity. Realistic young adult fiction (sometimes called "issues fiction") shows how teens like them cope with a variety of situations, emotions, and thoughts. Confronted by moral dilemmas, characters are forced to make the choices that define their identity, relationships, and place in society. Realistic fiction depicts a world that many teens recognize. They know about cliques at school and might wonder what it would be like to be in a school where cliques truly rule. They might also wonder what it would be like to be severely burned, or blinded, or maimed in an accident. Or to be orphaned, homeless, addicted to drugs, or locked up in juvenile detention. Or to be in an emotionally, physically, or sexually abusive relationship. Maybe they've heard of somebody with those problems. Maybe they know somebody with those problems. Maybe they are that person.

Like serious fiction written for adults, at its best realistic fiction written for teens is good literature, blending compelling subjects with perceptive, sometimes beautiful writing. First-person narration, or a third-person narration focusing on the protagonist, seals the reader's connection with the story. The appeal of realistic fiction is that it connects with the everyday lives of teens. A teen doesn't have to suffer from a mental illness to appreciate a novel about obsessive-compulsive disorder. All he has to experience are a few stomach-clenching bouts of anxious double-checking to make sure that today's homework is actually in his backpack.

During the late 1960s and throughout the 1970s, young adult fiction broke through the rosy mist of twentieth-century youth literature of teen romance, adventure, sports, mystery, and animal stories with novels that explored the social issues affecting teens' lives. These issues included class warfare, racism, drug abuse, poverty, sexual identity, dysfunctional families, and mental illness. The work of such writers as Richard Peck, M. E. Kerr, Walter Dean Myers, Norma Fox Mazer, Sue Ellen Bridgers, and others transformed books for teens into literature as complex and weighty as any written for adults. The trend toward realistic fiction also gave rise to the one-dimensional "problem novel," fiction driven not by characters but by the need to solve the "problem of the week" (Beers 2001, xix).

The didactic tone has a long pedigree in American literature written for young people. Puritan settlers in New England took education very seriously, mixing together the alphabet, vocabulary, cautionary tales, and theology to create *The New England Primer* (Hunt 1995, 103). The self-reflection that is characteristic of realistic young adult fiction's heroes and heroines today has its roots in Puritan writing (107). In the early 1800s, writers anchored their stories for young people in moralistic themes (106). Children in these stories learned to reverse their bad habits of willfulness, carelessness, and selfishness, and lead better lives. Later in the nineteenth century, writers depicted problems besetting youth in big cities: poverty, alcoholic parents who were neglectful or abusive, the lure of street life and crime, and hints about child prostitution (117).

Sound familiar? These were real social problems, and no more to be dismissed as mere Victorian-era hysteria than the problems revealed by 1970s realistic young adult fiction. Betty Carter notes that during the 1980s, writers continued to address teen problems, but in a less didactic and more novelistic style, through more fully developed plots, characters, and settings (Carter 2000, 9).

Michael Cart attributes some of the sanding down of the rough edges of realistic young adult fiction during the 1980s to publisher and bookstore preferences for middle-school reader titles over high-school reader titles. By the mid-1990s, however, he found that realistic young adult fiction had begun to regain its edge. Why? Because teens became one of the fastest growing segments of the American population, spending by public and school libraries increased, and publishers responded to the fiction needs of older teens by publishing more gritty fiction. Such innovative writing styles as novels in poetry, magic realism, novels in diaries or letters, multiple points of view, and multiple media have further transformed young adult fiction. And the globalization of young adult literature is reflected by an increased access by American teens to fiction written by Australian, British, Canadian, and other world authors (Beers 2001, xxi).

Let's examine some of the major themes of realistic young adult fiction, and how they appeal to teens.

Forming Identity

Reading Appeal: "Who am I?" Known in library literature as the "coming-of-age" novel, the teen bildungsroman supports as many subthemes as there are ways to grow up. These novels focus on self-perception and self-definition, while balancing responsibilities to others.

Examples: *Call Me Maria* (Cofer 2004), *Fat Boy Swim* (Forde 2004), *You Don't Know Me* (Klass 2001), and *Doormat* (McWilliams 2004).

Family

Reading Appeal: The first relationships teens build are with family members, and most teens have a family of some kind. Subthemes that appeal to teen readers include families that nurture teens, dysfunctional families, and families so battered that parents' and children's roles are redefined. Teens are shown individuating and pulling away from parental leadership or control. While sometimes fed up or self-centered, parents are shown chafing at their roles as breadwinner, housekeeper, chauffeur, and so forth. Teen characters can be astounded to learn that parents have (or want) identities apart from that of caregivers. Another recent theme is how the disappearance or death of a sibling affects a family. There can be depression after the family's loss, and also resentment on the part of remaining brothers and sisters, who feel neglected or smothered by their depressed or fearful parents.

Examples: *The Queen of Everything* (Caletti 2002), *Dead Girls Don't Write Letters* (Giles 2003), *Cuba 15* (Osa 2003), and *Run If You Dare* (Powell 2001).

Friends

Reading Appeal: Although their primary relationships remain with family members, teens bond fiercely with friends, helping each other through the storms of adolescence. The shadow side of friendship is explored in novels about teens who feel betrayed by their friends, or who befriend outcasts. Some turn out to be innocent victims of slander, while others prove to be just as bad as everyone said.

Examples: *Sisterhood of the Traveling Pants* (Brashares 2001), *Night Hoops* (Deuker 2000), *Feeling Sorry for Celia* (Moriarty 2001), and *Sevens* series (Wallens 2002).

Love and Sex

Reading Appeal: Just seeing a certain boy or girl makes a teen's heart beat faster. Realistic young adult fiction about love and sexual relationships often focuses on the risk of opening one's self to another person.

Sometimes the risk leads to the reward of a mutually nurturing relationship.

Examples: *Jason and Kyra* (Davidson 2004), *This Lullaby* (Dessen 2002), *Of Sound Mind* (Ferris 2001), and *Second Helpings* (McCafferty 2003).

Love Gone Wrong

Reading Appeal: Falling in love was so great. But now everything has gone wrong. The majority of "love gone wrong" novels depict a girl as an enabling victim and a boy as a controlling aggressor. Teens get hurt in these novels, but they usually start to recover.

Examples: *Dreamland* (Dessen 2000), *Breathing Underwater* (Flinn 2000), *Blind Sighted* (Moore 2003), and *Fault Line* (Tashjian 2003).

Am I Gay?

Reading Appeal: As teens begin to experience sexual feelings, some find themselves attracted to members of the same sex. Teens in these novels face the challenge of sorting out their sexual orientation—or that of their friends.

Examples: *Eight Seconds* (Ferris 2000) and *Kissing Kate* (Myracle 2003).

Gay/Lesbian Love and Sex

Reading Appeal: In a teen world dominated by images of heterosexual relationships, gay teens can feel doubly isolated: by their sexual orientation and by not knowing if they'll ever meet someone and fall in love. These novels reassure gay teens that their emotions are valid and that love is possible.

Examples: *Geography Club* (Hartinger 2003), *Boy Meets Boy* (Levithan 2003), *Keeping You a Secret* (Peters 2003), and *Rainbow High* (Sanchez 2004).

Teen Parenthood

Reading Appeal: Some teens see friends and young relatives with babies. For other teens, parenthood seems remote, impossible, and yet intriguingly intense.

Examples: *Hanging On to Max* (Bechard 2002), *Dancing Naked* (Hrdlitschka 2001), *First Part Last* (Johnson 2003), and *Chill Wind* (McDonald 2002).

School

Reading Appeal: Isn't it fun to read fiction set in a public library? (Not that there is much, unfortunately.) For teens, school is their workplace. School is their sunrise of new ideas, their dark night of social pressures—their social laboratory.

While many young adult novels include scenes at school simply because their characters are teens and go to school, others focus on issues that are particular to school. Novels set at school show teens taking their first steps toward finding their place in society. Then there are schools that are hell on earth, where harassment, peer pressure, assault, and even murder terrorize students. School is also the perfect setting for novels about teens in rebellion against the system. Teens are depicted as clever outsiders flying under the radar, avoiding toadies, kiss-ups, and bullies, while teachers and staff are usually depicted as officious yet clueless.

Examples: *Cheating Lessons* (Cappo 2002), *Double Dutch* (Draper 2002), *On the Fringe* (Gallo 2001), *Breaking Point* (Flinn 2002), and *Give a Boy a Gun* (Strasser 2000).

Physical Challenges

Reading Appeal: Car accidents, airplane crashes, and mass murder by political terrorists dominate the media. Teens are curious about these topics, and might speculate on what it would be like to rebuild their lives. Would they still be themselves, or would the accident or illness define them? Would their friends and other people pull away? Would they now be more dependent on their parents, just when they want to be more independent?

Examples: *Sweetblood* (Hautman 2003) and *Waiting for Sarah* (McBay and Heneghan 2003).

Illness and Death

Reading Appeal: In fiction about illness and death, relationships change under duress and characters emerge redefined by their experiences. These novels challenge teens to treasure each moment with people they love.

Examples: *When Dad Killed Mom* (Lester 2001), *Girlhearts* (Mazer 2001), *Both Sides Now* (Pennebaker 2000), and *Behind You* (Woodson 2004).

Substance Abuse and Mental Illness

Reading Appeal: Get good grades, rack up activities and community service for college applications, help out at home, keep the right friends and avoid those bad kids, be well adjusted, and so on ad infinitum. Are there any teens who *don't* feel overwhelmed sometimes? Realistic fiction depicts teens in the grip of anxiety, stress, or depression, a reflection of the high expectations laid upon teens today. Alcohol and drug abuse are depicted as symptoms of underlying emotional or psychological problems. Recent titles also depict teens coping with alcoholic parents. Teens are also curious about the extreme situations of such mental illnesses as obsessive-compulsive disorder and schizophrenia.

Examples: *Split Image* (Glenn 2000), *Not as Crazy as I Seem* (Harrar 2003), *Damage* (Jenkins 2002), *Cut* (McCormick 2000), and *Bottled Up* (Murray 2003).

Crime

Reading Appeal: Were you ever sent out of class to sit in the hall? Ever swipe a candy bar? Ever been falsely accused of something? For many teens, this is as close as they get to running afoul of the law. Novels about criminal activity allow teens to imagine what it would be like if their minor infractions had more serious consequences.

Examples: *Shattering Glass* (Giles 2002), *Silent to the Bone* (Konigsburg 2000), and *Handbook for Boys* (Myers 2002).

Religion and Spirituality

Reading Appeal: Teens may be grounded in a religious tradition, in rebellion against it, or exploring spiritual paths. Or they may have friends for whom religion is an important part of their lives. Some novels depict teen characters evoking their religious values to resolve moral dilemmas. In other novels, religion appears as a routine part of everyday life. Characters refer to attending church, synagogue, or other services, a reality that is seldom depicted in teen pop culture. And while teens may overhear profanity and notice crude behavior at school and elsewhere, that doesn't mean that all teens talk and behave crudely. And so some teens—and their parents—have learned to seek out teen novels published by Bethany House or other religious publishers, knowing they won't have to mentally screen out profanity or crude behavior.

Examples: *Diary of a Teenage Girl* series (Carolson 2000+), *Soul Searching: Thirteen Stories about Faith and Belief* (Fraustino, 2002), and *Buddha Boy* (Koja 2003).

Racial/Ethnic Conflicts and Immigrant Experience

Reading Appeal: Walk into many middle or high schools and you will be surrounded by the many peoples of America: African, Asian, European, Hispanic, and Native American. While they spend schooltime together, and time outside school, teens have also experienced racism, or they've heard their friends talk about it. They may enjoy reading about experiences grounded in their own culture, or other cultures besides their own.

Examples: *Who Will Tell My Brother?* (Carvell 2002), *Whale Talk* (Crutcher 2001), *Born Confused* (Desai Hidier 2002), and *First Crossing: Stories about Teen Immigrants* (Gallo 2004).

Sports

Reading Appeal: Writers often use sports as the setting for the exploration of personal dilemmas and social issues, such as testing oneself, competition, teamwork, overcoming interpersonal conflicts to achieve a goal, moral dilemmas, and cheating.

Examples: *Born in Sin* (Coleman 2001), *High Heat* (Deuker 2003), *House of Sports* (Russo 2002), and *Players* (Sweeney 2000).

Humor

Reading Appeal: After all the angst seething on the shelves, who wouldn't want to lighten up? Funny fiction offers teens a relaxed perspective on life and its weirdness. One of the joys of teen life is humor. Smart-aleck comebacks to put-downs, eyeball-rolling sarcasm, satiric running commentary to friends during school assemblies—you remember what it was like to unleash your brains, your attitude, and your mouth. Humor runs like a vein of gold through many novels, while others devote themselves entirely to getting laughs.

Examples: *Black Book: Diary of a Teenage Stud* series (Black 2001+), *Son of the Mob* (Korman 2002), *Sloppy Firsts* (McCafferty 2001), and *Gossip Girl* series (Von Ziegesar 2002+).

GENRE YOUNG ADULT FICTION

Like all readers, sometimes teens want to plumb the depths of human experience. Then again, sometimes they just want to be entertained, by a story that is familiar and instantly gratifying, with enough surprises to keep them turning the pages until the satisfying end. In genre fiction the scene is set, the characters take their places, the plot begins, and the writing style doesn't get in the way. Genre fiction written for younger teens tends to play it safe, sticking to plot and character conventions, giving adults a role to play in problem solving, and keeping the writing style light and smooth. Genre fiction written for older teens takes more risks, twisting up plots and characters, often leaving adults out of the picture, and employing a more complex writing style. In fact, some genre fiction written for older teens explores issues associated with realistic fiction.

Let's examine some of the major themes of genre young adult fiction, and how they appeal to teens.

Adventure
Survival/Rescue

Reading Appeal: Survival/rescue stories give readers fast pacing, plenty of action, and the depiction of teens who are strong, smart, and resourceful. In some stories, something that begins as a familiar experience or recreational activity—watching TV at home with friends, white water rafting, mountain climbing—turns into a fight for survival. In other stories, teens embark on journeys they know are dangerous in order to accomplish a task, or to simply survive.

Examples: *Overboard* (Fama 2002), *Underworld* (MacPhail 2005), *Takedown* (Sweeney 2004), and *Soldier X* (Wulffson 2000).

Teen Spies

Reading Appeal: This small but growing subgenre offers droll parallels to real life. Inside the classroom, teens are listening hard to find out what's going to be on the test. Out in the hall, they're dodging bullies. In teen spy novels, teen characters are listening hard to find out about gizmos. Out in the field, they're dodging killers. In real life and in fiction, teens and teen characters are developing skill sets in order to survive and thrive.

Examples: *Alias* series (various authors 2002+), *Alex Rider* series (Horowitz 2001+), and *Samurai Girl* series (Asai 2003+).

Mystery/Suspense
Crime-Solving Whodunits

Reading Appeal: Teens like to feel that their instincts, intelligence, courage, and grasp of right vs. wrong could help solve problems. The story begins when a teen protagonist notices that something has gone out of balance, doesn't add up, or doesn't fit. Eventually a crime is revealed and solved. These mysteries feature recognizable characters, settings, and dilemmas.

Examples: *Missing Persons* series (Rabb 2004) and *Sammy Keyes and the Search for Snake Eyes* (Van Draanen 2002).

Creepy Atmosphere

Reading Appeal: Teens like to feel they can not only solve problems, but also face unfamiliar or terrifying characters, settings, and dilemmas. Some suspense stories dig under the surface to explore psychological and social issues, crossing over into realistic fiction. The mystery is the frame story. The *real* story is what the "mystery" reveals about the characters.

Examples: *Shadow People* (McDonald 2000), *The Body of Christopher Creed* (Plum-Ucci 2000), and *Locked Inside* (Werlin 2000).

Dreams, Ghosts, and Other Unexplained Phenomena

Reading Appeal: What do dreams mean? Are ghosts real? Suspense novels that shimmer with the unexplained appeal to teens' imagination, and their willingness to be open to different ways of knowing.

Examples: *Kit's Wilderness* (Almond 2000), *Shades of Simon Gray* (McDonald 2001), and *Fingerprints* series (Metz 2001+).

Vampires, Witches, Werewolves

Reading Appeal: Whatever happened to teen horror fiction? You remember: horrid secrets that spawned gruesome, bloody, scary crimes. While teens continue to read horror fiction by such authors as Stephen King, Dean Koontz, and Clive Barker, teen horror fiction has morphed into other types of teen fiction. First, teen mysteries became creepier, as described in the Creepy Atmosphere subgenre. Second, the vampire revival in adult fiction kicked into turbo drive when *Buffy the Vampire Slayer* hit TV, and the teen fiction genre expanded to include witches, werewolves, and other children of the night. And third, realistic teen fiction began to explore the horror that can erupt into everyday life, such as bullying and harassment, sexual assault, incest, and addiction to hard drugs. Teen characters became more likely to encounter ghouls at school than in dark alleys.

Diana Tixier Herald (2003, 127) speculates that the real-life horror of recent events has also cooled interest in dead-teenager shockers. But some teens still like to be scared spitless, and so the horror of real-life tragedy is now displaced into the supernatural world.

The reading appeal of fiction about teen vampires, witches, and werewolves is obvious: power. These characters possess heightened intelligence, physical strength, emotions, and sexual allure. They obey no rules but their own. Parents and other authority figures are foils at best. And the transformation process these teen characters undergo mirrors the surging of growth and sexual hormones.

Examples: *Vampire High* (Rees 2003), *Cirque du Freak* series (Shan 2001+), and *Sweep* series (Tiernan 2001+).

Fantasy

Teens enjoy using their imaginations to envision other worlds and consider alternative lives. These other worlds are minutely described, and their rules clarified for the reader—in contrast with the shifting certainties of teen lives and the world.

Quests and Tests

Reading Appeal: Whether on a quest to save a kingdom, retrieve a talisman, or discover their true identity, teen characters learn to develop their strengths, compensate for their weaknesses, and find their destinies. Quest fantasy fiction appeals to teens' awakening to their life journey, and to their idealism.

Examples: *The Ropemaker* (Dickinson 2001), *The Sea of Trolls* (Farmer 2004), and *Treasure at the Heart of the Tanglewood* (Pierce 2001).

Magic and Sorcery

Reading Appeal: Is there a teen (or an adult) who wouldn't like to wave a magic wand? Like vampires, witches, and werewolves, teen wizards have great powers, and must learn to exercise them wisely.

Examples: *Abhorsen* (Nix 2003), *Circle Opens* series (Pierce 2000+), and *Harry Potter and the Half-Blood Prince* (Rowling 2005).

Time Travel and Parallel Worlds

Reading Appeal: How would you survive if you traveled back in time, or to a parallel world? Teens actually ask themselves the same question, when they start middle school, and later high school. These new environments force them to learn new rules quickly in order to survive.

Examples: *For All Time* (Cooney 2001), *Coraline* (Gaiman 2002), *The Grave* (Heneghan 2000), and *Pendragon: Journal of an Adventure through Time and Space* series (MacHale 2002+).

Retold Fairy Tales, Myths, and Legends

Reading Appeal: Retold fairy tales put new twists on familiar old stories. Sometimes the author transfers the old tale to a contemporary setting. In other novels, the author retells the old tale from a different point of view, such as a previously minor character, or reinterprets the tale itself. Teens especially appreciate funny, "fractured" fairy tales.

Examples: Retold fairy tales and myths by Patrice Kindl, Robin McKinley, Donna Jo Napoli, and Neal Shusterman, and retold Arthurian legends by Gerald Morris and Nancy Springer.

Animals with Unusual Powers

Reading Appeal: Teens' fondness for pets, their identification with outsiders, and their enjoyment of adventure/survival stories come together in novels featuring dragons, unicorns, mice, and other animals. Animals exemplify such appealing character traits as strength, cunning, wisdom, and loyalty—although sometimes animals revert to their wild natures.

Examples: *Hunting of the Last Dragon* (Jordan 2002), *Airborn* (Oppel 2004), and *Eragon* (Paolini 2003).

Romance

Reading Appeal: When teens look for a romance, what they usually want is something light and sweet, featuring recognizable characters facing familiar situations: crushes, falling in love, misunderstandings, making up.... Subthemes include friendship, trust, staying true to oneself, and understanding another person's point of view. Romance fiction is not without heartache—characters can experience rejection, and sometimes loss—but unlike realistic fiction about love and sex, romance fiction is seldom shadowed by anything more serious than communication mix-ups.

Examples: *Avon True Romance* series (various authors 2002+), *All-American Girl* (Cabot 2002), and *Girls in Love* series (Wilson 2002+).

Humorous Romance

Reading Appeal: Romantic comedy is a staple of teen movies, and is just as pleasant in fiction form.

Examples: *Truth or Dairy* (Clark 2000), *How Not to Spend Your Senior Year* (Dokey 2004), *Boy Meets Boy* (Levithan 2003), and *Flavor of the Week* (Shaw 2003).

Science Fiction

High Tech

Reading Appeal: Cell phones used to be "futuristic." Now they're in many teens' pockets. Generations of teens have grown up on tech: mechanisms change, but the fascination continues. High-tech topics in science fiction include space travel, artificial intelligence, genetic engineering, and other scientific advances.

Examples: *Feed* (Anderson 2002), *Mortal Engines* (Reeves 2003), and *Double Helix* (Werlin 2004).

Science Fiction in Everyday Life

Reading Appeal: This subgenre appeals to teens who enjoy tales of everyday teen life transformed by sudden, inexplicable weirdness.

Examples: *Things Not Seen* (Clements 2002), *Turnabout* (Haddix 2000), *Full Tilt* (Shusterman 2003), and *The Boy Who Couldn't Die* (Sleator 2004).

Aliens and Humans

Reading Appeal: He's not from around here, and this is his first day at school. Okay, he's kind of funny-looking, but don't make a big deal out of it. Be nice to him, show him around, introduce him to some of your friends. Make him feel at home.

Many teens have had the experience of seeing somebody new at school, or being asked to orient a new student. Sometimes that new student seems like he's from Planet X. The appeal of these novels is that the new guy *is* from Planet X. Science fiction focusing on alien/human interaction also appeals to teens' curiosity about outer space. If there's intelligent life forms on other planets, what do they look like? Could we communicate? Do they want anything from us? Like, Earth?

Examples: *Angel Factory* (Blacker 2002), *Singing the Dogstar Blues* (Goodman 2003), *Dancing with an Alien* (Logue 2002), and *Parasite Pig* (Sleator 2002).

Future Gone Bad

Reading Appeal: What if trends in society and advances in science led to oppression? What if the world as you knew it ended through an atomic blast, a plague, or other catastrophe? Would you succumb to social control or chaos, or would you rebel or rebuild? In these postapocalypse novels, part of the appeal comes from recognizing remnants of previous civilizations.

Examples: *Among the Enemy* (Haddix 2005), *The Last Book in the Universe* (Philbrick 2000), and *Memory Boy* (Weaver 2001).

Historical Fiction

Reading Appeal: Like fantasy and science fiction, historical fiction invites teens to put themselves into unfamiliar times and places. Studying history in school has familiarized teens with past times and a variety of cultures. The appeal of historical fiction, however, lies in its depiction of teen characters wrestling with many of the same issues as contemporary teens: forming identity, family, friends, and so on. Many historical novels are first-person narratives, and some are written in diary format. The *Dear America* diary series featuring girl protagonists, and the *My Name Is America* diary series featuring boy protagonists, transform history into personal stories.

Ancient World

Reading Appeal: The appeal of historical fiction about the ancient world can be summed up in three words: mummies, gods, and gladiators. Many teens have studied the history and culture of Ancient Egypt, Greece, and Rome. Some teens have also learned about ancient times among the Hebrews, Celts, Native Americans, Mongols, Pacific Islanders, Africans, and other peoples.

Examples: *Troy* (Geras 2001) and *Pharoah's Daughter* (Lester 2000).

Medieval Times around the World

Reading Appeal: Historical novels set in medieval times and places, like fantasy fiction, feature castles, knights, ladies, armor, codes of conduct, rumors of dragons and witchcraft, quests, and the struggle to become a hero or heroine under dangerous circumstances.

Examples: *Anna of Byzantium* (Barrett 2000), *Pagan's Crusade* (Jinks 2003), and *The Kite Rider* (McCaughrean 2002).

1500 Onward around the World

Reading Appeal: Teens study the Renaissance, the age of exploration, colonialism, and nineteenth- and twentieth-century history. In historical fiction, teens meet characters living in somewhat familiar times and places.

Examples: *The Convicts* (Lawrence 2005), *Beware, Princess Elizabeth* (Meyer 2001), and *An Ocean Apart, a World Away* (Namioka 2002).

United States

Reading Appeal: Like contemporary teens, the teens in these books struggle to form their identities as they meet such challenges as living on their own, living in community, making money, and discovering what is right.

Examples: *Fever 1793* (Anderson 2000), *Ashes of Roses* (Auch 2002), *Northern Light* (Donnelly 2003), *Fire in the Hole!* (Farrell 2004), and *The Land* (Taylor 2001).

U.S. Conflicts and World Wars

Reading Appeal: Historical fiction set during war allows teens to experience the extremes of oppression, danger, conflict, sacrifice, and destruction, and to imagine how they might have acted. Many of these novels show the impact of political and military conflicts back home, because that's where teen characters are most likely to be. Fiction about the Holocaust touches teens' sensitivity to oppression and suffering, and their desire for justice. The moral and physical challenges of war are also examined in fiction that takes place after military conflicts have ended.

Examples: *Daniel Half Human and the Good Nazi* (Chotjewitz 2004), *Soldier Boys* (Hughes 2001), *Just Jane* (Lavender 2002), and *Sarah's Ground* (Rinaldi 2004).

U.S. Civil Rights and Vietnam Conflict Eras

Reading Appeal: Mom and Dad and grandparents talk about those times. But what were they like for teens? These historical novels invite teen readers to experience "history" that was lived firsthand by people they know.

Examples: *Mississippi Trial, 1955* (Crowe 2002) and *Life History of a Star* (Easton 2001).

COMICS, GRAPHIC NOVELS, AND MANGA

Comics, graphic novels, and manga have emerged as popular reading choices for teens, combining the comic book conventions of action-driven drawings, dialogue and thought balloons, and sound and visual effects, with story lines from realistic and genre fiction, and topics from nonfiction. While comics typically feature science fiction, adventure, or fantasy story lines, graphic novels tackle such contemporary issues as family, friends, angst, humor, love, and social problems. Manga comics, published in Japan and Korea and translated into English and other languages, are inspired by Japanese anime cartoon series, whose heroes and heroines cope with superpowers, outer-space adventures, romance, and contemporary issues.

Parallels with young adult fiction abound, in books that mesh stories and pictures. The sense of imminent disaster hanging over the superhero in the comic *Origin: The True Story of Wolverine* (Jemas 2002) is created equally by the story line and dialogue, and the heavily shadowed drawings. The downbeat dialogue, teen angst, and humor of best friends Enid and Becky in the graphic novel *Ghost World* (Clowes 1997) is enhanced by the artist's downbeat visual style. The designer-clad girl bullies of the *Boys over Flowers* series (Kamio 2003+) are as fixated on fashion and clique status as their sisters in young adult fiction.

Comics, graphic novels, and manga feature many of the most popular themes and genres of young adult fiction and nonfiction (Herald 2003, 177).

Realistic Fiction

Examples: *Girl Got Game* series (Seino 2004+) and *Blankets: An Illustrated Novel* (Thompson 2003).

Humor and Weirdness

Examples: *Electric Girl* series (Brennan 2000+) and *Dragon Knights* series (Ohkami 2002+).

Adventures with Superheroes

Examples: *Ultimate Spider-Man* (Bendis 2001+) and *Mystique: Drop Dead Gorgeous* (Vaughan 2004).

Fantasy

Examples: *Rayearth* series (Clamp 2002+), *Castle Waiting: The Lucky Road* (Medley 2000), and *Inu-Yasha: A Feudal Fairy Tale* series (Takahashi 2000+).

Science Fiction

Examples: *Akira* series (Otomo 2000–2002) and *Dragon Ball* series (Toriyama 2000+).

Love and Romance

Examples: *Mars* series (Soryo 2003+), *Fruits Basket* series (Takaya 2004+), and *Kare Kano: His and Her Circumstances* series (Tsuda 1999+).

Historical Fiction and Nonfiction

Examples: *Usagi Yojimbo: Grasscutter II* series (Sakai 2002+) and *Persepolis: The Story of a Childhood* (Satrapi 2003).

CLASSIC LITERATURE

The extremes of human experience and emotion roil classic literature. What distinguishes classic literature and other great art from popular culture is its willingness to not stop at the surface of a story, but instead to continue drilling, drilling, drilling under the surface to extract maximum meaning. Teens are now at the point in their lives where they're discovering that despite the assurances of popular culture, there are no completely easy answers to life's big questions. They are ready to drill.

To identify classics with contemporary resonance, look for books that feature teens or young-20s characters with whom teens can empathize. Take *Adam Bede*, set in 1799 rural England (Eliot [1859] 1980). In one story line, Adam loves Hetty, who is young, pretty, and poor, and is flattered by the attention of rich boy Arthur. Pregnant, Hetty panics. Her dead baby is discovered, and Hetty is arrested, tried, convicted of murder, and condemned to be transported. Another story line follows Dinah, whose Methodist preaching stirs debates about women, power, and society. Their story lines converge when Dinah visits Hetty in her prison cell, prays with her, consoles her, and gives her the strength to face her exile. That was just old England, wasn't it? Not really. News stories about newborn babies abandoned in Dumpsters and restrooms show that some girls still believe they'll be ostracized for giving birth.

This brief list is intended to demonstrate how classics fit into the major themes of young adult realistic fiction. Take a look at the classics list distributed by your high school. How might those titles fit in with these and other themes?

Forming Identity

Examples: *Jane Eyre* (Bronte [1847] 1942), *The Song of the Lark* (Cather [1915] 1943), *A Portrait of the Artist as a Young Man* (Joyce [1916] 1976), and *The Red and the Black* (Stendhal [1830] 2002).

Family

Examples: *Go Tell It on the Mountain* (Baldwin [1953] 1963), *Metamorphosis* (Kafka [1915] 1981), *Nectar in a Sieve* (Markandaya 1954), and *Fathers and Sons* (Turgenev [1862] 1998).

Friends

Examples: *Cat's Eye* (Atwood 1988) and *The Little Prince* (Saint-Exupéry 1943)

Love and Sex

Examples: *Madame Bovary* (Flaubert [1856] 1957), *The Rainbow* (Lawrence [1915] 1961), *The Betrothed* (Manzoni [1827] 1984), and *Kristin Lavransdatter* (Undset [1922] 1955).

School and Social Pressure

Examples: *The Prime of Miss Jean Brodie* (Spark [1961] 1962) and *The House of Mirth* (Wharton [1905] 1997).

Physical Challenges, Illness, and Death

Examples: *The Plague* (Camus [1947] 1991), *The Magic Mountain* (Mann [1924] 1995), and *Of Human Bondage* (Maugham [1915] 1991).

Substance Abuse and Mental Illness

Examples: *The Sorrows of Young Werther* (Goethe [1774, 1787] 1993), *John Barleycorn* (London [1913] 2001), and *Temple of the Golden Pavilion* (Mishima [1956] 1959).

Crime

Examples: *Crime and Punishment* (Dostoyevsky [1866] 1993), *An American Tragedy* (Dreiser [1925] 2000), and *One Day in the Life of Ivan Denisovich* (Solzhenitsyn [1962] 1993).

Racial/Ethnic Conflicts and Immigrant Experience

Examples: *My Antonia* (Cather [1918] 1996), *Giants in the Earth* (Rolvaag [1927] 1999), and *Native Son* (Wright [1940] 1993).

POPULAR NONFICTION

As teens seek to understand themselves and others, as they encounter more life issues and challenges and discover new interests, their appetite for answers and insights explodes. When children have questions, they ask adults. When teens have questions, they still ask adults, but they also ask friends, and as their media use grows, they seek out answers in magazines, web sites, cable TV, and nonfiction books.

By building up and promoting the nonfiction book collection, young adult librarians help teens to see themselves as readers, overcoming the "nonreader" and "reluctant reader" labels that can be imposed on teens (and adults) who do not enjoy reading fiction. You are also helping teens to overcome assumptions about library collections, by showing them that the library has books to meet their interests. Both the topics and formats of nonfiction books can appeal to nonreaders and reluctant male readers (Abramson 2001, 88), as well as new English speakers (Jones 2001, 45). The popularity of magazines among teen girls suggests that girls also enjoy reading nonfiction.

In Chapter 1 you read about some of the reasons why teens may not feel like reading. Maybe they used to read as children, drifted away from reading to other activities, and now think of reading as something for little kids. Maybe they never read very well, and now associate reading with frustration and failure. Maybe they read well, but they have to read so much for school that they have little time for freely chosen reading. And when they do grab something to read, it might not be fiction: they'd rather read a magazine or a book about something that relates directly to their own lives, than a novel about made-up teens. However, fiction can spark interest in related nonfiction. For example, teens reading the *Sweep* series (Tiernan 2001+) may also reach for books on astrology, spells, and makeup. Teens reading the *Alex Rider* series (Horowitz 2001+) may also look for books on high tech and on martial arts.

Life skills nonfiction addresses some of the same issues as realistic young adult fiction, with books about identity, relationships, school, and the world beyond home and school. Personal interest nonfiction helps teens to pursue their interests and talents, with books on pop culture, sports, making things, and social issues. The appeal of popular nonfiction is that it relates to teens' real lives, and it tackles topics teens talk about with their friends. Often presented in short chapters and lots of pictures, teens can read these books in a few minutes at a time, between classes, waiting for a ride—the same way they read magazines.

By understanding the specific reading appeals of specific nonfiction topics, you will be better able to build and promote nonfiction book collections.

Self-Help

Reading Appeal: Teens are looking for answers to questions such as "Who am I? What do I want out of life? What's important to me? What's the right thing to do in this situation?" Self-help books are written in three formats. One format presents information and advice in essay and/or Q&A style, resembling a conversation with a caring adult. In a second format, real teens share their stories of challenge and hope. A third type of book offers quizzes, personality tests, and typologies, ranging from astrology to the Enneagram, which teens can ponder alone or share with friends.

These three nonfiction formats—guidance from adults, stories shared by peers, and information learned by teens themselves—appear in many categories of young adult nonfiction, but in no other category are they quite as pervasive as self-help books.

Examples: *Life Lists for Teens: Tips, Steps, Hints, and How-Tos for Growing Up, Getting Along, Learning, and Having Fun* (Espeland 2003), *Who Do You Think You Are? 12 Methods for Analyzing the True You* (Shaw 2001), and *Stay Strong: Simple Life Lessons for Teens* (Williams 2002).

Religion and Spirituality

Reading Appeal: As their minds and hearts open, teens begin to form personal values, ethics, and philosophies in which religious traditions and spiritual seeking may play a part. Religion also plays a role in teens' public lives. Debates and lawsuits have erupted over such issues as prayer at football games and graduation, prayer at flagpoles before class, the presence of the words "under God" in the Pledge of Allegiance, and the presence of Bible and other religious study groups on school property. Published books about Christianity and Judaism have been joined since the late 1950s by books about Buddhism and other Eastern religions, as well as Native American religions, and, more recently, Wicca and other prehistoric religions. Americans are also seeking to increase their understanding of Islam.

Examples: *Paths of Faith: Conversations about Religion and Spirituality* (Ford 2000), *Spiritualized: A Look Inside the Teenage Soul* (Healy 2000), and *Conversations with God for Teens* (Walsch 2001).

Physical Changes and Body Image

Reading Appeal: "Am I normal? Do I look okay?" For some teens, these questions have morphed into "Why can't I be perfect?" Body image is a big deal for many teens, because here's what's assailing them on a daily basis:

- unpredictable and uncontrollable physical changes (or not—another source of worry);
- self-consciousness due to exposure of physical changes in gym classes, locker rooms, and showers;
- media and peer drooling over buff young bodies;
- media hand-wringing over obese young bodies;
- peer sneering at obesity and other perceived physical imperfections;
- media pushing of high-fat, high-salt, and high-sugar processed foods;
- media pushing of "diets;" and
- fast food outlets, snacks, candy, and sugary soft drinks in schools and other teen-frequented locations.

Many teen magazine articles are about looking good. Books also offer help and hope.

Examples: *Born Beautiful: The African-American Teenager's Complete Beauty Guide* (Fornay 2002), *In Your Face: The Culture of Beauty and You* (Graydon 2004), *The Guy Book: An Owner's Manual for Teens* (Jukes 2002), and *Am I Weird or Is This Normal? Advice and Info to Get Teens in the Know* (Potash 2001).

Good Eats and Smart Moves

Reading Appeal: Quickie diets and exercise plans have been a staple of teen girl (and adult woman) magazines for decades. More recently, however, magazines and books for both girls and boys have emphasized nutrition and healthy eating over "diets," and a combination of aerobics, strength training, and stretching over "spot reducing."

Examples: *Teenage Fitness: Get Fit, Look Good, and Feel Great!* (Kaehler 2001) and *Fueling the Teen Machine* (Shanley and Thompson 2001).

Love and Sex

Reading Appeal: What do girls and guys ask their friends for advice about? What fills teen magazines and web sites? (Hint: It's not the SAT.) The appeal of books about love, sex, and sexual orientation is that teens can find out about sensitive topics in the privacy offered only by reading.

Examples: *GLBTQ: The Survival Guide for Queer and Questioning Teens* (Huegel 2003) and *Boyfriend Clinic: The Final Word on Flirting, Dating, Guys, and Love (Seventeen)* (Mannarino 2000).

Life Stories

Reading Appeal: Trying to figure out their own lives, teens can find inspiration in the lives of others, and their struggles, mistakes, setbacks, and triumphs.

Examples: *Geeks: How Two Lost Boys Rode the Internet Out of Idaho* (Katz 2001), *Soul Survivors: The Official Autobiography of Destiny's Child* (Knowles 2002), and *One Wild Ride: The Life of Skateboarding Superstar Tony Hawk* (Stewart 2002).

Family and Friends

Reading Appeal: While self-help books appeal to teens' need to understand themselves, books about family and friends appeal to their need to understand the primary people in their lives. Advice columns and articles in teen magazines cover similar topics: parents, siblings, family problems, best friends, cliques, and peer pressure.

Examples: *Can You Relate? Real-World Advice for Teens on Guys, Girls, Growing Up, and Getting Along* (Fox 2000) and *Pedro and Me: Friendship, Loss, and What I Learned* (Winick 2000).

School

Reading Appeal: As fifth or sixth graders, kids ruled elementary school. In middle school, suddenly everything is more complicated: classes, clubs, activities, and all those girls or all those boys.... Then it starts all over again in high school. Classes are more challenging, relationships are more complex, and then there's that "future" that adults are always yammering about. It helps to talk things over, but books offer help that is objective, disinterested, and private.

Examples: *Middle School, the Real Deal: From Cafeteria Food to Combination Locks* (Farrell and Mayall 2001), *Teenager's Guide to School Outside the Box* (Greene 2001), and *Super Study Skills: The Ultimate Guide to Tests and Studying* (Rozakis 2002).

What's Next? The Future

Reading Appeal: Eager, curious, and/or anxious about the future, teens may not realize just how much practical help they can get from books in the library. When these books are promoted to teens through displays or booktalking, teens check them out.

Examples: *101 Smart Questions to Ask on Your Interview* (Fry 2003), *Making the Most of College: Students Speak Their Minds* (Light 2001), and *Roadtrip Nation: Find Your Your Path in Life* (Marriner and Gebhard 2003).

Popular Culture

Reading Appeal: The appeal of books about popular culture is that they allow teens to explore contemporary music, movies, other entertainment media, and more.

Examples: *Reel Adventures: The Saavy Teen's Guide to Great Movies* (Lekich 2003), *Fast Food Nation: The Dark Side of the All-American Meal* (Schlosser 2001), and *Hip Hop Divas* (*Vibe* magazine 2001).

Sports

Reading Appeal: As athletes, friends of athletes, or spectators, many teens participate in sports. Playing on teams, they experience teamwork, camaraderie, and friendship. As individual athletes, they reach deep inside for their personal best. Teens are also curious about solo adventures: over the concrete on a skateboard, up a mountain face on spikes, and across the water on a surfboard or boat.

Examples: *Have Board, Will Travel: The Definitive History of Surf, Skate, and Snow* (Brisick 2004) and *Counting Coup: A True Story of Basketball and Honor on the Little Big Horn* (Colton 2000).

Fun Facts and Trivia

Reading Appeal: The biggest bug, the smallest gizmo, how to outrun killer bees—these books bulge with the fun facts that amaze and amuse teens.

Examples: *Book of Lists for Teens* (Choron and Choron 2002) and *Guinness Book of World Records* (Guinness 1963+).

Out There/Paranormal

Reading Appeal: The appeal of these books is that they confirm what every teen knows: things are not always what they seem. In fact, things are weird.

Examples: *Elements of Witchcraft: Natural Magick for Teens* (Dugan 2003), *That's Weird! Awesome Science Mysteries* (Haven 2001), and *Get Psychic! Discover Your Hidden Powers* (Wolf 2001).

Issues and Activism

Reading Appeal: While still influenced by family, other teens, and mass media, teens are beginning to think for themselves. Books on issues and activism help teens to explore the social, political, and environmental developments that impact their lives—and to find out how they can get involved. These books appeal to teens' growing empathy for others, and also to their expanding definition of themselves as citizens. Many high schools require students to perform community service, boosting the appeal of books on volunteering.

Examples: *Catch the Spirit: Teen Volunteers Tell How They Made a Difference* (Perry 2000), *With Their Eyes: September 11th: The View from a High*

School at Ground Zero (Thoms 2002), and *Teen Rights: A Legal Guide for Teens and the Adults in Their Lives* (Truly 2000).

Making Things

Reading Appeal: Thinking for themselves, teens are also eager to make things for themselves. The appeal of these books is that they foster the independence and self-reliance teens want and need.

Examples: *Manga Mania: How to Draw Japanese Comics* (Hart 2001), *Teen Feng Shui: Design Your Space, Design Your Life* (Levitt 2003), and *Crafty Girl: Slumber Parties* (Traig 2002).

In My Own Words

Reading Appeal: Forming their identities, building relationships with others, exploring the world: teens have a lot on their minds, and poetry and other forms of writing give teens ways to share their thoughts and feelings. The appeal of books written by teens is that they offer peer support as well as inspiration for teens' own writing.

Examples: *You Can Write Song Lyrics* (Cox 2000), *Teen Ink: Our Voices, Our Visions* (Meyer 2000), *YELL-OH Girls! Emerging Voices Explore Culture, Identity, and Growing Up Asian American* (Nam 2001), *Wachale! Poetry and Prose about Growing Up Latino in America* (Stavans 2001), and *Teen Angst? Naaah: A Quasi-Autobiography* (Vizzini 2000).

FINDING BOOKS
Talk with Teens

Just asking teens what kinds of books they like to read is a basic method for building collections. This is not exactly a news flash—like asking customers what products they like to buy—but it's worth repeating. Turn readers' advisory and reference conversations into opportunities for collection development. While helping a teen find more books to read for fun, ask what other types of books she likes, and does she usually find them at the library, or not. After finding information for a school project, ask, "So do you have any time to read stuff that you want to read? Read anything good lately?" Visiting schools to perform booktalks, take advantage of the natural opportunities to talk with teens about books they enjoy and would recommend. Talking about music and TV is also instructive. To many adults, contemporary rock music sounds angry and discordant, reflecting the shock of youth at discovering that life and the world are not the nice, orderly places they seemed to be when they were children. That shock is also the basis of much of realistic young adult fiction. On TV, both fictional and "reality" series address many of the same real-life challenges explored in young adult fiction and nonfiction.

Talk with Library Staff Members

As the young adult librarian, you are not the only staff member serving teens. Ask the rest of the library staff what types of books teens ask for and check out. Ask what types of books never seem to get checked out. Look at the young adult books on shelving carts. Shelve young adult books. Create and distribute a survey, asking library staff to evaluate the popularity of different types of young adult fiction and nonfiction among teens. During two successive summers I sent surveys about nonfiction and fiction to the twenty-seven libraries that make up Timberland Regional Library. Book categories resembled those delineated in this chapter's sections on fiction and nonfiction. I asked the youth services librarian at each library to rank each book category's popularity on a scale of one to four: high demand, popular, some interest, or marginal interest. I visited libraries, and we sat down and discussed teen reading interests and book titles. What emerged was a portrait of the reading interests of each library's teens, which I then combined into a portrait of the reading interests of teens throughout the library district.

While far from exact and scientific, the results did offer guidelines for collection development. Some staff members annotated their surveys with notes about books that were especially popular at their libraries. Under "Family," one librarian asked particularly for fiction about "abducted teens, teens who never came home, runaways on the street." Under "Animals," several librarians asked for fiction about teens and horses, while another added, "no more dead dogs, though." Humorous fiction was identified as "easy to sell."

Community

School media specialists and teachers are a great source of information about reading preferences of teens, whether the books are assigned, read for Accelerated Reader (AR) or another reading testing program, or freely chosen. Contact school media specialists to find out about assigned titles, and if reading testing programs are being used in their schools. If so, request a print copy of their test title list, and find out if the schools post their lists on their web sites. Check to ensure that your collection offers a sufficient and balanced representation of assigned or tested titles. School media specialists and teachers can also tell you what individual titles, or themes, genres, and nonfiction topics, are popular reading choices among their students.

Bookstore owners and employees can tell you what's popular with teen customers. While teen picks on Amazon.com and other bookselling web sites give some clues about national reading preferences, there's nothing like knowing what teens in your town are buying. Looking for graphic novel and manga guidance? Stop by your local comics bookstore and ask the staff what's popular with teen customers.

Magazine Content

By reading teen magazines' articles, columns, and personal narratives, you can pick up clues about teen interests, and use that information in building collections. *Teen People* addresses such topics as embarrassing moments, dating disasters, smoking, peer pressure, summer jobs, room decorations, and relationships with family members and friends. *Seventeen* also explores family, friends, and romance, as well as academic and athletic achievement. *Dirt Rider* focuses on dirt bike maintenance and moves, interviewing young riders about their dreams, disappointments, and achievements. A cruise through *GamePro* reveals high interest in computer games driven by action, whether the game's story is played out as adventure, crime, fantasy, horror, or science fiction. Humor is always identified by reviewers as an added value to any game. These are just a few examples. Whatever the magazines read by teens in your library, they will address teen interests that you can also meet in the book collection.

Resources and Reviews

Both collection development and readers' advisory resources—print and electronic—help young adult librarians to anticipate as well as respond to teen reading interests. The particular collection-building strength of readers' advisory resources is their emphasis on linking together books of similar appeal.

Check Amazon.com's teen page to find out what's flying off the warehouse shelves. Check web sites of local bookstores, both chain and independent. Books or web sites that include actual booktalks are good resources because, generally speaking, booktalkers focus their efforts on books they are fairly sure they can sell to teens. Collection development resources include book reviews, "best books" lists, and reference resources. For a list of the books referenced in this chapter, please see Appendix I. For a list of print and electronic resources and reviews, please see Appendix II.

Now that you're building up the collection, where are you going to put all of those books? In Chapter 4, we'll find space for books—and for reading.

REFERENCES AND SUGGESTED READINGS

Abramson, Marla. 2001. "Why Boys Don't Read." *Book*. (January/February): 86–88.

Beers, Kylene, and Teri Lesesne, eds. 2001. *Books for You: An Annotated Booklist for Senior High*. Urbana, IL: National Council of Teachers of English.

Carter, Betty. 2000. *Best Books for Young Adults*. Chicago: American Library Association.

Herald, Diana Tixier. 2003. *Teen Genreflecting: A Guide to Reading Interests*. Westport, CT: Libraries Unlimited.

Hunt, Peter, ed. 1995. *Children's Literature: An Illustrated History*. Oxford, UK: Oxford University Press.

Jones, Patrick. 2001. "Nonfiction: The Real Stuff." *School Library Journal*. (April): 44–45.

King, Stephen. 2000. *On Writing: A Memoir of the Craft*. New York: Scribner's.

Nichols, C. Allen, ed. 2004. *Thinking Outside the Book: Alternatives for Today's Teen Library Collections*. Westport, CT: Libraries Unlimited.

4

SPACE FOR BOOKS, SPACE FOR READING

By creating a teen space, your library tells teens that they have their own space in the library. By actively managing that space, your library communicates to teens that the teen space is not simply warehouse shelving for teen collections, but an integral part of library services.

All teen spaces have the potential, whatever their size, to promote reading and books to teens, by providing books, displays, such print promotions as booklists, and comfortable seating for reading.

A teen space is...

- a place to house teen collections;
- a place where teens can find and use teen collections;
- a place where teens can receive library services, and participate in activities and events;
- a place where teens can hang out by themselves or talk with a friend or two;
- a place where teens can study or work on school projects;
- a place where teens see library staff providing teen services (making displays, arranging books, posting fliers, adding bookmarks, etc.);

- a place where teens can talk with library staff; and ...
- a place where teens can read books.

Teen spaces vary in size and function, ranging from one shelving range of young adult materials to multipurpose spaces gleaming with neon lights, computers, chairs and sofas for reading and socializing, and listening and viewing stations. This chapter will focus on how you can use your teen space to promote reading and books to teens.

GOING PLACES

When they were kids, if teens wanted to go somewhere besides school, an adult had to take them. Dependent on adults for transportation to such places as parks, recreation centers, malls, places of worship, restaurants, and public libraries, they were also supervised by adults.

It's different now. By public transportation, bike, skateboard, foot, a friend's car, or their own car, teens are going places on their own, by themselves or with friends. Going to a place such as a restaurant, alone or with friends, signals teen independence (Sheridan 2003, 36). Free from adult supervision, teens are stretching their social muscles, finding things they need, and enjoying experiences they want.

While home serves as the first place for most people, and the workplace as second, sociologist Ray Oldenburg (1989, 16) identified the locale that is conducive to unstructured activity and conversation as the "third place." People gather in the third place by choice, not because it's required. Sitting around and talking on park benches or in coffeehouses, bookstores, and other gathering places, people meet on neutral ground, free of the definitions and restrictions of home or the workplace. Good conversation rules: bores and bullies are not tolerated. Some people become "regulars" for a time, before they move on and are replaced by new regulars. Third places are also the traditional refuge of the artist. What writer—teen or adult—hasn't sighed with longing at the thought of scribbling in a café in Paris (Hemingway 1964) or Taos, New Mexico (Goldberg 1990)?

The teen space in a public library has the potential to be just such a third place. It's not home. It's not school, that is, the teen workplace. For some teens, the public library is an extension of the workplace, where they go to get materials for school projects. Or they've been told by their parents to go to the public library after school. Still, for many teens, the public library is a place where they gather because they want to be there. Teens can encounter one another on neutral ground, away from their identification with particular schools or cliques, as noted by a teen who frequents Teen Central at the Phoenix Public Library (Kendall 2003, 380). They can enjoy the library as a physical space where all people are welcome. And despite the decentralization of information storage and the expansion of entertainment media, there's just no substitute for going to the library to talk with friends and to look at books and magazines. Libraries and teen spaces are not sanctuaries set apart from their communities and its problems (Bernier 2003, 198–199). But for many people of all ages and interests, the public library continues to be "an island of tranquility, balance, sanity, and reason... the entrance to other worlds, thoughts, times, and minds" (Kniffel 1999, 34).

The teen space meets a community need. Many after-school programs and recreation facilities do a good job in offering activities that are planned, structured, result-oriented, and adult-directed, such as homework help, sports, and opportunities in the arts. The teen space offers unplanned, spontaneous, open-ended, and teen-determined activities, such as sitting around talking with friends or playing cards or board games. While maintaining family relationships, teens are also expanding their social circle, with friends, acquaintances, and boyfriends or girlfriends. Friends do things together, including going places in groups (Vaillancourt 2000, 6). Many teen spaces, therefore, feature tables for group study, work on shared projects, or board games, and lounge seating for relaxation and conversation. And because groups of people of any age tend to generate more noise than the same number of self-contained individuals, a teen space can keep teen energy focused and contained, lessening its impact on other library users (Jones 1998, 34).

But let's not forget that teens are individuals, too. In fact, the teen years are first and foremost a time for asking, "Who am I?" and developing an identity (36). In order to develop an identity, a person needs time alone—to think, to dream, to feel—independent of the opinion and judgment of others, including friends. "YAs need not so much physical space, as psychological space. The most basic thing any library can provide is a place for people to sit and think. Sometimes that is all a YA really needs and wants from us—a place for time alone" (37).

It is important to plan for the space needs of teens who visit the library by themselves. Teens' weekdays are spent in public spaces with groups of teens: school bus, school, streets, stores, parks, and recreation centers. All day long, they are herded into group activities, judged by peers, and graded by school personnel. They are constantly told to use their time "constructively," that is, in structured, adult-directed activities such as school, sports, service or academic clubs, music practice, and the like.

After school, some teens can go home, to a private space, their own space. Many cannot, and must remain in shared public spaces until late afternoon or early evening. Some teens who visit the library every day after school are not allowed to be at home alone. Other teens would rather not be at home. Maybe it's noisy, with younger brothers and sisters, blaring TV, and busy adults. And so there are teens who are looking for a little peace and quiet after the nonstop noise of school all day, a break from the constant aural and visual stimulation, a respite for the requirement to be "on stage" for others. The public library can be a place that offers quiet and privacy. Teens can leaf through magazines, check their e-mail, study, write in their journals, draw, listen to music through headphones, read, or just stare out the window without anybody telling them to do something else. It's okay for teens to be by themselves sometimes. Being alone does not make a teen an outcast, a depressive, a loser, a failure, or a future suicide or killer. In the quiet of a comfortable chair or study carrel, teens can hear themselves think. And because they can think, they can better become themselves: independent and free human beings, not simply members of a group called "teens." And it is in the quiet space that teens can read.

VISIBILITY

Walk into your library through the front door. Can you see where the teen space is located? Can you see the space itself, or its sign, or a sign directing patrons to different spaces in the library? Just where is your teen space?

Adults assume that the public library is set up to accommodate their reading and information interests. They may grimace at the long waiting list for a bestseller, or maybe the library isn't updating its computer manual collection frequently enough for their needs. But it doesn't occur to adults who use public libraries that there might not be books and other collections for adults, and places around the library to look at them.

Similarly, children brought to the public library by parents or by other adults learn that the library dedicates spaces, collections, staff members, activities, and events to children. The children's space can be the largest specialized space in the public library, clearly marked by such indicators as brightly colored signs, bookshelves, murals, bulletin boards, big stuffed animals, and computers. Adults and library staff help younger children choose materials, while older children find materials on their own.

Like adults, teens use collections and equipment located all over the library—reference books, adult fiction, adult nonfiction, magazines, audio and visual materials, computers—as well as study spaces at tables and individual carrels. Like children, teens use collections unique to them: young adult fiction, nonfiction, and magazines. Unlike adults and children, however, teens walking into the library for the first time may not assume there's a space designated to meet their needs and interests. So it's important that they see either the teen space itself, or a sign, from the front door, and ideally, from multiple points in the building.

Visible from multiple points in libraries, neon signs have become a popular choice, as documented in the "YA Spaces of Your Dreams" articles appearing each month in *Voice of Youth Advocates*:

- **"Teen Lounge"** glows yellow, white, and green in the corner of the teen space of the Pinellas Park Public Library in Pinellas Park, Florida (Hollingsworth 2002, 178).
- A blue-green neon sign proclaiming **"teens"** lets teens know that they have their own space in the Scott County Public Library in Georgetown, Kentucky (Burnside 2003, 32).

Also, imaginative lighting distinguishes the second-floor Teen Lounge in the L. E. Phillips Memorial Library in Eau Claire, Wisconsin. Colored sheaths cover all the lightbulbs, creating a special glow that attracts teens (Tvaruzka 2003, 294).

LOCATION, LOCATION, LOCATION

In real estate, the three most desirable characteristics of a house or commercial building are location, location, and location.

The question of where to locate the teen space mirrors one of the inner conflicts of teen life, between teens' new need for independence and their continuing need for inclusion. Teens are seeking out and testing independence. At the same time, their rapidly developing social radar is quick to tell them when they are not being included. A remote location in the middle of nowhere meets teens' need for a room of their own. But if the teen space is located in nowheresville, how easily can they find materials shelved elsewhere in the library? Or computers? Or the librarians for assistance? Or bathrooms?

The ideal location encompasses as many of the following characteristics as possible:

- Visible from the front door, whether by location or signage
- Near public service desks, or within sight lines
- Near computers
- Near nonfiction collection
- Near reference collection
- Near adult fiction collection
- Away from quiet reading area
- Away from large print area
- Away from children's space

Teens queried about library services in a study conducted between November 1998 and May 1999 named "a place of our own" as a desirable feature of a public library (Meyers 1999, 44). In the same survey, some teens complained that library staff members sometimes ignore them. Locating the teen space near public service desks, or at least within sight lines, allows teens to seek and get assistance more easily. This proximity also balances teens' enjoyment of their space as a third place with the library's need to not let the teen space mutate into a private party zone (Taney 2003, 9).

Think about the other collection and service spaces in the library that teens are most likely to use, when choosing a location for the teen space. A teen space adjacent to computers makes it easier for teens to check e-mail, find and print articles from databases, find books and other materials, and type up reports. A teen space located near the reference collection facilitates its use for school assignments, and also offers interesting collection promotion possibilities. For example, you can create displays that promote such teen-appeal reference resources as college, university, and trade school directories and catalogs, and job and career resources. Add such materials as educational loan applications, job application worksheets, and pathfinders about education and career databases and web sites. Serving as a transitional space between the teen space and the rest of the library, the reference collection, tables, and chairs show how teens' growing real-life information needs can be met by the library.

A teen space adjacent to the audiovisual, adult fiction, and adult nonfiction collections makes it easier for teens to browse for materials. Some libraries feature listening stations in the teen space. Others may have found it prudent to locate audiovisual collections and listening stations within the immediate view of staff in order to discourage theft by adults and/or teens. Proximity to adult fiction collections makes it easier for teens to browse for fantasy, science fiction, thrillers, romance, mysteries, and other teen-appeal adult books, while proximity to adult nonfiction facilitates finding books that address educational, informational, and personal interest needs.

Inadvisable adjacent locations include the quiet reading area, large print area, and children's space. In the quiet reading area, there are people—including teens—who are trying to read, and are sitting in there because it provides an oasis of old-time library quiet. Patrons browsing quietly for books in the large print area are not compatible with teens unwinding after being in school all day. When it comes to proximity to the children's space, teens have cited the presence of noisy children as a reason they avoid going to the public library (Meyers 1999, 44). Moreover, teens do not want to be thought of as children themselves (Vaillancourt 2000, 31). Teens want and need their own space as they move away from childhood. A teen space located away from the children's space—even around a corner—meets the needs of all library users.

There is an advantage to a teen space that is a bit remote from other library activity centers. In a remote location, teen cafes, focus groups, book discussion groups, open mic readings, and booktalk events present minimized disturbance to other library users. Another advantage is that there are teens who feel more comfortable attending events in a teen space—with porous borders—than events in a meeting room. They can wander near the teen space and participate on the edges, rather than having to venture all the way into a meeting room, with no way of escaping without everybody looking at them.

Wherever the teen space is located, it is desirable to take into account its multiple uses by teens, and the best way to keep the area acoustically separated yet not isolated from the rest of the library.

INSIDE THE TEEN SPACE
Floor Plan

Following the signs, teens find themselves inside the teen space, which ideally appears to have been created just for them (Taney 2003, 8). Everything in the space should say *teen*: collections, displays, furniture, décor, posters, fliers, bookmarks, and electronics. It's okay (and desirable) to mix in a few young-20s items, such as posters for music or arts festivals or sports events, because they advertise the milieu to which teens aspire. (Posters for local events for 10-year-olds are best displayed on general-interest bulletin boards, or in the children's space.)

Teen spaces come in many shapes and sizes. Floor plans include circles, squares, oblongs, and elongated serpentines. What successful floor plans have in common is their ability to support the multiple functions of a teen space in a cohesive fashion, that is, to store books, to promote books, and to facilitate reading.

Shelving

Shelving serves to store and display books. Shelving can also be used to define the borders of the teen space, by serving as walls. The side of the wall facing into the teen space houses teen collections, while the outward-facing side houses other collections.

The amount of shelving available to the teen space influences the number of collections that will fit into it. In some libraries, the size of the teen space and the amount of shelving are large enough that they can house and display all types of teen collections: young adult fiction, teen magazines, young adult nonfiction, young adult books recorded on CDs and audiocassettes, and DVDs and videos. In other libraries, the size of the teen space and the amount of shelving oblige young adult librarians to trim collections down to print only, or fiction and magazines only, or fiction only. If the teen space is not large enough to house all teen collections, it is important to tell teens where other teen collections are located and describe how to get there. If the collection is just outside the teen space, a few words will suffice. Another option is to create a poster of the library floor plan with a YOU ARE HERE icon in the teen space, and signs or arrows indicating the location of other collections, such as CDs. Such a poster accomplishes three objectives: (1) it helps teens find what they're looking for; (2) it shows that the teen space is linked to the rest of the library; and (3) it tells teens that the library cares enough about their needs to anticipate them.

Whatever the amount of shelving, shift or weed collections to free up space for face-out displays of books at the end of each shelf. If you have limited shelf space, shift and weed so you can use the eye-level shelf on each shelving range for face-out displays.

Furniture

Many teen spaces are large enough to include tables and chairs for groups of teens. Other teen spaces are small.

Once only study tables, hardback chairs, study carrels, and maybe a lounge chair or two sat in the teen space. They've been joined by teen-painted study tables, round coffeehouse-style tables, low living room–style tables, and end tables. Seating options include rock-back chairs, bean bags, floor rockers, comfortable chairs, sofas, and modular sofas. The proliferation of furniture styles reflects the library's recognition of the many ways in which teens use the library. To the uses of the library for solitary study or reading have been added the group activities of socializing, group study, music and video enjoyment, computer use, activities, and events.

Comfortable chairs tell teens that the teen space is not simply an after-school study hall. It's also a place to sit down, relax, and read for pleasure. If the teen space is so small that it has room for only one piece of furniture, make it a comfortable reading chair, with enough room next to it so teens can drop a backpack without blocking access. After all, if you want to promote reading, you need to make it physically possible. Add an end table, and you've created the same comfortable arrangement that teens encounter in other public spaces, such as bookstores, dentists' offices, and the teen spaces described in "YA Spaces of Your Dreams" articles:

- Three overstuffed chairs upholstered in the same blue-violet and gold colors glowing from the **Young Adults** neon sign cluster around two round end tables in the Young Adults Area at the Orrville Public Library in Orrville, Ohio (Lombardo 2002, 426).
- Two coffee tables and four comfortable chairs range along windows in the **Teen Lounge** at the L. E. Phillips Memorial Public Library in Eau Claire, Wisconsin (Tvaruzka 2003, 294).

Fixtures

Books, a comfortable chair, room on the floor for a backpack, an end table . . . What else do teens need for reading? Good light! To find out if there's enough light for teens to read, grab some books of various print sizes and some teen magazines, and sit down to read in different places in the teen space, between 2:15 p.m. and closing. During the afternoon, depending on the location of the teen space, the square footage of nearby windows, and the time of year, the combination of indirect sunlight and overhead artificial light may be sufficient. When natural light is in short supply due to the time of day or year—or nonexistent, in teen spaces located far from windows—the work of lighting the teen space shifts entirely to overhead artificial light, commonly fluorescent lamps. However, a floor lamp or a table lamp placed on an end table will help to make up for the light deficit (Lushington 2002, 175–179) and will add more atmosphere than institutional-style ceiling light fixtures. If you can read easily and without strain at different times of the day, chances are good that teens will be able to read, too.

Don't forget to get teen input. If teens ask you, "What are you doing?" tell them that you're testing the light for reading. And then ask, "Is there enough light for you to read in here? How about at night?" If they don't ask what you're doing, take the initiative and ask them about the light. By asking teens for their input, you will not only find out about lighting, but will also be showing teens that the library cares enough about facilitating their use of the library to ask them their opinion.

Fixtures for promoting reading and books include bulletin boards, wall poster holders, sign holders, book easels, and literature holders, all of which will be described in more detail in Chapter 5.

KEEP IT CLEAN

Try to avoid the perceived extremes of neglect by library staff and nonuse by teens, by keeping the teen space clean—and then mussing it up a little.

Periodically, remove the collections and printed materials, and dust and clean the shelves and fixtures. Put the books and printed materials back, create a book display, refill all printed material holders, and push the chairs up to the tables. The teen space looks cared for. Now muss it up a little. Pull some shelf ends to the right in order to create a few gaps on the shelves, as though some books have been checked out. Remove a few books from the book display, and don't replace them. Remove some of the booklists from their holders and drop one or two on an end table. Pull out a chair and angle it slightly away from the table. Make it look as though teens actually use the teen space.

Ever go apartment or house hunting? When you walk into an apartment or a house and like it, you might not notice details. Instead, you get an overall first impression. "This is clean, comfortable, but not uptight. There's stuff here, but it doesn't look cluttered. It looks like people live here. I could live here." When a teen walks into your teen space, he might not notice details. Instead, he gets an overall first impression. "This is clean, comfortable, but not uptight. There's stuff here, but it doesn't look like a mess. It looks like teens hang out here. I could hang out here."

So keep the teen space clean—but not antiseptic. The worst impression teens can receive is that the teen space has been ignored. Dust has congealed into grime. The books are old, faded, in bad shape, with loser covers. A few lonely bookmarks rattle around in a literature holder. One poster clings to a pockmarked bulletin board. There are few signs of teen life. The second worst impression teens can receive is that the teen space is so manicured to perfection that no teen ever touches a book or sits down to read it. A faint smell of cleanser hangs in the air. The books look as though they've never been taken off the shelf. Every literature holder is crammed to the gagging point with booklists and bookmarks that nobody has picked up. Posters and fliers cover the bulletin board in rigid geometric lines. There are few signs of teen life.

SPACE FOR READING
Reading in the Teen Space

The presence of a few comfortable chairs in the teen space promotes reading. When the library stocks bookmarks, it's easier for readers to mark their place in their books. Think of the times that you have wandered into the teen space and found two or three teens studying at a table, and one or two other teens reading in comfortable chairs. The studying teens may be talking, but the reading teens are able to tune them out. After all, it's a lot quieter in the teen space than anywhere else they've been all day long—except perhaps the school library.

Reading Outside the Teen Space

Then again, if one or two groups of teens have taken over the teen space, teens will look for other places in the library to read, where it's quiet and where they'll feel comfortable and safe. Good places to read include the quiet reading area (a space sometimes assumed to be of interest only to adults), comfortable chairs scattered around the library, and study carrels. Many bookstores divide their floor space into discrete subject areas, using shelving to create cozy corners furnished with comfortable

Comfortable chairs for reading outside the TeenZone at
Tumwater Timberland Library.

chairs so that customers can sit down and read. Libraries that follow the
model of creating quiet, private spaces within large, public spaces are
promoting reading by making it physically possible.

Besides bookstores, another good model to follow is the school library,
which ideally combines comfortable chairs, windows, natural light, plants,
private study carrels, and "a quiet hum of human activity" (Bush 2003,
438). Public libraries are public places, not safe havens. Anyone can walk
in, including adults who bother teens and teens who target other teens. By
reading within sight and sound of other library service areas, teens know
that they are not isolated and vulnerable. The quiet hum reassures teens
that other people are nearby. That quiet hum is the sound of the third
place.

Ask teens which are good places to read in the library, and what makes
them good? Make sure that teens know you're interested in making space
for them to read wherever they like, in the teen space and elsewhere in the
library.

Look, an Adult—Reading a Book!

While walking around the library, observe adults. They are variously hunched over computer screens, standing at the photocopier, picking up tax and other brochures, looking for children's books, cruising the new books shelves, trawling the shelving trucks for just-returned DVDs and videos, standing at checkout, and so on. Maybe a few adults are taking a break from the frenetic pace of twenty-first-century life and are actually sitting down, reading books.

Here's a way you and other library staff can promote reading: by showing teens—and everybody else in the library—that adults read, too. Spend a few afternoon work breaks a week reading a book, not hidden away in the staff lounge, but out there in the library where you can be seen. It's true that a library patron—an adult, a teen, or a child—might see you and ask for assistance. That's why it's advisable to limit your public space reading; we need our breaks from library work. There will also be times when library patrons will see you but will leave you alone, *because you are reading a book.* I know that this suggestion runs counter to a concern about a public perception that all library staff members do all day is sit around and read. But to show teens that people do read books, take a risk and be seen reading.

Reading expert David Bouchard (2003, 63) makes the point that public school administrators need to become readers themselves if they are to truly influence the parents and teachers who want children and teens to read. He advocates such practices as presenting short booktalks at staff meetings, inviting local dignitaries to read aloud in classrooms, and instituting Sustained Silent Reading (SSR). By reading out in the library where you can be seen, you're showing teens that SSR is not just a school thing. It is a life thing.

CREATING TEEN SPACES

There are many ways to promote reading and books in teen spaces, whatever their size.

Let's say all you have is one bookcase housing teen fiction and some teen nonfiction. That's it. No floor space, no wall space, no furniture, no nothing. Weed the fiction and weed or relocate the nonfiction, and shift the collection so that you can remove a couple of shelves at eye level. Now you have a promotional space. In the center of the shelf, place a half-sheet poster ($5\frac{1}{2} \times 8\frac{1}{2}$") in a poster holder that reads something like, "Teens!

Finding what you're looking for? If not, please ask the library staff at the (location of your service desks)." This poster establishes a link among teens, collections, and staff. It communicates to teens that teen services are not limited to simply warehousing some teen books in a bookcase. Fill the rest of the space with bookmarks, booklists, and brochures in literature holders, and one or two face-outs of teen fiction with colorful, attention-grabbing covers.

If you have two or three bookcases, you have more room for display space. Create a bulletin board space by weeding and/or relocating collections and removing two or three shelves from the bookcases to create a promotional space in the center of the shelves. Get some foamboard, cover it with bulletin board paper, and tape it into place from behind using sturdy book tape. Now you have a bulletin board.

If you have a corner or other floor space, add furniture and fixtures, such as a comfortable chair or two, a small round coffeehouse-style table, two chairs, a poster, a reading lamp, maybe a plant. Choose a teen-appeal poster, featuring a teen celebrity or other reasonably cool individual. Periodically replace the poster, as teen celebrities can quickly become so five minutes ago.

Teen spaces are not and should not be static. This is not simply a question of replacing a teen celebrity poster. Book collections grow, magazine collections grow, other collections join them, reading promotions expand. Things change. Ideally, the teen space changes, too. Working with your existing floor space, shelving, furniture, promotional areas, and collections, there are ways to keep the teen space responsive to changing needs.

GENRE LABELS AND SHELVING

"Do you have any good mysteries?"

"Where're the fantasy books?"

"I just want some action adventure."

Help teens find books they want to read by adding genre spine labels to books. Help teens find those books quickly by shelving titles by genre, like genre sections in a bookstore. Genre spine labels are available from Demco, Gaylord, and other supply companies.

Deciding to shelve titles in a genre together may be influenced by the size of your YA collection, and whether or not it is possible in your library to create new young adult fiction collection codes. Ideally, when teens find a book in the catalog, the location is given as YA-FIC-MYSTERY-AUTHOR, instead of YA-FIC-AUTHOR. If the location code includes the genre, teens can go right to the relevant shelving section. If it does not include the genre, teens will need to know something about the book, so that they can guess where it is shelved, and keep looking if they don't get the right section the first time. Teens who want to browse for titles in their favorite genre prefer genre shelving. Teens looking for specific titles recommended by friends, and who look them up in the catalog, may prefer alphabetical-by-author shelving. Organize your YA titles according to the way best supported by your catalog and according to the way teens usually look for books.

Here's a way to genre-label a young adult fiction collection and sort it into genre sections. Start at "A," weed worn books, and sort titles into genres onto book trucks. Keep realistic fiction on the shelf, shifting those titles to the left. They will eventually form their own section, which you might call "Realistic Fiction: Issues and Challenges." Recruit teen volunteers to help fix genre labels on the book spines, secured with clear label protectors. When the books go back up on the shelves, they'll look new, because you've simultaneously weeded out the ragged-looking books, and affixed colorful genre labels to the spines. In order to fit the genre collections back on your shelves, however, you may need to intershelve some related genres together. Whether devoted to one genre or intershelving two or three related genres, within each shelving range or series of shelves, shelving is alphabetical by author.

Here's how it worked out at Tumwater Timberland Library:

Genre Shelving, Stage One

Ranges 1–2:	Everyday Life
Range 3:	Mystery, Suspense, and Horror
Range 4:	Romance (top three shelves)
	Humor (fourth shelf)
	Classics (fifth shelf)
	Short Stories (sixth shelf)
Range 5:	Fantasy, Fairy Tales, and Science Fiction
Range 6:	Adventure and Historical Fiction
Range 7:	Teen Magazines
Range 8:	Teen Magazines
Range 9:	Bulletin Board and Printed Materials

Genre Shelving, Stage Two

Ranges 1–3:	Everyday Life
Range 4:	Adventure (top two shelves)
	Classics (third shelf)
	Fairy Tales and Graphic Novels (fourth shelf)
	Humor (fifth shelf)
	Short Stories (sixth shelf)
Range 5:	Fantasy and Science Fiction
Range 6:	Historical Fiction
Range 7:	Mystery, Suspense, and Horror
Range 8:	New Fiction (shelves 1–3)
	Romance (shelves 4–6)

Two years later, the young adult fiction shelves were bulging. We wanted to keep the fiction collection together. So we moved the magazine collection around the corner to a wall that was visible from the teen space. We replaced the magazine slant-shelving with regular shelving, and shifted the genre collections into their new space.

As mentioned above, while some teens liked the genre shelving, others didn't. They'd hear about a great book from a friend, but because they didn't know the genre, they couldn't find it and walked out without the book. For this and other reasons, we decided to return the collection to an alphabetical-by-author shelving sequence. Because we've retained genre labeling, teens can still pick out books of the type they like to read. And because the young adult fiction is intershelved, teens can also make discoveries outside of their reading preferences.

With a teen space for reading and books, there's room for displays. In the next chapter, we'll look at ways to promote reading and books through displays in the teen space, and throughout the library.

REFERENCES AND SUGGESTED READINGS

Bernier, Anthony. 2003. "A Library Director Speaks Out: The Case against Libraries as 'Safe Places.'" *Voice of Youth Advocates.* (August): 198–199.

Bouchard, David. 2003. "Improve Student Literacy: Pick Up a Book and Read." *Teacher Librarian.* (February): 63.

Burnside, Patti. 2003. "YA Spaces of Your Dreams." *Voice of Youth Advocates.* (April): 32–33.

Bush, Gail. 2003. "Safe Haven." *Voice of Youth Advocates.* (February): 438–439.

Goldberg, Natalie. 1990. *Wild Mind: Living the Writer's Life.* New York: Bantam Books.

Hemingway, Ernest. 1964. *A Moveable Feast.* New York: Charles Scribner's Sons.

Hollingsworth, Arline. 2002. "YA Spaces of Your Dreams." *Voice of Youth Advocates.* (August): 178–179.

Jones, Patrick. 1998. *Connecting Young Adults and Libraries: A How-to-Do-It Manual.* New York: Neal-Schuman Publishers.

Kendall, Karl. 2003. "YA Spaces of Your Dreams." *Voice of Youth Advocates.* (October): 380–381.

Kniffel, Leonard. 1999. "Soothing Words Often Begin with 'L.'" *American Libraries.* (November): 34.

Lombardo, Cindy. 2002. "YA Spaces of Your Dreams." *Voice of Youth Advocates.* (February): 426–427.

Lushington, Nolan. 2002. *Libraries Designed for Users: A 21st Century Guide.* New York: Neal-Schuman Publishers.

Meyers, Elaine. 1999. "The Coolness Factor: Ten Libraries Listen to Youth." *American Libraries.* (November): 42–45.

Oldenburg, Ray. 1989. *The Great Good Place: Cafes, Coffee Shops, Community Centers, Beauty Parlors, General Stores, Bars, Hangouts, and How They Get You through the Day.* New York: Paragon House.

Sheridan, Margaret. 2003. "Mad Cool: Appealing to 21st Century Teens Begins by Understanding Their World." *Restaurants and Institutions.* (June 15): 35–38.

Taney, Kimberly Bolan. 2003. *Teen Spaces: The Step-by-Step Library Makeover.* Chicago: American Library Association.

Tvaruzka, Kati. 2003. "YA Spaces of Your Dreams." *Voice of Youth Advocates.* (October): 294–295.

Vaillancourt, Renee J. 2000. *Bare Bones Young Adult Services: Tips for Public Library Generalists.* Chicago: American Library Association.

5

✧◈✧ ✧◈✧ ✧◈✧

ON SALE NOW! CREATING BOOK DISPLAYS AND BULLETIN BOARDS

Previous chapters about reading, merchandising, collections, and library spaces have filled in the background on promoting books to teens. With this chapter, you're stepping into the foreground. It's time to start moving the inventory, by creating book displays and bulletin boards that grab teens' attention and keep their interest. You do not have to have a degree in design or art in order to make aesthetically pleasing displays. In fact, you probably know more about design principles and design elements than you think, simply by having been alive long enough to absorb the pattern and harmony of the world around you. You already recognize attractive and effective displays when you see them in stores, museums, trade shows, and other venues. By examining such topics as the reasons why displays work, how to plan and locate displays, design principles and elements, and display fixtures, you'll learn more about *how* they work, and will be better able to create your own promotions—with a big boost from your own love of young adult books and your caring for teens. And like everything else, methods of visual communication are always changing, and so the chapter concludes with some suggestions on how to keep visually up-to-date.

WHY DISPLAYS WORK

Few people have the time, interest, or stamina to examine every piece of clothing on every rack, every CD in every bin, or every electronic gizmo on every shelf. Some teens do, but most do not. Teens are busy. And they don't all own cars and so they are not all in control of their own transportation. Unlike children brought to the library by their parents or caregivers, or adults on their own schedules, teens may not always have the time to browse the collection for books at their leisure. First they have to study or do research. Then they have to catch the bus or subway, or be ready to be picked up by a parent after work.

And as noted by Sharon L. Baker (1986, 315–329), readers' advisory and collection management expert, library users can become overwhelmed by the array of choices available to them. They see so many books that they don't want to look at any of them. Displays are welcome oases in a desert of a zillion grains of sand, and if the library is so small that it has no room for a separate teen space, displays show teens that the library offers collections and services just for them (Nichols 2002, 73).

There are four basic reasons to create displays of young adult books.

First, displays are a quick way for teens to find good books. Maybe they need a good book, quickly, and an eye-grabbing display gives them what they need—fast. Or maybe they weren't looking for a book at all, but saw a display, and the impulse-shopping response kicked in.

Second, books on display speak for your entire collection. Convince teens that the library has plenty of good books to read by putting *really* good books on display, because those books will project quality onto the rest of the collection.

Third, the very creation of displays signals that library staff members are working for teens. The importance of service made visible cannot be overemphasized. Everything we do—or don't do—communicates a message. Teens walk into libraries and see big, colorful book displays and bulletin boards for children. The "new books" display is for adults. Why would teens think that the library has anything for them? Displays communicate the message that the library cares about teens.

The fourth reason to create displays is to increase your knowledge of the collection. Finding books, skimming back-jacket blurbs, and arranging books in displays all build up your knowledge of your collection, for readers' advisory services and collection management. For example, while pulling books off the shelf for an adventure display, you may come across just the right mystery for that teen boy who told you how much he likes mysteries. Now you have another book to tell him about. When you looked for romances to put in a display, all you found were a few dozen tattered series paperbacks. Now you know that you need to rebuild the genre, by replacing well-read titles and buying new titles.

PLANNING DISPLAYS

You know you should put some books on display. But you never seem to have enough time, so you fall into the what's-for-dinner-there's-nothing-in-the-fridge panic, and just like grabbing any old thing off the super-market shelves you're grabbing any old thing off the young adult fiction shelves. You know you should freshen up the bulletin board. But you never seem to have enough time. And now you realize that the blue butcher paper has been covering the bulletin board for months, it's faded, and it's riddled with pushpin holes, so you race around and look for a poster, any poster—anything to fill up the space.

Scheduling Displays

Instead of waiting for inspiration to strike, schedule displays in advance on the master calendar where you schedule programs, school visits, meetings, and so on. There are three types of book displays you can schedule:

- Ongoing displays of new books, teen-recommended books, "good books," or materials not shelved in the teen space, such as adult nonfiction, CDs, DVDs, and videos
- Short-term displays of books that relate to a nonfiction topic or a fiction theme
- Short-term displays of books that relate to a library event, community event, media or entertainment event, the school year, the seasons, and the like

Plan to have at least two displays up at all times: one ongoing, and the other short-term. Two displays double the probability that teens will find something to read. If they ignore the ongoing display, maybe they'll glance at the short-term display, and vice versa. For example, a summer reading display will be up from mid-June through the end of August. During the summer, short-term displays promoting such upcoming events as journal-writing workshops, book discussion groups, and art workshops will be up for two to three weeks.

If you've scheduled a school visit, schedule a follow-up book display made up of the books you booktalked, copies of your booklist handout, and a poster declaring, "Hey! I heard about that book at school!" with a graphic of an astonished teen. Keep the display up for two or three weeks.

Perhaps you've scheduled a journal-writing workshop for the twentieth of the month. Schedule a display to go up on the seventh. Include workshop handouts and journal-writing materials: books, CD-ROMS, and the like. Leave it up until the twenty-seventh, giving teens who were unable to attend the workshop a chance to find materials on the topic. No school visits or events coming up? Schedule book displays, for example, "Theme display: Fantasy" on the first and "Topic display: Music Biographies" on the sixteenth. No schedule is set in stone. If you suddenly get a great idea and are inspired to whip up a display on something, great. If teens are suddenly talking about an issue, a movie, or something else, respond to that interest. Be spontaneous. In the meantime, plan for having no time to be spontaneous by being spontaneous in advance. By actively planning displays in advance rather than reactively throwing them together, you will be able to create more displays, promote more areas of the teen book collection, and thus promote books to more teens.

Short-term displays stay fresh by virtue of their two to three week duration. With ongoing displays, remember that the point is to display the books, not warehouse them. If teens see the same old fading wallflowers week after week, they'll receive an impression of stasis that they can project onto the entire library collection—and staff members. So change those books before their expiration date, or they'll spoil the rest of the collection!

Display Locations

While the premiere location for display of teen books is the teen space, teens also spend time in other areas of the library. In fact, they may never reach the teen space. They may stop at the information desk on their way in, continue on to the computer area or study table area, walk back to the rest rooms and drinking fountain, and then stop at the circulation desk on their way out the front door. They may gather in the foyer waiting for a ride or for the bus, with not much to do except stand around.

Anywhere teens stop can be used as a display location. By creating displays of teen books in these additional locations, you can "cross-merchandise" teen materials (Nichols 2002, 53). Moreover, seeing teen books on display outside of the teen space tells teens—and other library users—that service to teens is an integral part of the library's service, rather than a tacked-on "extra" confined to one area of the library. And while the focus of this book is on promoting reading and books to teens, alerting parents and other adults about teen services reinforces that effort.

Display locations include the following:

- *Public service desks.* Place a teen book in a book easel, next to a poster holder describing it as the "Teen Book of the Day." Change the book daily, and replace it if a teen checks it out.

- *Computer space.* Create a display of books, magazines, and CD-ROMs about computer programs, codes, the Internet, and the like. Or create a display of just one book or magazine next to a poster holder listing all of the library's computer magazines.

- *Audiovisual collections.* Place several CD or audiocassette recordings of teen books in display holders next to a poster holder asking, "Teens: Heard any good books lately?"

- *Reference space.* Create displays that feature materials relevant to the reason why teens are sitting at study tables. A "Study Smarts" display highlights books on study skills, reading improvement, term paper writing, and test preparation. A "Going to College" display includes guides to choosing colleges, college catalogs, and financial aid applications. A "Get a Job" display features books on resume writing and workplace success, DVDs and videos on interview skills, brochures on your state's labor laws for youth, and suggestions for where to find jobs in the community.

Change the books' location codes from ON SHELF to DISPLAY TEEN SPACE, DISPLAY INFORMATION DESK, DISPLAY CDs, and so on. This means that if a library patron or staff member looks up a book in the catalog, he or she can see the location, and find the book.

Displays should be located in spaces that allow teens to stop and look at the books without feeling crowded or rushed. A good rule of thumb is to place small displays in small spaces and big displays in big spaces. Place small displays at public service desks, where teens wait for service. Place large displays in large spaces, away from traffic flow and with plenty of space around them. Unlike service desk locations, there is no reason to stop in a large space with a display, except to look at the display, and so the display needs to grab teens' attention, with backdrops, posters, theme-related objects, and colorful books.

THEY SEE IT BEFORE THEY READ IT

Teens see a book display or bulletin board from a distance before they're close enough to look at the books or read the posters. They will first experience a display or bulletin board in purely visual terms, as a cohesive design constructed of color and shape, before they experience its content. A brief review of design principles and design elements can help you to recognize what works in book displays and bulletin boards, and then to apply that knowledge in your library. Design principles—unity, balance, contrast, focal point—are the concepts that guide the creation of a design. Design elements—color, shape, graphic, line, font—are the visuals that express those concepts.

Design Principles
Unity

Also referred to as harmony, consistency, or cohesion, unity helps the viewer to see a display of books as cohesive and purposeful, pulled together by a coherent theme rather than assembled at random for no reason. Unity transforms a bulletin board from a hodgepodge of posters and fliers into a cohesive presentation of activities and events.

In graphic design, the underlying structure of a design is called the grid (Peterson 1997, 62). The grid is what gives structure to the arrangement of color, shape, and graphic in a book display or on a bulletin board. To "see" the grid on a table or shelf used for a book display or a bulletin board, mentally superimpose a checkerboard.

A display need not be uniform in order to be unified. Remove a book or two from a line of book easels, or a few posters from a bulletin board. The eye still perceives the grid, "filling in" the blank spaces, and the display retains unity. Your eye knows what looks "right."

- How unity works in a book display:
    1. A display of books is unified by inserting the same teen booklist in every book.
    2. An entire book collection is unified by placing a small poster holder at the end of the fourth shelf in every shelving range.

- How unity works on a bulletin board:

  1. An eclectic bulletin board of posters is unified by variations on a single theme, such as information about components of summer reading, or a single color that appears on all of the posters.

  2. Individual fliers fill the bulletin board in a unified layout, whether positioned an equal distance apart in squares of the grid, bunched together in the center of the board, or lined up along the top, bottom, or side margins of the board. The idea is to make the fliers appear to have been arranged as a group, rather than tacked up randomly.

Balance

Balance is a way to pull together disparate books or posters to make a single impression (White 2002, 65). In a display that is out of balance, the viewer sees only the disparate parts rather than the unified whole (White 2002, 65). Symmetrical displays achieve balance by positioning same-sized books or posters an equal distance apart from one another. Symmetry projects efficiency, organization, and stability. Symmetrical displays can also look predictable, perfunctory, and dull. Asymmetrical displays achieve balance by presenting different-sized books or posters in such a way that their mass—the amount of space perceived by the viewer—balances. An asymmetrical display projects spontaneity and creativity. Unless maintained, however, asymmetrical displays can look careless and neglected.

- How symmetrical balance works in a book display:

  Position a poster holder between two countertop display shelves and fill the shelves with books.

- How asymmetrical balance works in a book display:

  Position a poster holder between a large book easel and a countertop display shelf. Add a small poster holder to the right of the display shelf. Place an oversized book in the book easel, and fill the display shelf with books. The visual mass of the oversized book is asymmetrically balanced by the display shelf and the small poster holder.

- How symmetrical balance works on a bulletin board:

  Post same-sized posters at an equal distance from one another, or mirror the two sides of the bulletin board so that different-sized posters and fliers match up.

Asymmetrical book display at Tumwater Timberland Library.

- How asymmetrical balance works on a bulletin board:

    Post a large poster in the lower right quarter of the bulletin board, a cluster of small fliers in the upper left corner, and scatter graphics cut out from more fliers around the bulletin board. The visual mass of the large poster is asymmetrically balanced by the smaller fliers and the even smaller graphics dripping over the rest of the bulletin board.

Contrast

Juxtaposing different design elements—color, shape, graphics, line, and font—gives a display contrast (Peterson 1997, 57). Further, throwing a design out of balance creates tension, spontaneity, surprise, and the unexpected (54). As the viewer's eyes race around the display, looking at this, that, and the other thing, the display picks up movement and dynamism.

- How contrast works in a book display:

    Contrasting book sizes, book cover designs and colors, and print and audio formats enliven a display and also project their multiplicity onto the entire collection.

- How contrast works on a bulletin board:

    Deep jewel or neon colors in paper or fabric on a bulletin board contrast with white or pastel posters or fliers—and vice versa.

Focal Point

Every display has a focal point, defined by its color, shape, the open space around it, or sheer double take-inducing weirdness. The focal point grabs teens' attention—from a distance or close up—and serves as the entry point into the rest of the display (White 2002, 63). Give teens one thing to look at, and they'll see the rest.

- How focal point works in a book display:

    A big graphic novel, a self-help book with a quirky title in big type, two or three neon-colored book covers clashing together, a big CD-ROM, an old athletic shoe or other theme-related object—all of these things can serve as the focal point of a book display. In some displays, objects unrelated to the theme are added precisely to provoke the question, "What is *that* doing there?" so that teens will take a closer look at the rest of the display.

- How focal point works on a bulletin board:

    Once teens finish reading the big poster advertising a statewide teen readers' poll on good books, they may stick around to read postcard-size fliers describing the books.

Design Elements

Color

Color communicates to the viewer before he or she stops and becomes a reader. In Marshall McLuhan's three-level "hierarchy of communication," color registers first with viewers, signs and symbols register second, and words register third (White 2002, 67). Colors themselves communicate different meanings associated with their hues—warm or cool—and their intensity—light, medium, or dark. One color may dominate a book display or bulletin board, with or without accents of other colors. Conversely, many colors may crowd together, producing impressions ranging from cornucopia to claustrophobia.

The primary colors are red, yellow, and blue. The secondary colors are orange, green, and purple. The tertiary colors are orange-red, yellow-orange, yellow-green, blue-green, blue-violet, and red-violet. Complementary colors are colors on opposite sides of the color wheel, for example, blue and orange. Analogous colors are next to each other on the color wheel, for example, blue, blue-green, and green. Triadic harmonies are achieved by combining three colors equidistant on the color wheel, for example, yellow-orange, red-violet, and blue-green. Depending on their proximity to red or blue, colors are classified as warm or cool. Warm and cool colors combine well, because each enhances the other, literally filling in from the other side of the color wheel. For example, orange combines well with blue, and also with blue-violet, and blue-green. Warm colors jump forward, while cool colors hang back (White 2002, 67). Gardeners apply this fact of visual life by planting bright yellow daffodils behind cool blue pansies.

Color intensity is varied by shade (add black) and tint (add white). When the colors in a multicolored book display, bulletin board, print piece, or web page share the same intensity, they blend as beautifully as a flower garden or a watercolor, because the intensity or value is the same (Peterson 1997, 128).

To identify colors with teen appeal, look at teen magazines. Computer, gaming, and skateboarding magazines offer a palette of burnished metallic colors—olive, brown, dull red, dark blue, ochre, pumpkin, dull silver—with lots of black. Fashion, celebrity gossip, and girls' advice magazines feature a palette of bright tints and neons—hot pink, hot turquoise, hot yellow, watermelon, lime, tangerine, and cool violet—with lots of white. Check the colors of cell phones, iPods, and computers and their tints and shades: metallic, hard candy, nail polish, and faux industrial. All of these are hues that color teens' world.

- How color works in a book display:

    Include books whose cover art features complementary colors, or at least a mix of warm and cool colors. If all the books in a theme display turn out to have the same color cover, make a virtue out of necessity with a poster that says, "Same color cover—different books inside!" You can also bring color to a display by covering a table or backdrop with paper, craft materials, or fabric.

- How color works on a bulletin board:

    Go beyond the primary colors and look for paper, fabric, or other coverings in bright, glowing secondary and tertiary colors. Triadic harmonies make vibrant backgrounds.

Shape

Shape is any element that defines form (Peterson 1997, 38), such as a backwash shading, illustration, photograph, object, border, or block of type. Everything in a display is a shape, including empty space. The viewer registers different shapes differently: shapes that are big and dark, intense, or bright register as more important, while shapes that are small and pale register as less important (White 2002, 71). This differentiation was probably imprinted on human consciousness at an early date: when we saw that woolly mammoth charging toward us, we might not have paid much attention to the little bunny rabbit sitting under a tree. Empty space on a page gives the eyes space around text and graphics, as a relief from feeling crowded and pressured. Empty space in a display of books or on a bulletin board gives the viewer's eyes a place to rest, and the viewer's mind an opportunity to assimilate what he or she has been looking at.

- How shape works in a book display:

  The standard size of most teen hardcover fiction is $5½ \times 8½$ inches, for a percentage of width to height of 64 percent; most paperback trade nonfiction measures 6×9 inches, for a percentage of width to height of 66 percent; and most fiction paperbacks measure $4 \times 6¾$ inches, for a percentage of width to height of 59 percent. Within recent years, however, sizes have begun to vary. Books measuring $5\text{-}¼ \times 7\text{-}¼$ inches, for example, look stubby and square-shaped because their percentage of width to height is 72 percent. Books recorded on CD go all the way to square proportions: 100 percent. Graphic novels come in all sizes, as do many nonfiction books.

- How shape works on a bulletin board:

  Posters and fliers can be cut into many different shapes. Create 10×10 inch posters, because in a paper world dominated by $8½ \times 11$ inch posters, anything else stands out. Create fliers sized 5×5 inches—like CDs. Overlap flier corners to create chains that undulate across bulletin boards. Empty space around a poster draws attention to it.

Graphics

As the second of McLuhan's three levels in a communication hierarchy, the signs and symbols conveyed by graphics add another dimension to displays. Graphics can reinforce the message in two ways: by "match-ing" the headline and text with a related picture, or by creating an ironic, humorous commentary on the display with a seemingly unrelated picture. Teens are beginning to understand that all is not always as it appears to be, and are able to see the irony and humor in such juxtapositions.

What kind of graphics have high teen appeal? Avoid stereotypical teen graphics. "Anything that includes a skateboarding scene kind of worries me," notes Michael Moore of Teenage Research Unlimited. He added that simply throwing hot music genres, celebrities, and extreme sports motifs into advertisements is "sort of an outdated model" (Tschorn 2003, 42B).

Choose graphics that reflect ongoing teen interests and activities. You know what they are. Two friends talking. Teens talking in groups, walking, lounging, drinking lattes, or chowing down. Sports. Reading. Studying. Instant messaging and cruising the Internet. (Okay, and skate-boarding.)

- How graphics work in a book display:

    Use a graphic of a teen reading in a hammock to promote sum-mer reading: it's free time, it's relaxation, it's fun.

- How graphics work on a bulletin board:

    To promote a book discussion event, use a graphic of a table of teens talking and drinking coffee or hot chocolate. There's no need to show the books: what you are promoting is an event where teens can relax and talk.

Fonts

Fonts will be described in Chapter 6, including details on their use in book display posters and larger posters for bulletin boards.

DISPLAY FIXTURES

Display fixtures range from small and essential items that work in any-sized teen space, to large and optional items that work in large teen spaces. Whatever you buy, make sure it is sturdy, functional, attractive, and can be used to display different sizes of books, as well as books recorded on CD or audiocassette.

If you can buy only one type of display fixture, make it a book easel—in different sizes and quantities. Everywhere they're placed—at shelf ends, on display tables, on public service desks, on top of four-foot shelving ranges, next to computers—they hold up books so they can be seen. Book easels are made of wire, plastic-covered wire, molded acrylic, and other materials.

Poster holders, also molded from acrylic, are available in many sizes and styles, and can be used in a variety of ways. Place a poster holder measuring 4×6 inches at the end of a book shelf and insert a small poster with an attention-grabbing graphic. Place a small poster holder next to a book, and insert a copy of a review of that book by a teen (Nichols 2002, 91). Poster holders measuring 8½ × 11 inches can be used to promote book displays, book-related events, book discussion groups, and contests or polls.

Different poster holder styles are better suited to different locations. Because of sight lines, it's easier to read a poster holder that tilts back when it's placed on a table or other surface below eye level. It's easier to read a poster holder that is vertical when it's placed on a book shelf or slatwall at eye level. Other poster holder styles are designed to be fastened to walls, and range upward in size to hold big posters. Additional styles feature boxes for related brochures, so that the poster holder both promotes a book display and offers a related booklist.

Like book easels, countertop display shelves are versatile, attractive, and inexpensive. They are made of wood, molded acrylic, and other materials. Measuring 18 inches or longer, they can hold up to two dozen books in a display. Used in combination with book easels and poster

Poster holders alert teens to special collections at Tumwater Timberland Library.

holders, they can anchor your book displays. And for appearance—that is, service made visible—they sure beat propping up two dozen books between scabrous metal bookends.

Cork bulletin boards are available in many sizes and colors; some include dry-erase whiteboard sections or other features. Posters and fliers can also be displayed on posterboard or foamboard set up on an easel, or fastened to the end of a shelving range. You can also cover foamboard with paper or fabric, remove two or three shelves from the young adult shelving range, and insert the foamboard to create a bulletin board—and a display area on the shelf underneath.

Slatwall paneling is made by fastening 4-inch slats of Formica-finished wood, $2\frac{3}{4}$ or 4 inches wide and $\frac{3}{8}$ of an inch apart, to a backing. The $\frac{3}{8}$ inch gaps serve as grooves, into which specially designed book easels and poster holders can be hooked. Slatwall shines on range ends, because books from the range can be displayed without impeding foot traffic, hinting at riches in the stacks. Slatwall can also be used to cover or create walls, making an instant teen space (Nichols 2002, 77).

Shelving units that back up against range ends can hold plenty of books, but can also be expensive. Bookstore "dumps" are end-of-range shelving units made of cardboard and covered with advertisements. They are sometimes available to enterprising young adult librarians who stride into bookstores and ask for them once they're to be replaced (Nichols 2002, 87).

Freestanding display units can measure as much as 7 feet tall, 4 feet wide, and 2 feet deep, which allows for a foot of display shelving on either side. Wire display units, similar to those found in computer games stores, cost quite a bit less than units made out of wood or wood products.

Look for more fixtures and containers in craft supply shops, gardening shops, department stores, and farmers' markets. That big basket or milk crate could hold some books, and that bizarro bright green frog pot could hold the book of the day. Have some fun—go shopping!

For a more thorough description of display fixtures, please consult "Fixtures for Merchandising," in *Merchandising Library Materials to Young Adults* (Nichols 2002), which also includes a generous listing of library equipment vendors.

BOOK DISPLAYS

Book displays, whatever their location in the library, comprise three elements: a poster describing the display, books, and aesthetics. For some displays, a booklist is recommended; for others, it is optional.

Posters

A poster tells teens three things: the theme of the display, so that they know what they're looking at has a purpose and is not just a random jumble of books; that they can check out the books (especially if the poster says, "These books can be checked out"); and that library staff members care enough about teens to put together book displays.

Posters are generally composed of a headline, a graphic, and a line or two of explanation. Avoid using the word "information" in posters promoting nonfiction. Words that are ubiquitous blend into the woodwork. For example, "Health News You Can Use" makes a stronger statement than "Health Information."

As visual representations of ideas, graphics reinforce the message of headlines. Graphics can match up with headlines—lipstick kisses on a poster for a romance display—or they can conjure up a mood. For a display of weepie teen fiction, try a graphic of the sun behind a cloud. (Or come to think of it, how about a theme-related object—like a box of tissues?) Once you stop expecting to find an exact match between headline and graphic, your mind will open up to images that express the concept of the display.

A line or two of text is all you need to explain the contents of the display. I like to run a line at the bottom of the poster, in small italic type, reading, "This display of (whatever) has been brought to you by (first names), your friendly librarians at (your library)." The italic type looks handwritten, the text is whimsical, and the message is that real people are working for teens.

Books

Include all formats in book displays: books, books recorded on CD or cassette, and relevant magazines. Check the display to see if you need to replace books that have been checked out, or to swap out stale books for fresh books. Replace or exchange single books on display—at public service desks or at the ends of shelves—as needed. Or don't, and allow the empty book easel to mutely witness the fact that a teen checked out the book that was on display.

Aesthetics

What are the aesthetics of a book display that promotes reading and books to teens? Simply, make it neat, but not too neat. Make the book

National Poetry Month display at Tumwater Timberland Library includes poster promoting poetry events, books, and poetry-themed monthly teen newsletter. One of the easels is empty.

display solid, but insert a random element. Place six books in six book easels on a table. Remove the fourth book. Now it looks as though one of the books was so good that a teen checked it out. Let that impression remain for a couple of days, then replace the fourth book. Remove a book from another easel. Muss up that neat stack of booklists a little so it looks as though teens picked some up. The impression you want to leave is that library staff members put together a display of good books, and teens are checking them out.

Print Promotions

An accompanying booklist or bookmark is a good idea for displays of books that you booktalked during a school visit or featured at a library event, and optional for other displays. Print promotions will be described in more detail in Chapter 6.

BULLETIN BOARDS

For some young adult librarians, creating attractive bulletin boards is easy. Maybe they worked in children's services and learned how. Maybe they studied design or art. Or maybe they have a good eye and know what they're doing. And then there are those of us whose brains freeze solid at the sight of an empty bulletin board, and it's all we can do to tack up a few posters. If your bulletin boards make even your eyes glaze over, for sure they'll be invisible to teens. By following a few basic guidelines, however, you can create better bulletin boards.

Like book displays, bulletin boards comprise three elements: a sign describing the bulletin board; posters, fliers, and other materials; and aesthetics.

Signs

Signs tell teens what they're looking at. Let's say there is one large bulletin board in the teen space, measuring 4×6 feet. One way to handle the space is to divide the bulletin board into three 4×2 foot sections, and label them "Teen Services," "Teen Reading," and "Teen Events." Now teens know what they're looking at. Similarly, if the teen space features two or three bulletin boards, each bulletin board can promote a single aspect of teen services.

Then again, you could post a sign reading, "It's all for teens" slightly off-center. Stretch out mylar strips from the sign, connecting it to posters scattered all over the bulletin board. What gives teens a reason to look at the individual posters is the sign telling them that everything on the bulletin board is for them.

Print Promotions

Posters and fliers that promote reading and books to teens include lists of popular teen books, posters advertising book-centered activities and events, book reviews by teens, newspaper articles about local teen writers, magazine articles about regional or national teen writers, and posters published by library promotions companies and publishers.

Aesthetics

Bulletin boards are designed to be effective at a distance, as well as to be a showcase for bits of information at reading distance. By designing bulletin boards with unity, as cohesive wholes, you give them their due as purely visual entities. There is no more powerful visual element than color. Cover the surface with neon colors to attract the eye, with rich jewel colors to please the eye, or with white, which is the background color of many teen magazines and web sites. For bulletin boards made by inserting paper or fabric-covered foamboard into shelving ranges, bright colors compensate for the shadow cast by overhanging shelves. Look for color combinations around the twelve-hued color wheel, and use more than one color to cover your bulletin board. If you use one color, say, red, add a touch of red to posters: color provides the unity that pulls your bulletin board together.

As with book displays, schedule your bulletin boards. For example, sometime in August, have a plan for removing all of the summer reading publicity materials from your bulletin boards. By "plan" I mean not just thinking about it, but creating a new design and stockpiling paper, fabric, new posters, and other things, so that you're ready to make the change on September 1.

HOW TO KEEP VISUALLY CURRENT

As librarians, we work in a world defined and dominated by text. Print surrounds us: on computer screens, in books and professional journals, and in reading at home. Our immersion in text makes it even more important for us to nurture our need—as human beings as well as librarians—for color and design. Immerse yourself in color and design, by looking at nature and gardens, and at displays in retail outlets, museums, banks, grocery stores, and restaurants, to see how products and services are merchandised to customers.

Take a break from text. Leaf through teen magazines, looking at colors and page layouts for book display, print promotions, and bulletin board ideas. Pick up some books and magazines on commercial graphic design, focusing on color photographs of advertisements, posters, menus, and other print materials. These are color palettes designed to look good up close. Look at theater and opera magazines for color photographs of visually striking stage productions. These are color palettes designed to look good at a distance.

Visit libraries to look at book displays and bulletin boards. At a library conference or trade show, examine vendor displays for product presentation as well as the products themselves. Which presentations attract your eye? Which products, services, and sales literature kept your attention? Keep looking at the world around you.

Book displays and bulletin boards attract teens to books and book-related activities and events. The next chapter explores how young adult librarians can promote reading and books through bookmarks, booklists, newsletters, brochures, fliers, and posters.

REFERENCES AND SUGGESTED READINGS

Baker, Sharon L. 1986. "Overload, Browsers, and Selections." *Library and Information Science* 8 (October 1986): 315–329.

Nichols, Mary Anne. 2002. *Merchandising Library Materials to Young Adults*. Greenwood Village, CO: Libraries Unlimited.

Peterson, Bryan. 1997. *Using Design Basics to Get Creative Results*. Cincinnati, OH: North Light Books.

Tschorn, Adam. 2003. "How to Tickle the Fickle: Grabbing the Attention of Teenagers in an Advertising-Saturated World Requires a Fresh Approach. One Thing That Isn't Hard to Motivate Them to Do: Spend Their Cash." *WWD*. (August 25): 42B.

White, Alex W. 2002. *The Elements of Graphic Design: Space, Unity, Page Architecture, and Type*. New York: Allworth Press.

6

❖❖❖ ❖❖❖ ❖❖❖

PRINT PROMOTIONS

Like sales literature and magazines, library bookmarks, booklists, and other print promotions can sell mood, experience, and lifestyle. Look at an advertisement for jeans. It is designed to make the viewer think that if he wears those jeans, he can have that cool life. Similarly, the graphics described in Chapter 5—of a teen reading in a hammock, or a group of teens talking—sell the blissful experience of reading in comfort, or the exhilarating experience of talking with friends.

Sales literature conveys two messages: denotative and connotative. The denotative message expresses the primary meaning of the advertisement; for example, "this is a list of books" or "this poster gives information about the time and place of a library event." The connotative message expresses the appeal of the product or service conveyed through design choices in color, graphics, language, font, and page layout (Landa 1998, 30). Through these design choices, teens are thus encouraged to think that "the library has good books for teens like me," or "this event will attract cool people." A booklist printed on bright neon paper sends a connotative message that "these books have teen appeal." Conversely, a poster for a book discussion event featuring graphics of dorky-looking teens or teens from another era sends a connotative message that "the people at this event will not be cool—and so the event will not be cool."

Different types of print promotions play different roles in promoting reading and books to teens. Bookmarks, booklists, and nonfiction guides bring order out of the seeming chaos of all those books on the shelves. They offer shortcuts to the themes and genres of fiction, and the topics of nonfiction discussed in Chapter 3. Newsletters can promote new books, book discussion groups, author visits, and writing workshops. As for general brochures about library services, they offer an opportunity to promote reading and books to teens as well as to their parents. Posters can also be used to promote reading and books.

Before plunging into library print promotions, however, we'll study some commercial sales literature and teen magazines. I'm not advocating that you violate copyright by duplicating advertisements; rather, I'm advising that you examine their design and content for content and design ideas when creating your own sales literature. Studying advertisements can also be helpful when creating your library web page, which will be explored in Chapter 7.

SALES LITERATURE

Whatever the product or service it advertised, the sales literature I picked up at the mall had one thing in common: all of it was visually pleasing and informative. These print promotions are designed to appeal to teens and to motivate them to spend. Teens are spending $158 billion a year (*Know Your World Extra* 2004, 14). Obviously, it pays to advertise.

From the tropical hues advertising PacSun clothing to the earth tones advertising Starbucks, sales literature offers attractive palettes. However, there is currently one item that has been defined by teen pop culture as both cool and necessary to teen life—for both girls and boys: the cell phone. Of all the sales literature I picked up at the mall, the brochures for cell phones were the most attractive and informative. Cell phone manufacturers and service providers spend huge sums on sales literature. Let's analyze what they get for their money, and how libraries can create similar print promotions. Just as when we toured teen-appeal stores in Chapter 2, the purpose of this analysis is to understand how to extract design ideas from whatever happens to be hot at the moment, rather than to adopt one style and use it ad infinitum.

The brochures feature an overall look that is very clean, open, and light, by using white clay-surface paper and lots of blank space.

- How to get the clean look in library print promotions:

    Suppress the save-money instinct to describe as many books as possible in a booklist so that it will be useful for five years. Resist the temptation to cram text and graphics into every square inch of a poster. Instead, allow for open space so the reader or viewer can focus on what's important. The cell phones themselves are photographed like works of art: small, sleek, platinum, beautiful. The sleek look is reinforced by sans serif fonts and a limited color palette: metallic gray, gray, shocking pink, and blue.

- How to get sleek images and clear colors in library print promotions:

    If you can use photographs, strive for as crisp a reproduction as possible. Dots per inch (dpi) is a measure of print resolution, referring to the number of dots of ink per linear inch (Webopedia 2005). The standard resolution for photographs in print promotions is 300 dpi, meaning 300 dots across and 300 dots down, or 90,000 dots per square inch. (Newsprint photographs require fewer dots per square inch because the coarser surface of newsprint allows the ink dots to bleed and blend together: 150 dpi does the job.) If you can't use photographs, use graphics, and keep the edges clean and sharp. Color palettes are usually limited by the cost of four-color printing. Consider using two-color palettes: white paper, black ink for text, and an accent color for graphics and backwashes behind selected text blocks. Or use white paper and one dark color ink.

    The young 20s in the photographs look as though their lives are fun, exciting, smart, and full of wonderful friends of both genders and all ethnic backgrounds; some are even wearing glasses! In fact, now that they're connected by cell phones, their lives look even more perfect. This is the connotative message par excellence.

- How to show teens enjoying library products or services in library print promotions:

    If you can't find photographs or graphics of cool-looking older teens or young 20s, avoid making do with dorky-looking or old-fashioned teens. Instead, use crisp graphics related to the topic of the print promotion.

Information about each product feature is conveyed by a small graphic of each feature's opening screen, a headline describing it, and a one- or two-sentence description.

- How to use small graphics in library print promotions:
  Use icons or small graphics to illustrate explanatory text.

Technical information about the product is conveyed in a "Detailed Specs" list.

- How to use a list in library print promotions:
  Promote library card registration on a bookmark featuring a bulleted list of such card benefits as the following: realistic fiction themes; popular fiction genres such as fantasy, thrillers, and humorous romances; manga and graphic novels; and nonfiction books about extreme sports, crafts, how to start a band, and so forth.

A good place to find design ideas is on the covers of recent young adult books. The covers of the Orca Soundings imprint of Orca Books, for example, offer a palette of blurry tropical colors, evocative photos, and edgy layouts.

MAGAZINES

Sales literature gets teens' attention. But what they really *read* is magazines. Both local and national teen reading surveys show that magazines rank high as a reading format. Among teens who participated in a Teenage Research Unlimited (TRU) survey, 67 percent reported that they spent time reading magazines; 57 percent spent time reading books for pleasure (Zollo 2004, 258). Magazines cater to teens' developing individual interests, while at the same time creating and promulgating a shared teen pop culture. The short articles and dramatic visuals fit perfectly into the busy teen lifestyle. Magazines are photo-splashed, and giddy with graphics, sidebars, quotes, and other informational appetizers. Like sales literature, magazines are selling a lifestyle, the perfect teen lifestyle. (Whether or not teens are totally buying it is another question.)

By studying magazine content, you can learn about teen interests, and apply that knowledge to building teen collections. By studying magazine design—color, graphics, font, language, and page layout—you can learn to design print promotions. When doing my research, I focused on such magazines as *GamePro* (video game reviews and news), *Rockergrl* (women in rock music), *Seventeen* (fashion, makeup, friends, boys), *Teen People* (celebrity news), *Thrasher* (edgy skateboarding), and *Wizard* (comics and related media reviews and news). I also looked at *American Cheerleader*, *Breakaway* (Christian teen boys), *Brio* (Christian teen girls), *Sister to Sister* (African American teen girls' fashion, makeup, friends, boys), *Teen Voices* (high school girls), *Transworld Skateboarding*, and *Young Money* (high school, college, first job), as well as music magazines like *Right On*, *Spin*, and *Word Up*. I looked at some teen web magazines, like *Latinias* (Latina teen girls). While I didn't find the content of *Wired* and a few other young-20s magazines to always be directly teen-related, their sophisticated design elements reflected the cool independence to which teens aspire.

Color

Color palettes reflect magazine content. *GamePro*'s colors mirror the dark, muddy colors of video games: black, silver, dark blue, brown red, and olive. On these dark backgrounds, text is printed in white, in tiny 8- or 6-point type. *Wizard*'s bright, clear colors reflect those found in comics: black, white, fire-engine red, royal blue, yellow, emerald green, ochre, brown, and midnight blue. White backgrounds, black type, and color photos predominate in rock music and skateboarding celebrity magazines like *Rockergrl*, *Spin*, and *Thrasher*.

Fashionista flavors rule in *Teen People*: shocking pink, bright turquoise, cantaloupe, neon yellow, mauve, chartreuse, rose, pumpkin, dark blue, and pastels such as pale blue, pale lilac, pale aqua, and pale pink.

Color is used to highlight key words and phrases in text blocks in both *GamePro* and *Teen People*. Both magazines occasionally run a neon-color highlight line over key words and phrases—just like using a highlighter in a textbook.

Ideas for using colors in print promotions include the following:

- "Brand" teen print promotions by establishing a distinctive color palette that you use only for those materials.
- On a poster advertising a drawing or cartooning workshop, use the bright, clear colors of comics and graphic novels: royal blue, fire-engine red, emerald green, and the like. Or evoke the pages of a manga comic with a black-and-white design in the manga style.

- On a poster advertising a jewelry or cosmetic making workshop, use the fashion world colors of shocking pink, bright turquoise, lilac, and so on.
- Print a nonfiction guide featuring books about jobs, college, military service, and careers. Use silver-gray paper with one dark accent color, underscoring the serious, real-world nature of these topics.
- Print booklists and bookmarks on a wide variety of colors, expanding from the standard pastels to such hues as salmon, apple green, lilac, and mauve, and neon everything. Neon and strong colors reflect the emotional intensity of teen fiction, and the fun and thought-provoking intensity of teen nonfiction.
- On posters and fliers, print neon backwashes behind text blocks or phrases.

Images

The majority of images in teen magazines are photographs. Many libraries cannot afford to illustrate everything with color photographs, and rely on black-and-white photographs and graphics instead. Whether you use photographs or graphics, avoid dated images of teens; instead, choose images of objects, settings, or sentient beings that are attention-grabbing, quirky, bizarre, intense, or sleekly well-designed. Sometimes a plethora of images works best, reflecting a variety of teen interests met in a booklist. Sometimes, one large image gives a print promotion focus, definition, and intensity.

- For a book discussion group or focus group, show teens sitting around a table, drinking hot chocolate or coffee (fall and winter), or smoothies or sodas (spring and summer). If you can't find cool-looking teens, enlarge the drinks so that they completely fill the poster.
- Enlarge a cell phone and print program information on the screen.
- For a summer booklist, pair a graphic of a giant open book with a graphic of a diving board, with words like fantasy, mystery, adventure, and romance as the splashes.

In *Teen People*, many pages are stamped with a tiny stencil-style rectangle of shocking pink, asking teen readers if they want to "CONTRIBUTE to *Teen People*." All teens need to do is to visit the *Teen People* web site listed on the stamp and download an application to be a "Trendspotter," somebody who alerts the magazine about what's hot and what's not in their communities.

- How to use a "stamp" logo:

  Write a short survey under the headline, "Speak up about teen services!" In the survey, ask teens about collections, services, events, the teen web site, and ways to promote the library to teens. Distribute paper copies of the survey. Design a stamp logo, including the headline and the URL, for your teen web site. Include the stamp logo on all print promotions: posters, bulletin boards, newsletters, bookmarks, booklists. Sprinkle the logo around your teen web site with the caption, "Got something to say about teen services at your library? Click here and speak up!" Print or post the stamp logo in different places on print promotions and the web site so it doesn't blend into the background.

Fonts

Fonts are crucial elements in the headlines and texts of print promotions. Display font styles are often used to convey connotative messages about content. For example, serif fonts (those with tails, such as Times Roman, Garamond, and Palatino) look stolid and traditional. Sans serif fonts (those without tails, such as Arial, Tahoma, and Verdana) look clean-edged and contemporary. Jagged fonts look edgy and alternative. Cursive fonts look artistic and imaginative. Block fonts look down-to-earth and practical. To facilitate readability, text font styles are usually more straightforward and less artistic in design. Examples of display fonts with suggested uses related to booklist and poster content, and text fonts in common use appear on the next page.

To find teen-appeal headline fonts, look at teen magazines and teen web sites, then see if you can find an exact or close match in your design software.

Language

Getting your message across while avoiding the pitfalls of too-bland or too-clever writing is a challenge. The goal is to communicate the content of the print promotion—the denotative message—as well as how it could make a teen think or feel—the connotative message. Even if you could

---

Teen-Appeal Fonts

Headline fonts used to characterize the content of printed materials include the following:

Andy (Creative and journal-writing books and workshops)

Bradley Hand ITC (Creative and journal-writing books and workshops)

Chiller (Creepy books, activities, events)

Curlz MT (humorous books, comedy workshops, anything fun)

Impact (Extreme sports and rock music books and events)

Jokerman (Humorous books, comedy workshops, anything fun)

Lucinda Handwriting (Calligraphy and card-making books and workshops)

Mistral (Teen book review forms, creative and journal-writing workshops)

Snap ITC (Weird books, activities, and events)

Text fonts for maximum readability in printed materials include the following:

Arial

Comic Sans MS

Times New Roman

Verdana

---

keep up with teen slang, using slang is like spicing a dish. A pinch of spice perks it up: too much spice ruins it. Few things are more off-putting to teens than adults mouthing what they think is teen slang. Alan Adamson, managing director at a brand identity consulting firm, cautions against grabbing the hot word of the nanosecond and overusing it. The worst form of marketing, he says, is to think that you can "catch the wave" simply by parroting the hot word or idea. "This could actually damage a brand because it's so me-too," he notes (Petreca 2000, 16).

Okay, if you're going to avoid slang, isn't there something you can do to punch up your writing? Sure! You can listen to teens, noticing the words they use a lot. You can read teen magazines, noticing the words that appear a lot. While slang words are specialized and can be used to convey different meanings, words in current use that basically mean

---

Hot Books for Cold Days

Never mind the cold, the rain, the damp, the dark. Books that thrill can chase away the chill. Wander in to the library's TeenZone, slide into a mug of hot chocolate, and relax. Kristine Mahood, Timberland's Young Adult Librarian, will talk up books—mysteries, thrillers, romances, fantasy, tales of teen life, and true books about what's real—and get you and your friends raving about books you like, too. *Refreshments provided by the Friends of the Tumwater Timberland Library.*

- Here's what's going on: Winters in the Pacific Northwest can be cold, wet, and dark. Find out about good books at this event.
- Here's why it's worth your while: Hot chocolate, probably some cookies, and hearing about books that friends and other teens like. This event happens after school, when you and your friends are in the library anyway, and it's been a long time since lunch.
- Here's what's a little weird: Thrill, chill . . . and sliding into a mug of hot chocolate.

---

what they say give writing a dynamism, like a current rippling through water.

Examples of words I've heard teens use repeatedly in the Pacific Northwest, and which I've also seen in teen magazines, which suggests nationwide use, include

- nouns: Bud/buds, issues, rants, raves, stuff, tunes.
- verbs: Chill, visit web sites ("surf" is so 90s).
- adjectives: Angsty, annoying (used a lot), intense, scary, total snore, weird.

You can also write in a lively, humorous style that depicts teens as active participants in library activities, rather than as passive recipients of assistance. And give the facts. In a TRU study, teens were presented with a list of rules for advertising to teens and asked to assemble their own lists. 65 percent of teens included "be honest," 52 percent included "make me laugh," and 45 percent included "be clear" (Zollo 2004, 402). Honesty is the best policy. As for humor, one or two humorous words or phrases are all it takes to liven up a bookmark or a poster. Tell too many jokes, however, and you undercut the validity and truthfulness of the message. Tell teens what's going on, make it worth their while, add a little weirdness, but you don't have to hit them over the head. They'll get it.

An example of an event description appears on the previous page.

Page Layout

Page layout pulls together color, graphics, fonts, and language.

The page layouts in *Wizard* and *GamePro* adhere to a standard review media style. In *Wizard*, reviews are crammed into three-column pages and highlighted by a few full-color thumbnails from comics. *GamePro* layouts position the review in the center of the page, surrounded by thumbnails of screens from the game.

- How layouts work in library print promotions:

  The "Picks: Must-Read Books" reviews in *Wizard* begin with the title of the comic, followed by a pithy "Why It's Cool" evaluation, and close with a plot summary. Reversing the usual book review format of title, plot summary, and critique, this format begins by giving a teen the reason why he'd want to read the comic, and only then follows up with the plot. On a poster advertising a teen event, headline the title of the event, follow with a brief text explaining "why you want to be here," and conclude with a short description of the program.

Teen People uses more open, free-flowing layout styles, with occasional use of hand-drawn arrows (and handwriting) for a spontaneous look. Text blocks float on white backgrounds, jostling for space with headlines and subheads, photographs, dialogue balloons, sidebars printed on pastel or medium color backwashes, and pop-ups. The magazine looks like a scrapbook, a bulletin board, or a refrigerator door, and the connotative message is lighthearted and open.

- How a scrapbook layout works in library print promotions:

  Throw a jumble of text blocks, graphics, sidebars, scribbled notes, and your stamp logo into a brochure describing teen services or onto a poster promoting an activity or event.

DESIGN SOFTWARE AND PAPER

Many print promotions can be produced in Microsoft Word, using available fonts and clip art. Other design programs include Microsoft Publisher and Pagemaker. Photoshop handles images and special effects, and can be used to create custom designs. More graphic design programs are Freehand, Illustrator, and InDesign. Liquid Library (formerly Dynamics Graphics) is a subscription resource for clip art and photos.

Library print promotions are typically produced on bond paper, clay-surface paper, and card stock. Available in many colors, 20- to 50-bond paper is commonly used for booklists, brochures, and fliers. Like bond paper, clay-surface paper is available in many colors and weights. The clay coating gives the paper a smooth finish, allowing ink images to retain crisp edges, and showcasing brilliant colors. Clay-surface paper is commonly used for brochures, bookmarks, fliers, and posters. Card stock, available in 90-pound weight, with uncoated or clay-coated surfaces, and recycled formats, is commonly used for bookmarks.

Many booklists are printed on $8 \frac{1}{2} \times 11$ inch or $8 \frac{1}{2} \times 14$ inch paper, and folded to a width of about $3 \frac{1}{2}$ inches with two or three folds. One approach has been to create booklists in the shape and size of CDs. Young Adult Library Services Association's (YALSA) "Outstanding Books for the College Bound" (1999) booklists were printed on 5×10 inch clay-surface paper, which are then folded into 5-inch squares.

Chicago Public Library went the other direction, however, with striking results. "Reading for High School: GREAT READS for 6th, 7th, and 8th Graders" is printed on chartreuse clay-surface paper, with pumpkin and white accents, measuring $11 \times 25 \frac{1}{2}$ inches and letterfolded into $8 \frac{1}{2} \times 11$ inch size. There's plenty of room for seven annotated booklists on themes ranging from overcoming adversity to understanding variant points of view.

GENERAL LIBRARY BROCHURES

Brochures describing library locations, hours, collections, services, and programs, while not designed to highlight teen services, nonetheless present you with an opportunity to promote reading and books to teens—and parents. When general brochures turn to youth services, they typically focus on services to young children: toddler and preschool storytimes, early literacy support, and abundant materials. As you saw in

Chapter 1, reading is a skill that develops over a lifetime. The library's role in fostering teen reading—through access to books, magazines, and audiobooks as well as book discussion groups and other activities—is important. It is also important that these brochures do not limit their descriptions of teen services to educational support, as though the public library serves simply as an after-school study hall. Instead, promote the full range of teen services, collections, activities, events, and volunteer opportunities.

BOOKMARKS AND BOOKLISTS

Bookmarks and booklists promote reading and books to teens by making it easier for them to find books to read. Bookmarks and booklists also promote teen books to library staff members, who are able to refer to these print promotions when advising teens about books they might want to read. Like book displays, bookmarks and booklists can promote general categories of teen books—fiction about contemporary teen life—as well as highlight themes, genres, and formats. They can pull together titles in categories that teens already know and like, such as fantasy. They can also highlight types of books teens may not know about and might like, such as real-life memoirs by young 20s about their teen years.

Bookmarks and booklists must be seen to be picked up. Try to avoid laying them flat on tables, bookshelves, or windowsills. Instead, purchase literature holders and fill them up with booklists. Slip bookmarks into books on displays, like flags. Purchase one-slot literature holders, and embed bookmarks and booklists in the teen fiction shelves. Give circulation staff members a supply of bookmarks and ask them to slip one in the top book checked out by teens. If your library includes self-checkout stations, place a one-slot literature holder nearby with a small sign encouraging teens to pick up bookmarks. Give out bookmarks and booklists during readers' advisory and reference conversations, during casual conversations with teens, during booktalking visits to schools, and while sitting at a table in the school cafeteria hawking library ware. Send your middle and high school media specialists a supply.

Public agencies and organizations have sent you brochures to distribute in the library. Ask if you can send them some teen booklists, which promotes not only reading and books for teens but also the entire library. Retail outlets such as bookstores, coffeehouses, and music stores may also accept bookmarks and booklists.

Production

While teens do read hardcover books, paperbacks are extremely popular. So it makes sense to print bookmarks on card stock, sized to fit paperbacks (2¾ × 7 inches). Sixteen titles (title/author/subject headings) will fit onto a bookmark this size. I know that it can be more cost-effective and convenient to print bookmarks four-up on 8½ × 11 inch card stock, but—convenient for whom? As with any communication piece, product, or service, design bookmarks with the end user in mind.

The number of titles that will fit on a booklist varies, depending on the size of the paper and the length of the annotations. The size of the print run will depend on the anticipated length of time that print materials will be used, and the size of your library.

One way to get the most out of printed bookmarks is to turn them into annotated booklists on the teen web site. Add the URL of the teen web page at the end of the bookmark, encouraging teens to visit it to see full descriptions of these books—and more books as well.

Topics

Bookmark and booklist topics include the following: fiction themes and genres, nonfiction subjects and topics, tie-ins to community concerns and events, media tie-ins, books that were booktalked during class visits, and summer reading lists. Some bookmarks and booklists will be made up entirely of fiction, some of nonfiction, and others will include both. For sample topics, please see Chapter 3.

By starting file folders for fiction themes and nonfiction topics, you can start collecting all those book titles that you run across in review journals, listservs, your own and colleagues' reading, from your work in the teen book collections, and from new books arriving in your library. I keep files on topics of ongoing interest, such as "Adventure," "Asking Questions, Listening for Answers" (religion), "Boy Books," "Countries and Cultures," "Fantasy," "Free Time" (hobbies and pastimes), "Girl Books," "Good Books about True Stuff" (all nonfiction), "Historical Gals and Guys," "Horrors!," "Issues," "Love," "Mystery/Suspense," and "Sob Stories." I toss in notes, articles, and lists of fiction and nonfiction. When I need to update or create a bookmark or a booklist, I look in the file folder that would most likely include titles on that theme or topic.

Many fiction and nonfiction bookmarks and booklists focus on one theme or topic. Multi-topic nonfiction bookmarks and booklists promote

Reality Checkouts

So what's on those shelves numbered 000–999.999? Here's the basic breakdown of where you'll find what you're looking for in nonfiction.

Look in the **000s** for...

...UFOs, unexplained weirdness, computers, Internet, and zines.

Look in the **100s** for...

...philosophy, psychology, astrology, and self-help.

Look in the **200s** for...

...religion and spirituality.

Look in the **300s** for...

...teen life, teen legal rights, school success, fairy tales, and world customs.

Look in the **400s** for...

...English and other languages.

Look in the **500s** for...

...math, chemistry, physics, plants, and animals.

Look in the **600s** for...

...body info, sex info, health, cars, cookbooks, makeup, and getting jobs.

Look in the **700s** for...

...how to draw, art, music, theater, movies, and sports.

Look in the **800s** for...

...writing, poetry, plays, and world literature.

Look in the **900s** for...

...adventure, travel, and history.

If you're not finding what you're looking for, let us know up at the Information Desk. We like to find books for people!

(Your library's name)
(Your library's web site address)

areas of the collection that will appeal to teens, whether they are pursuing personal interests or doing research for school assignments. An example of a multi-topic bookmark appears on the previous page.

Where to Find Titles

There are lots of places to find titles. Ask teens about books, and add their suggestions to your files. Appendix II lists print and electronic resources on collection development, readers' advisory, and booktalking. YALSA's web site includes such awards lists as Best Books for Young Adults, Printz Awards, Quick Picks, and more—current winners, previous years' winners, and the current year's nominees. Many libraries' teen web sites include their own booklists. Virtual YA Index: Public Libraries with Young Adult Web Pages, located at http://yahelp.suffolk.lib.ny.us/virtual.html (accessed April 21, 2005), is a major resource. Favorite Teen Angst Books, TeenReads.com, and other teen book web sites offer booklists in an awesome range of categories, and will be explored in further detail in Chapter 7. Middle and senior high school library web sites also link to booklists, and some include recommended or required reading for each grade. Your own reading and colleagues' reading are more resources. Finally, cruise the shelving trucks, and browse your collection. Many gems do not make it onto awards lists or into readers' advisory resources.

Look for titles that connect with the bookmark or booklist theme in unexpected ways. The search for identity and the desire to be accepted is a popular theme of realistic fiction. You'll also find that theme explored in such books as the following: *Firegold* (Calhoun 1999), a fantasy novel in which Jonathan struggles to reconcile his dual tribal heritage; comics featuring identity-challenged heroes like Spider-Man and Wolverine; and true adventure/survival stories depicting teens facing their fears, discovering their strengths, and finding acceptance.

Headlines

Some bookmarks and booklists are best described with denotative headlines, such as "Diaries and Journals," which tells teens that these books could be about writing diaries and journals, or that they're written in those forms. "I Wrote about It in My Journal" invites teens to write journals—and it brings teens into the experiences of the fictional characters.

A quick look around the Internet yields such imaginative headlines as

- "For Real" (realistic fiction), "No Fear" (adventure), "Out and About" (fiction featuring gay and lesbian characters), and "Never to Forget" (books on the Holocaust) (Bay County Library System, Bay County, Michigan, located at http://www.baycountylibrary .org/TeenPage/booklist.htm, accessed February 1, 2006).
- "Fanging Around" (vampire novels), "Bare Bones" (weight and eating disorders), and "Nail Biters" (teen psychological thrillers) (Reading Rants, located at http://tln.lib.mi.us/~amutch/jen, accessed April 21, 2005).
- "Believers and Doubters" (faith), "Hip-Hop," "Thrillers and Mysteries for the Adrenaline Junkie" (Carnegie Library of Pittsburgh Teen Reads, Carnegie Library of Pittsburgh, located at http:// www.carnegielibrary.org/teens/read/teenlists.html, accessed April 21, 2005).

Annotations

With limited space, titles on bookmarks can be "annotated" by the specificity of the genre or subgenre, and possibly by a few descriptors. A serviceable format is:

Title in Boldface

Author in Regular Type

(Descriptors in Italicized Type)

Booklists' greater space allows librarians to craft one- to three-sentence annotations, plus subject headings and notes on audio formats, sequels, and similar books. Include the name of the protagonist, and his or her age, indicated by numerical age or a reference to middle or high school. Name and age are important to teens who want to read books featuring characters "like me." The third crucial piece of information is the action or plotline of the book. Scan the back cover for clues (Nichols 2002, 113), because its job is to encapsulate the appeal of the book and sell it to teens.

Mary K. Chelton advises librarians to pose the following five questions, and from the answers to craft an annotation (Vaillancourt 2000, 115–116). Let's answer the questions, assemble information, and write an annotation for *Godless* (Hautman 2004).

Question: Who is the central character? Usually, the protagonist is identified by gender, age, and other characteristics that will pique the reader's interest. Chelton points out that the character with the most teen-appeal may not be the protagonist.

Answer: Sixteen-year-old Jason: sarcastic, overweight, alienated, and attracted to Magda.

Question: Who are the significant others? They could be family, friends, people at school, nature—whoever the protagonist becomes involved with.

Answer: Best friend Shin is quiet and obsessive, Magda is cute and adventurous, and Henry is edgy but unexpectedly insightful.

Question: What is the setting? It could be home, neighborhood, school, or further away in a big city, wilderness, another country, or outer space.

Answer: Smalltown, USA.

Question: When does the story take place? It could be in the present, past, or future—or in more than one time frame.

Answer: Present day.

Question: What is the character's challenge? This is the reason why the book was written, and why it will be read. The challenge can be a change in the status quo, a break in the continuity, and the characters' leap—or shove—out of their comfort zone.

Answer: Bored with Mom and Dad's church, the church youth group, and everything else in his small town, Jason makes up a new religion centered around the town's water tower. Best friend Shin takes the new religion way too seriously, while Magda and Henry use it as an excuse for dangerous pranks.

Godless

Pete Hautman

Sixteen-year-old Jason is just joking when he makes up a new religion centered on the town's water tower. Cute Magda and edgy Henry think it's a blast. Best friend Shin becomes a true believer—even a fanatic. (Friendship, Family Problems, Religion) Audiobook available.

This annotation describes the new religion, Jason's relationships, and the conflicts the new religion creates among the four characters. Because the annotation is written from Jason's point of view, his relationships with the three characters are telegraphed through their adjectives. He's attracted to "cute Magda," he's wary of "edgy Henry," and Shin is his "best friend." Conflicts among the four teens are conveyed by the con-trasts among Jason's attitude ("just joking") and the attitudes of Magda and Henry ("it's a blast") and Shin ("true believer—even a fanatic"). A volatile situation is set up, and it is neither necessary nor desirable to conclude the annotation with a phrase like, "...with unexpected results" or "...which ends in tragedy." Subject headings reinforce the two principle themes—friendship and religion—and introduce a third theme: family problems. I've also added "Audiobook available," signaling that the book is also available in CD or audiocassette formats.

NEWSLETTERS

A monthly newsletter reflects ongoing service to teens. The newsletter may be written and produced by the young adult librarian, with contributions from teens. Or the newsletter can be taken on as a teen advisory group project, under the guidance of the young adult librarian (Nichols 2002, 110). If you have access to a computer or typewriter and a photocopier, you can produce a teen newsletter.

Teen newsletter content can include the following:

- Reviews of new books, fiction and nonfiction. You have a good chance of seeing new young adult books as they arrive. Teens may not. By reviewing new books, the teen newsletter fosters equity of access. (You can also include teen reviews—see below.) Earlier in this chapter I referred to a book review style used in *Wizard*, a magazine that is made up almost entirely of 80- to 100-word reviews of comics and related media. Each word counts, so the writing is vivid, action-filled, and humorous—like many comics. I'll repeat my description of the reviews in the "Picks: Must-Read Books" section: they state the comic title, briefly explain "why it's cool," then close with a plot summary. Reversing the usual book review format of plot summary followed by critique, this format first gives the reader the reason why he'd want to read the book, and then follows up with the plot.

- Reviews of "oldies but goodies." With a few exceptions, both the publishing and library worlds spend the majority of their promotion time, money, and energy on new titles. Throw in a review of an oldie or a "recentie."

- Book reviews by teens. Many teen web pages include book reviews by teens submitted online. Not every teen enjoys 24/7 access to the Internet. So pull two or three short reviews off your web page and include them in the monthly newsletter. Teen book reviews will be discussed in more detail in Chapter 10.

- Reviews of book-related web sites. Review teen book sites and adult book sites in teen-appeal categories such as fantasy and science fiction. Other book-related sites to review include bookstores' teen web sites, which include book reviews by teens, advance promotion of upcoming titles, and author interviews.

- Surveys and quizzes. Print a short survey at the bottom of the newsletter and encourage teens to clip it and turn it in as a coupon for a prize drawing. Or ask teens to fill out a longer survey available in the teen space and online. Reading interest surveys and quizzes will be discussed in more detail in Chapter 10.

- Advertisements for book-centered activities and events. These include book discussion groups, bookmark contests, book-making workshops, writing workshops, author visits, and library book sales.

- Lists of books that were recently booktalked in schools.

- List of teen books found on shelving trucks.

- Quick theme, genre, or topic booklists. List five or ten good search-for-identity novels, thrillers, books about contemporary music, and so forth.

- Issues built around a theme. The September issue can highlight nonfiction guides to success at school—and teen fiction that tweaks school life. The October issue can focus on Teen Read Week activities, events, and prizes. The January issue can encourage teens to start the year off on the right foot with reviews of self-help books. By March, it's time to start promoting books about outdoor sports. The April issue can focus on poetry: teen novels written in poetry form, books about writing poetry, and collections of poems written by teens. Summer issues can celebrate free reading. Devote an entire issue to books recorded on CD or audiocassette, or books that have been made into movies.

- Additions or changes in the teen space. If your teen space has added a significant quantity of new books, a new collection (such as graphic novels, comics, or audiobooks), or has undergone a remodel, promote it in the teen newsletter.

- Reminders about readers' advisory and reference services. Create an advertisement reading, "Is there anything good to read around here? Sure! Pick up bookmarks and booklists, or ask your friendly library staff members. They'll be happy to dig into the collection with you."

Newsletters can be distributed in various ways. Insert a copy in a poster holder so that teens can see it, and stack the rest in front. Hand out copies during readers' advisory and reference conversations, and at teen activities and events. Build mailing lists or e-mail lists from registrants for activities, events, or contests (Nichols 2002, 110) and from summer reading participants. Add more names at every opportunity: at teen activities and events, during school visits, and while providing readers' advisory or reference service. Create a postcard-size form to distribute in the teen space—and other library locations—and post it on the teen web site, asking teens if they'd like to receive the newsletter by surface mail or e-mail. Mail or e-mail the newsletter to middle and high school media specialists. Bear in mind that school library collections—and selection policies—may vary from those of public libraries. Your newsletter promotes books to teens of all ages, and your middle school media specialist may not feel comfortable distributing a newsletter that reviews books that he or she has not selected for the school library, judging them more suitable for high school teens. That is his or her decision, and should not influence the types of books that you—and teens—review in the public library's newsletter.

POSTERS

Commercial sources for posters and bookmarks include ALA Graphics, Demco, Inc., Gaylord Bros., and Highsmith, Inc. Many publishers produce posters and bookmarks promoting upcoming titles, generally for the bookstore market; check publishers' web sites for the availability of their print promotions. You can also create your own posters, using software programs mentioned in the section above about design software and paper. What can you create that might appeal to teens? Remember, honesty, humor, and clarity top the list of what works in advertising directed to teens. Here are some ideas:

- "High Circ Books" is a list of high-circulating young adult fiction. Wait a minute. Outside of library land, nobody understands what we mean when we say "circulation," let alone "circ." Instead, let's call the list something like, "Teen Favorites" or "Popular Picks." The graphic could be a stack of books with little lines radiating from them, or lightening bolts.

- "Keep Your Brain Buff—Read!" In the upper right corner, there's a happy, well-toned brain reading a book. In the lower left corner, there's a dripping, disintegrating, nonreading brain sliming across the floor.
- "They Read It, They Liked It." Retype some of the teen book reviews from your teen web page and glue them onto a big sheet of paper.

Print promotions help young adult librarians promote reading and books to teens in many ways. Teens can find books on their own by using bookmarks and booklists. Library staff can provide more knowledgeable readers' advisory service. The library can advertise its core product—books and other materials—in the community. The biggest advertising space, however, is on the Internet. In the next chapter, we'll examine how you can use a new communication technology—the Internet—to promote a very old communication technology: books.

REFERENCES AND SUGGESTED READINGS

ALA Graphics. Located at http://www.alastore.ala.org/ (accessed February 1, 2006).

Calhoun, Dia. 1999. *Firegold*. Delray Beach, FL: Winslow Books.

Demco, Inc. Located at http://www.demco.com (accessed April 25, 2005).

Favorite Teen Angst Books. http://www.grouchy.com/angst/ (accessed April 25, 2005).

Gaylord Bros. Located at http://www.gaylord.com (accessed February 1, 2006).

Hautman, Pete. 2004. *Godless*. New York: Simon & Schuster for Young Readers.

Highsmith, Inc. Located at http://www.highsmith.com (accessed April 25, 2005).

Jones, Patrick. 1998. *Connecting Young Adults and Libraries: A How-To-Do-It Manual*. New York: Neal-Schuman Publishers.

Know Your World Extra. 2004. "Get Your Bling On . . . But Don't Break the Bank!" (January 30): 14–16.

Landa, Robin. 1998. *Thinking Creatively: New Ways to Unlock Your Visual Imagination*. Cincinnati, OH: North Light Books.

Nichols, Mary Anne. 2002. *Merchandising Library Materials to Young Adults*. Greenwood Village, CO: Libraries Unlimited.

Petreca, Laura. 2000. "Going to Extremes: Excesses of X's; Marketers Are Testing the Limits of Hot Teen Buzzword." *Advertising Age*. (July 24): 16–17.

TeenReads.com. Located at http://www.teenreads.com (accessed April 25, 2005).

Vaillancourt, Renee. 2000. *Bare Bones Young Adult Services: Tips for Public Library Generalists*. Chicago: American Library Association.

Webopedia. Located at http://www.webopedia.com/TERM/d/dpi.html (accessed September 6, 2005).

Zollo, Peter. 2004. *Getting Wiser to Teens: More Insights into Marketing to Teenagers.* Ithaca, NY: New Strategist Publications.

7

WEB IT

"Teen Life Online," a study conducted by the Pew Internet and American Life Project in 2001, surveyed 754 American teens aged 12 through 17. According to the study, 73 percent of teens used the Internet, and about half of high school teens and a third of middle school teens reported that they used the Internet every day (Lenhart 2001, 13). Of those online teens, 94 percent used the Internet for schoolwork (5). But the Internet means much more to teens than help with schoolwork. Online, teens can stay connected with friends via instant messages (IMs) and e-mail, explore interests and pastimes, find out more about who they are, and learn new things (10).

If you didn't know already, from these and other data about teens and the Internet, you can see that American teens are online, they're online frequently, and they're online in ways that reflect the basic developmental tasks of adolescence: establishing identity, connecting with others, and exploring the world. The finding that 76 percent of teens responded that they would miss Internet access "a lot" or "some" should it disappear (3) is a gauge of how established the Internet has become in the lives of many teens. What teens value about the Internet is social connection, entertainment, and information (14). As a section of your library's teen web site, the teen book site ideally offers social connection (book reviews by teens, book blogs, and online book discussion groups), entertainment (quizzes, surveys, and polls), and information (booklists and links to book sites).

While the focus of this chapter is on the teen book site, it will also refer to the teen web site as a whole. We'll begin with a review of web design basics. Moving into content, we'll start with library-created content, including booklists, book features, and newsletters. Next, we'll explore opportunities for teens to create content through booklists and book reviews. Then we'll review promotion methods, run a maintenance check—and plan for future renovation.

TEEN BOOK SITE CONSTRUCTION

Planning the teen book site, as a section of the teen web site, builds on the answers to three questions:

- What is the site about, and what is its purpose?
- What are your resources of time, expertise, and online capacity?
- Who is its audience?

Answering these questions in some detail will help you to plan the teen book site. The more detailed the plan, the less time it takes to build and maintain the site, because decisions and details have been worked out in advance (Vander Veer 2004, 13).

Book Site Plan

What is the site about, and what is its purpose? The teen book site is about reading and books, and its purpose is to inspire teens with the joy of reading and to connect them with books that will foster that joy. Ideally, the teen book site design and its content will reflect both the library's mission statement and the interests of its intended audience: teens (Itzkovitch and Till 2003, 20). Keep your library's mission statement in mind when designing your teen book site, writing out the ways in which the teen book site will help achieve that mission (14).

What are your resources of time, expertise, and online capacity? How much time will you be able to spend on the teen book site? For example, a "New This Week" book feature sounds great, but given available time, maybe a "New This Month" book feature is more feasible. Who will do the web work? Library web sites are variously created and maintained by in-house webmasters or communications departments, outsourced design firms, or library staff members. And the online capacity of teens connecting to your library's teen web site varies between broadband and dial-up, factors that can influence decisions on images and animation.

Who is its audience? As with any type of communication, find out about the audience you want to reach. Researching studies, journal articles, books, and web site resources helps, but what about teens who use *your* library? Find out what they like to read, and what they're looking for on a book web site. If your library has a teen advisory group, web site design is a great project. Bring printouts of teen web sites, preferably in color, for the group to critique. If your library does not have a teen advisory group, bring up the teen book site whenever you get the chance. Ask about it when talking with teens, visiting schools, or facilitating library activities or events.

As discussed in Chapter 6, design a stamp logo that links to an online survey about teen services and sprinkle it liberally around the teen web site. Distribute paper copies of the survey in your library's teen space, computer area, and service desks. Send the survey's URL to middle and high school media specialists, distribute paper copies of the survey to schools, and distribute the survey's URL—or paper copies—to teens on your electronic and surface mailing lists.

Online and paper surveys are useful, but keep in mind that many teens have so much paperwork for school that the last thing they want to do is to fill out something that looks like a worksheet. So keep talking with teens and asking them about the teen web site and its book section, whether casually or with a clipboard of your surveys so that you can fill them out on the spot.

Web Design Basics

Many of the same design principles and elements we examined in the context of teen spaces, displays, and print promotions apply to the web. The Internet is simply a new way to convey information. At the same time, there are design principles and elements that are particular to the Internet. Young adult librarians are principally web content specialists (Vander Veer 2004, 347), while web designers develop the visual and navigational components. For in-depth technical details about web design, you will need to refer to resources focusing on HTML coding, and such web design programs as Dreamweaver, Flash, Front Page, and Java Script.

The Look

The look of the teen web site is created by consistently featuring layouts, colors, images, and fonts that create a "brand," so that teens know exactly where they are when they arrive—and so do adults (Braun 2002, 51). Supporting the consistent look of the web and book sites is a consistent theme (Itzkovitch and Till 2003, 36), that is, reading and books. This means that no matter where teens go on the teen web site, they can easily link up with books, magazines, and graphic novels, and they will see images of cool-looking teens reading and talking about books.

Layout

The ideal web page design is a balance of image, text, and open space. A standard page layout comprises a Page Header Area across the top, a Sidebar Text Area along the left margin, and a Text Area in the middle. The Page Header Area features such images as the name of the teen web site, the name of the library, and a frieze of teen-appeal graphics or photographs. The Sidebar Text Area is often used as the site map or table of contents. The Text Area on the main page welcomes teens, while text areas on sub-pages (such as the teen book site) are for content. A Navigation Bar runs along the top, bottom, or one side of the page, linking to such informational sections as the library's home page, locations, hours, catalog, and contacts. A line along the bottom of the page lists copyright information and site update dates, and includes contact links for visitors' comments.

Remember the "underlying grid" that we examined in Chapter 5? The grid is as important in web design as it is in display design. The brain seeks order and consistency. When the eye perceives a consistent underlying design on home pages and subsequent sub-pages, the brain doesn't have to wear itself out bringing order out of chaos and can focus on content. Web page layouts also use angles, curves, and images as grids. Angular grids connote edgy, cutting-edge content, while curvilinear grids suggest free-flowing content. Choose clarity and legibility over overpowering background images, so that information is not subordinated to images: rather, they complement and enhance one another (Vander Veer 2004, 49).

Looking at teen web sites, two main page layout styles stand out: a big picture dotted with images that link to sections of links, and a rectilinear design of three or more columns of print, some stationary and some scrolling independently.

The advantage of the big picture layout is that it instantly communicates a mood and a purpose, and teens can easily find images or words to click on so they can get to content. Some big picture layouts also include a thumbnail of the big picture on all sub-pages, so that the mood and purpose of the site are sustained. A good example of the big picture layout is BPL Teens of the Burlington Public Library in Ontario, Canada, located at http://www.bpl.on.ca/bplteens/thezone.htm (accessed April 21, 2005).

The disadvantage of the big picture layout is that it can take "forever" to load, that is, up to 10 seconds or longer. "A slow loading page is an instant turn off, and most browsers won't stay, even if the page is worth the wait" (Kyrnin 2004). Also, if the picture layout is too big, there might not be room for much else besides a few button links and the navigation bar. There's less room for such teen-appeal interactive features as surveys, book discussion group news, and books on display.

The advantage of the multi-column layout is that it allows you to pack two or three web pages into one, as each column can be searched independently (Vander Veer 2004, 62). Even without the scrolling feature, the multi-column layout can burst with lively content: surveys, news about books and library events, reports from the teen advisory group, book reviews, and so forth. A good example of the multi-column layout is the Teen Zone of the Plymouth District Library in Plymouth, Michigan, located at http://plymouthlibrary.org/ya.htm (accessed April 21, 2005).

The disadvantage of the multi-column layout is that there can be so much going on that the page can lack focus, and come across as a confused grab bag. There's just too much crammed onto the page and no way to know what's important.

Layouts that balance image, text, and open space, setting the mood with a picture or two and previewing sub-page content, are visually pleasing and mentally stimulating. Two examples of balanced layouts are TeensPage, at the Loudon County Public Library, Loudon County, Virginia, located at http://www.lcpl.lib.va.us/teens/index.htm (accessed April 21, 2005), and Teen Zone, at the Calgary Public Library, Alberta, located at http://www.calgarypubliclibrary.com/teens/welcome.htm (accessed April 21, 2005).

Make sketches of what you'd like the main pages of the teen web site and teen book site to look like. Attach examples of teen book sites you like, to give the web designer an idea of what you envision (Itzkovitch and Till 2003, 24). Attach also examples of teen-appeal commercial sites you like. For example, Nokia.com, located at www.nokia.com (accessed April 21, 2005), exemplifies the sleek, modern look, while Hottopic.com, located at www.hottopic.com (accessed April 21, 2005), exudes cheeky splatterpunk. You can also find ideas, instruction, and inspiration in such books as *Building a Web Site for Dummies* (Crowder 2004), *Web Site Design with the Patron in Mind: A Step-by-Step Guide for Libraries* (Davidsen and Yankee 2004), *Faster Smarter Web Page Creation* (Millhollon 2003), and *Creating a Web Page with HTML* (Castro 2005). And keep checking for newer titles, magazine articles, and web sites, to keep up with changes in web design.

It All Starts at Home

The home or main page of the teen web site serves as the model for all other pages. Keep a book presence on the main page, and you will convey the connotative message that books and reading are important. Just as the teen space in the actual library is the primary display area for teen reading and books, so also is the main page of the teen web site the primary online display space. Include at least one book-related feature at the top of the home page, such as a book survey, book of the month, book group news, and so on.

When it comes to designing the teen book site, retain the look of the teen main page by using the same layout. But there's more to it than following the grid. If the spirit of the main page is upbeat, tough-minded, yet whimsical, keep it that way on the opening page of the teen book site. If teens leave a lively main page by clicking on "Books," and arrive at a book site that lists booklists or book links but lacks news and interactive features or images, they may feel let down.

As in other communication forms, open space is a place for the eyes to rest so the brain won't feel overwhelmed. Open space also serves to showcase text and images, much the same way a Japanese-style landscape of raked gravel showcases a few special plants or rocks. People are accustomed to scrolling down a screen, and it's preferable to leave some open space than to cram everything into the top half of the opening page. Use layout and colors to help visitors make their way through your site (Itzkovitch and Till 2003, 147). Keep the same type of information in the same spot, and color-code live links from the main page to sub-pages. Teens, however, are often accustomed to visual complexity—news crawls, split screens, and pop-ups—so don't be too spare.

Color

Establishing a teen-specific color palette is a good way to brand your teen web site. There are fourteen colors—coded by hexadecimal strings—that appear the same in all browsers. They are black, silver, gray, white, maroon, purple, fuchsia, green, lime, olive, yellow, navy, teal, and aqua

(Vander Veer 2004, 47). Bright turquoise, hot pink, lime, melon, metallics, and black appear often in teen magazines and web sites. Color choices drive connotative messages (79): red conveys excitement, passion, and power; blue conveys calm, reason, and ethics; and cool grays, taupes, and browns suggest balance and tradition. Some colors, however, are not recommended: using red, green, black, and other dark background diminishes your site's accessibility to visually impaired teens.

Before drenching your teen book site in color, remember that the mission of the site is not only to attract teen eyes but also to keep them on the page long enough to absorb some content. Use colors that harmonize rather than compete (83). Good combinations are secondary and tertiary groups from the color wheel. For a cooler look, go with a range of tints and shades of the same color, or two or three colors.

Think about surprising teens with color. For example, while retaining the same page layout for a seasonal reading promotion, such as summer reading or Teen Read Week, induce double-takes with a temporary color palette change. Change your usual lime and orange to a bright fuchsia and violet palette that will pop the page right off the screen.

Think also about branding all teen services through color: teen space décor, display fixtures, print promotions, and the teen web site. Keep in mind, however, the amount of time it will take to coordinate a color scheme for all teen services, and the time that will pass before you can change it—as some color schemes may quickly become dated.

Images

In Chapter 6, you saw how a booklist can carry both a denotative message (list of books = these are good books) and a connotative message (image of teens reading and sipping lattes = cool teens read books). Choose images that reflect the subject and purpose of the teen web site, such as those of teens in a library setting reading, talking, studying, playing board games, making things. Images that send a connotative message that reading is pleasurable and exciting include

- a teen sitting in a big comfortable armchair with a book and a mocha latte;
- a teen lounging poolside with a book and a cold drink;
- teens sitting around a table strewn with books, and talking about books; and
- a teen standing at a mic declaiming or reading poetry (or prose).

Web page images are of two types: graphics and photographs. GIF images (Graphic Interchange Format) are graphics that are often used as icons, buttons, backgrounds, line art, and animation (Vander Veer 2004, 66). JPEG images (Joint Photographic Experts Group) are photographs. Although JPEGs are not usable as animation or background images, their color range is tremendous—16.7 million colors—and their presence on a web site instantly upgrades it. There's nothing like cool, crisp photos to impart a sophisticated and intelligent look (Itzkovitch and Till 2003, 42).

Images take longer to load than text, so avoid weighing down the teen web site with large, complex background images or myriad small images. Eighty-three percent of teens go online from home (Zollo 2004, 360), and many of those home connections are dial-up, not high-speed broadband connections. Complex images, animation, Flash, and other features slow down loading even more. So go easy on the images on the main page, and consider using them on content pages as teens are drawn further into the web site (364). Be aware that you must obtain permission from the copyright owner before you scan and display copyrighted web images or images from magazines, books, and other materials (Vander Veer 2004, 69).

Libraries promote reading and books, and one way they do it is by displaying book covers and author photographs on their web sites. Book cover images are copyrighted and owned by book publishers. If your library uses a web-based catalog interface, check the terms of your licensing agreement to see if it includes the use of book cover images in locations on your web site besides the catalog. If your agreement does not include such use, you will need to contact publishers and request permission to display their book covers on your web site. Even if your agreement includes such a use, remember that book cover images are copyrighted and owned by book publishers, and as a courtesy it is recommended that you contact publishers for permission. To contact a publisher, visit its web site, find the link to rights and permissions guidelines, and follow their procedure. Some publishers include book cover images on their web sites that can be downloaded.

As for author photographs, they may be obtained by contacting authors, explaining that you wish to promote their work on your teen web site, and asking for digital photographs to download or print photographs to scan.

Ask your web page designer about the feasibility of "random images," a program that shows different images each time anyone visits the teen web site. Find or create a series of related photos for the page header area. Then again, if the teen web site and the teen book site already offer a lot of variety—including features that change periodically—random images may be disorienting. After all, what you want is for teens to know where they've landed, not to look around in confusion.

Fonts

Arial and Verdana are easy fonts to read; the latter font was created expressly for the web. These and other san serif fonts are used extensively as text fonts, and also as display fonts, particularly on navigation bars and site maps. The look they impart is clean, cool, and modern.

Using serif fonts for display text brings more visual interest to web sites, as well as to the same connotative messages used in print promotions. For example, using a handwritten-looking font like Mistral as a button link to teen book reviews conveys the excitement of dashing down a note to a friend, raving about a book.

Resist the urge to reduce the text font size below 10 point. Teens of all visual abilities need to be able to read what's on the screen. At the same time, avoid enlarging the text font size so that it resembles the print in a child's beginning reader. Keep headlines and other nontext fonts larger than text, but not so large that the site looks top-heavy. Use fonts from the same family to promote cohesion and credibility, while including a few fun fonts for variety. Contrast large, bold typography (for headings) with small, regular type for sentences or paragraphs. As with other design decisions, it's all about balancing eye appeal with clarity.

Accessibility

As we saw in the section on color, accessibility means many things. It means that red, green, or other dark backgrounds make a web site less accessible to visually impaired teens. Tiny print and patterned backgrounds are also difficult to read, whatever one's visual capacity. However cutting-edge and cool these visual choices may seem, they effectively reduce accessibility. Also, if your teen web site uses Flash, accommodate teens without Flash capability by offering a non-Flash version as well. And because many teens go online from handheld devices and cell phones, you might consider testing your library's web site accessibility from a variety of electronic devices (Firestone 2004, 133).

LIBRARY-CREATED CONTENT

The teen book site offers tremendous opportunities for young adult librarians to showcase their library's collections, services, and events for teens. Teen book sites have been enriched with booklists, promotional features, teen book reviews, reader advisory services, and book event news. By creating content, you show teens that their library truly plans and works for them. You are also contributing to what makes the Internet the fabulous resource that it has become.

Booklists

No paper, no ink, no waiting for the press, no problem! The Internet has liberated information from the bounds of paper. There are a staggering number of teen booklists online: on sites sponsored by public and school libraries, publishers, bookstores, other organizations, and individuals.

To create booklists for the teen book site, follow the steps outlined in the section on booklists in Chapter 6. Forward the file to your computer services department, to be posted in the booklist section of the teen book site in text and/or PDF format. Red-flag more recent lists with a "New!" graphic and/or a parenthetical note of the season/year or month/year of the booklist. There are different ways to arrange booklists: in reverse chronological order; alphabetical by author or title; in theme, genre, or subject lists; and graphically, with related images to click on that link to lists. Where possible, post book titles as live links to your catalog, so that teens can check to see if copies are available or, if not, they can be requested.

There are so many teen booklists on the web that it is impossible to list more than a tiny fraction of them:

- Good Books and More, at the Champaign Public Library, Champaign, Illinois, located at http://www.champaign.org/teens/goodbooks.html (accessed April 21, 2005). Booklists include "Record Label Dreams: Music Fiction and History," "Airing Dirty Laundry: The Secrets of Family and Friends," and "You're Friends with Who? Unexpected Friendships."

- Great Reads, at the Beaverton City Library, Beaverton, Oregon, located at http://www.beavertonlibrary.org/teens/reviews (accessed February 1, 2006). Booklists include "Books for Boyz," "Chick Lit," and "La Vida Latina: Titles for Teens about Latino Culture."

- Teen Zone Booklists and Reviews, at the Pike's Peak Library District, Colorado Springs, Colorado, located at http://library.ppld .org/YoungAdults/Pages/TalkAboutBooks/Brdefault.asp (accessed

April 21, 2005). Booklists include "Dark Humor/Mystery," "Fantasy/Humor," "Life's Tough," and "Tear Jerkers."

Displays

Maximize your teen web site's capacity to promote reading and books to teens with one or two eye-grabbing display features located just under the home page's Page Header Area. When teens click on the display, they'll arrive at the teen book site—and the display will be in the same spot it occupied on the home page.

Possible displays include the following:

- "Book of the month." On the home page, feature a thumbnail of the book cover and the book title. On the teen book site, feature the thumbnail with a *Wizard* magazine-style review, that is, a short review under the heading "Why you want to read it."

- "Author of the month." On the home page, feature a thumbnail photograph of the author and a few of the titles he or she has written. On the teen book site, feature the thumbnail, and link to the author's homepage.

- "Monthly book review/teen newsletter." Post your monthly book review/teen newsletter on the opening page.

Blogs

According to Perseus Co., a maker of web-surveying software, 52.8 percent of the world's approximately 38 million blogs are published by people 19 years old or younger (MacDonald 2005, 11). Perseus Co. further states that the typical blogger is a teenage girl who uses her blog to keep in touch with five to ten friends. Libraries have adapted this communication medium as a way to keep library patrons of all ages current on services, collections, and programs. Some library blogs serve as teen services' newsletters, in which library staff review books, promote activities and events, sponsor book chats and book discussion groups, and post general library news. Teen Blogmatic, sponsored by the Framingham Public Library in Framingham, Massachusetts, is located at http://fplya .blogspot.com (accessed September 6, 2005), and functions as just such a newsletter. Parma Public Library Blog Spot for Teens, sponsored by the Parma Public Library in Hilton, New York, is located at http://pplya

.blogspot.com/ (accessed September 12, 2005) and advertises itself as a place for teens to express their views on books, music, and current events. More library blogs—public and school—have been compiled by Amanda Etches-Johnson at blogwithoutalibrary.net, located at http://www.blog withoutalibrary.net/?page_id=94 (Oatman 2005, 39).

Libraries sponsoring blogs that are open to teen input use such sites as Blogger, located at http://www.blogger.com (accessed February 1, 2006), and Live Journal, located at http://www.livejournal.com (accessed September 6, 2005).

TEEN-CREATED CONTENT
Book Reviews

Just as the Internet has expanded libraries' ability to promote books through online booklists and readers' advisory, so also has it empowered teens to share their opinions about books. Teen book review sites are sponsored by public and school libraries, online teen magazines, bookstores, and other entities. Reviews can be short and to the point, or long and detailed, and many use a rating system from five points (fabulous) to one point (forget it).

To solicit teen book reviews, work with your web page designer to create an online book review form. Data fields can include title, author, review, rating, reviewer's first name, reviewer's age, and library (if part of a multibranch system). The review form can include a prompt to spark teen writing, such as

- "This book was (numerous adjectives, check all that apply)..."
- "I liked this book because..."
- "The reason you want to read this book is..."
- "This book is about..."

Post the book review form and scatter button links to it throughout the teen web site. The presence of button links labeled "Write a Review" and "Reviews by Teens" promotes reading, books, and teens who read, by giving attention to teens who are reading. Promote online book reviews off-screen by printing up the form, making photocopies, and distributing them in the teen space, at service desks, and during school visits.

The reviews on the "Reviews by Teens" page on your teen book site can be arranged in reverse chronological or alphabetical order, by author, or by title. If possible, make each title a live link to your catalog so that teens can reserve copies, whether they are currently available on the shelf or checked out. Teens can also contribute booklists on various themes, genres, or nonfiction subjects. Want to know what books teens would recommend to other teens? Just ask at your next book discussion group meeting. Encourage teens to share their interests and expertise—and they will!

LINKS

Teen book sites show teens who read that they are not alone, that other teens like to read, and that other teens like some of the same books they like. Peer-to-peer marketing is powerful. Scanning teen bestseller lists on bookstore sites, teens find out what's hot. Reading booklists and book reviews written by teens, and jumping onto blogs to comment about books, is the next best thing to hearing about books from friends. Teen book sites abound on sites sponsored by public libraries, school libraries, authors, publishers, bookstores, and colleges and universities. Follow the "three-click rule," so that a link is no more than three clicks away from your teen book site's home page:

Teen book site home page

List of sites of book reviews by teens

Book review site

Public Library Book Sites

Here are just a few of the many public library book sites on the Internet:

- Books Reviewed by Teens for Teens, St. Louis County Library, Missouri, located at http://www.slcl.org/teens/reviews/index .html (accessed February 1, 2006).
- More Book Reviews by Teens, Johnson County Library, Kansas, located at http://www.jocolibrary.org/index.asp?DisplayPage ID=1163 (accessed April 21, 2005).
- Reader's Club: Teen Corner, Public Library of Charlotte and Mecklenberg County, North Carolina, located at http://www.readers club.org/category.asp?cat=4 (accessed April 21, 2005).

Teen Book Sites

Public and school library web sites aren't the only places where teens can find booklists and book reviews. Teen book sites are springing up to meet all kinds of reading interests. Here are just a few:

- Favorite Teen Angst Books, located at http://www.grouchy.com/ angst (accessed April 21, 2005). Teens can find books about personal problems and self-discovery, send in comments about books, and read reviews by teens and articles by authors.
- Gilmore Girls: Rory's Book Club, located at http://www.the wb.warnerbros.com/web/o_genericfeedback.jsp?id=GG-Rory% 27s+Book+Club (accessed February 1, 2006). Rory's reading list includes classics and new books. Teens can also sign up for a newsletter, send in reviews, and post messages on a discussion board.
- Guys Read, located at http://www.guysread.com/ (accessed April 21, 2005). This site aims to connect guys with books they'd like to read.

Readers' Advisory Sites

Many high school teens and some middle school teens are reading adult books: bestsellers, literary fiction, classics, and nonfiction. Often, teens know about one or two authors of a favorite type of book—for example, Stephen King and Dean Koontz for horror—but that's it. Links to readers' advisory sites help teens to keep reading more books like the last book they liked so much. If your library's web site includes a readers' advisory site or portal, provide a link to it. Link also to such sites as the Alex Awards, located at http://www.ala.org/ala/yalsa/booklistsawards/ alexawards/alexawards.htm (accessed April 21, 2005). The Alex Awards are given each year by the Young Adult Library Services Association to adult books of great interest to teens.

Author Sites

Find out which authors are popular by talking with teens and library staff, by asking school media specialists, and by looking at shelving trucks. An ongoing "Author of the Month" feature on the teen book site validates teens' reading choices. However, try to avoid turning the author feature into an endorsement for a few highly popular authors. Instead, establish the monthly feature as a place where favorite authors can be found, then start mixing in less well-known authors. The monthly feature can include a photograph of a book cover or the author, and links to his or her web site, blog, book reviews, and the author entry in your library catalog, so that teens can easily find books. Definitely feature authors who come to your area for a book tour, or a school or library visit. You will need to obtain permission to use photographs of the author or book covers.

School, Publisher, Bookstore, and College Sites

Include links to your middle and high school libraries' web sites, and encourage them to link to your web site. School library web sites can include such information as assigned school reading lists, Accelerated Reading lists, and summer reading lists. An example of the latter is Boston Public Library's "Boston Schools Summer Reading Lists," located at http://www.bpl.org/kids/summerlists/index.htm (accessed December 28, 2005).

Links to publishers, bookstores, and college and university sites show teens that the culture of reading extends to the world of adults. Many of these sites highlight the social aspects of reading, by reporting book group news, hosting blogs, or posting site visitors' book reviews. Some sites support teen pages. HarperTeen, located at http://www.harperteen.com/ (accessed April 21, 2005), features a poll, an author spotlight, book reviews, and a bestseller list. The "Reading Community" button links to such features as e-newsletters, advice on starting a reading group, and information about receiving review copies. Some bookstores sponsor teen book groups or events, such as author visits. Others get involved in schools' and public libraries' summer reading promotions, or they may sponsor their own. Local and regional bookstores also serve as good gauges of reading interests. For example, the teen book site of Powell's City of Books in Portland, Oregon, located at http://www.powells.com/psection/ChildrensYoungAdult.html (accessed April 21, 2005), features new arrivals, top ten selling teen books in the Portland area, and staff reviews. Teen book sites sponsored by chain bookstores reflect national reading interests. Barnes and Noble's teen web site, located at http://www.barnesand noble.com (click on "Children," and then "Teens") (accessed April 21, 2005), features reviews of new books, top five selling teen books, and numerous links to featured authors, favorite series, and book categories.

While you may have already linked to local and regional colleges and universities from a "life after high school" section of the teen web page, consider also linking to campus libraries, bookstores, and Humanities departments. Older teens may want to check out campus sites for author visits, bookstore sales, or other book-related news. Other links of interest to teens include college or university freshman reading lists. Contact the relevant academic department, ask for the reading list web address, and add it to the teen book site.

INTERACTIVITY

Teens value social connection and communication. 87 percent of U.S. teens aged 12–17 use the Internet (Lenhart, Madden, and Hitlin 2005, ii), 45 percent own a cell phone (ii), and 33 percent have used a cell phone to send a text message (ii). To keep in touch with friends, 51 percent of teens report using the telephone most frequently, while 24 percent use IMs (iii). Of IM-using teens, 50 percent report including links in messages (iii). Teens are online, they're communicating, and they're sending files. The Internet's interactive character fosters teens' interests. Standard features of commercial web sites include FAQs about products and services, polls and surveys, results, Q&A contacts, product reviews by customers, and press releases (Vander Veer 2004, 12). Depending on available staff time, the teen book site can offer teens a variety of interactive features.

Quizzes, Surveys, and Polls

Teens enjoy learning about themselves in entertaining ways, responding to magazine and online quizzes, surveys, and polls. They also like to share their opinions. Young adult librarians can create interactive features such as

- "Tell me about five good (name of theme, genre, or subject) books for teens." Teens link to a list of five chatty shelf talks.
- "Vote for the book of the month." Teens link to an online ballot of five titles.
- "What kinds of books do you like? Take this quiz and we'll tell you about some good books!" This feature is more complex to construct and maintain than shelf talks or polls. Teens link to a quiz of ten multiple-choice questions, crafted from information about appeal

characteristics, follow-up questions, and other material covered in Chapter 3 on collections and in Chapter 8 on readers' advisory. Unless you program this quiz for instant results, you will need to ask for an e-mail address to which to send a response.

E-mail

Some teen-oriented commercial web sites offer e-mail notification of sales and product arrivals. Maintaining an equivalent service—e-mail notification of new books and other news—can be very labor intensive (Braun 2002, 26). Instead, consider offering e-mail sign-up to receive an existing publication, such as your teen newsletter. Similarly, if you invite online readers' advisory questions, you'll need the staff time to provide the service in a complete and timely manner (Firestone 2004, 127).

Forms for teens to fill out and submit via e-mail can include the following: book reviews, top ten favorite books ballots, questionnaires, book recommendation/purchase requests, web site recommendations, and activity/event evaluation forms (sent to registrants/participants only). Use the same e-mail address for all of these forms (Vander Veer 2004, 24), and add a "Contact Us" button to every page. Always ask if teens would like to receive e-mail, rather than assume that because teens like online communication, they must also like unsolicited e-mail. Ever heard of spam? Teens told researchers at Teenage Research Unlimited (TRU) that if there's one thing they abhor, it's unsolicited e-mail (Zollo 2004, 381).

Online Book Discussion Groups

Online book discussion groups allow teens to communicate about books free from the constraints of time and space. An easy way to facilitate a group is to select a book, post it as the "book teens are talking about," and invite teen comments via the teen book review form. Collect comments as they come in. Other ways to sponsor online book discussion groups include joining online book clubs, setting up blogs, and sponsoring online discussion boards.

By joining the Teen Book Club at DearReader.com (http://www.dear reader.com, accessed February 5, 2006), you will receive chapters of a book by e-mail, which you can forward to an e-mail list of interested teens. Teens can post their comments to book club forums, read by subscribers all over the United States (Jones 2004, 284). Yahoo! Group pages can be created by anyone with a Yahoo! account, and set up as chat rooms, enabling teens to meet in cyberspace and chat about books. Teens will need access to a personal computer with Windows 95, 98, NT, or 2000, plus Microsoft Internet Explorer (4.0 version or later) or Netscape Navigator (4.08 version or later) (287). Libraries can also sponsor a web discussion board by buying requisite software, enabling discussion group members to post and read messages. Once purchased and installed, this software opens possibilities for other discussion forums, whether for adult reader services or internal staff development (285).

Information about facilitating and promoting book discussion groups appears in Chapter 10.

PROMOTION

Promote the teen book site inside the library by printing up copies of its main page, in color if possible. You can also create a simplified poster by using the teen book site address as the headline, the dominant book site image as the graphic, and a bulleted list of book features. Laminate and display these posters in the teen space, on bulletin boards, in book displays, and on book shelves. Post them in the computer area and at service desks. Include the teen book site address in all teen print promotions.

Promote the teen book site during school visits, writing the address on the board and talking about the booklists, the book reviews by teens, and how easy it is to send in reviews. Include the address on the booklists you distribute. Promote the teen web site to other youth-serving agencies by sharing the address with parks and recreation departments, health and human services departments, hospitals, and such youth organizations as the Boys and Girls Club. Alert service organizations to the library's commitment to teens with a letter describing the teen web site and an invitation to add it to the "community resources" section of their web sites.

Finally, add the teen web site address to your e-mail signature, so that individual correspondents and e-mailing list subscribers will see it, too.

WEB PAGE MAINTENANCE

Answering the three questions about site purpose, staff time, and audience helped you to plan and carry out web site construction. Construction, however, is just the beginning. Now comes maintenance: checking links, updating links, and remodeling the site. Periodically check that all links lead to viable sites, and make sure that interactive links lead to their respective e-mail, book review, blog, or survey forms. Periodically view your site on Windows, Mac, and Linux to ensure that it's still getting through to all three operating systems (Itzkovitch and Till 2003, 28).

Such regularly updated features as surveys, book or author features, new booklists, and new links to book sites keep the site lively and engaging. At the same time, try to avoid changing the layout and content categories too frequently: visitors want dependability as well as novelty (Firestone 2004, 141). They like finding the same thing in the same place so they don't have to waste time looking for it. "New!" printed on a bright red or yellow paint splotch is a fun way to tell teens that a site has just been added. The "freshness date"—which usually appears at the top or bottom of an updated page—reassures visitors that the site is dynamic, not static. Many teen-appeal entertainment, commercial, and information sites display the current date or week, which conveys currency, but only if content is updated daily or weekly. You need to know how much time you will have to devote to updates. If the date changes daily but the content changes only monthly, why hint at currency through the daily date only to disappoint with content that does not change as frequently?

Extreme Makeover

Perhaps your teen web site was designed a while ago, and it's time for a change. It may need only a bit of redecoration: same layout, new colors, different graphics. It may need some remodeling: new links categories. Then again, it may need . . . an extreme makeover: new layout, new colors, new fonts, new graphics, new categories, new links, new everything. What to do?

Revisit public library, school, and teen-appeal web sites. Look at current layouts, colors, fonts, graphics, sections of links, and language. Get ideas from new books on web design, and web magazines. Send sketches and favorite web site designs to your web site designer. Meanwhile, start thinking about updating your sections. Maybe you have six broad sections with eight subsections of links each. Think about reshuffling sections, maybe ending up with ten sections with fewer subsections, so that teens can more directly see what's available on the teen web site. For example, your existing teen web site might include both advice and volunteering sites in a "Real Life" section. Make them more visible by splitting them into new sections, such as "Get Help" and "Give Help." Remove tired links and edit the remaining site annotations.

Look for new links for the new categories, and new links for existing categories. While you've been developing content—floor plan, frame, and furniture—the web site designer has been developing the visual and navigation components—the interior and exterior decoration. Soon you'll be able to put everything together, for a teen web site that's as good as new.

Like many teens and adults, I love, love, *love* the web. But sometimes, when you're looking for help finding a book like the last book you liked so much, you don't want to trawl through a thousand books on the shelf, or pick up books from a display and then put them back. You don't want a printed booklist, and you don't want a web site. You want a person. You want someone who will listen to what you have to say, and make some suggestions. As a teen, you might not know what to call that kind of help. But as librarians, we do. We call it readers' advisory.

REFERENCES AND SUGGESTED READINGS

Braun, Linda W. 2002. *Teens.library: Developing Internet Services for Young Adults.* Chicago: American Library Association.

Castro, Elizabeth. 2005. *Creating a Web Page with HTML.* Berkeley: Peachpit Press.

Crowder, David A. 2004. *Building a Web Site for Dummies.* Hoboken, NJ: Wiley.

Davidsen, Susanna, and Everyl Yankee. 2004. *Web Site Design with the Patron in Mind: A Step-by-Step Guide for Libraries.* Chicago: American Library Association.

Firestone, Tracy. 2004. Nothing but Net: A Virtual Collection Young Adults Will Want to Use. In *Thinking Outside the Book: Alternatives for Today's Teen Library Collections*, ed. C. Allen Nichols Westport, CT: Libraries Unlimited.

Itzkovitch, Avi, and Adam Till. 2003. *Design-It-Yourself Web Sites: A Step-by-Step Guide.* Glouster, MA: Rockport.

Jones, Patrick, Michele Gorman, and Tricia Suellentrop. 2004. *Connecting Young Adults and Libraries: A How-To-Do-It Manual for Librarians.* New York: Neal-Schuman Publishers.

Kyrnin, Jennifer. *If You Build It . . . Will They Come? Tips to Promote Your Web Site.* Available at http://webdesign.about.com/library/weekly/aa032398.htm (accessed November 29, 2004).

Lenhart, Amanda, Lee Rainie, and Oliver Lewis. 2001. *Teenage Life Online: The Rise of the Instant-Message Generation and the Internet's Impact on Friendships and Family Relationships.* Pew Internet and American Life Project (Washington DC, June 2001). Available at http://www.pewinternet.org/ (accessed November 17, 2004).

Lenhart, Amanda, Mary Madden, and Paul Hitlin. 2005. *Teens and Technology: Youth Are Leading the Transition to a Fully Wired and Mobile Nation.* Pew Internet and American Life Project (Washington DC, July 2005). Available at http://www.pewinternet.org (accessed December 17, 2005).

MacDonald, G. Jeffrey. 2005. "Teens: It's a Diary. Adults: It's Unsafe. Blogs Are a Fun Forum of Self Expression for Adolescents. But Might Blogging Be Dangerous?" *Christian Science Monitor.* (May 25): 11.

Millhollon, Mary. 2003. *Faster Smarter Web Page Creation.* With Jeff Castrina. Redmond, WA: Microsoft Press.

Oatman, Eric. 2005. "Blogomania!" *School Library Journal.* (August): 36–39.

Vander Veer, Emily. 2004. *Creating Web Pages: All-in-One Desk Reference for Dummies.* New York: Wiley.

Zollo, Peter. 2004. *Getting Wiser to Teens: More Insights into Marketing to Teenagers.* Ithaca, NY: New Strategist Publications.

8

TELL ME ABOUT A BOOK
THAT YOU'VE READ
AND ENJOYED—OR
HOW ABOUT A MOVIE?

It's one of the oldest questions in library land.

"I'm looking for a book to read. What do you recommend?"

Through readers' advisory service, you can directly promote reading and books to teens—one teen at a time. Not only does readers' advisory allow you to make the connection between teens and books, but it also gives you and teens the opportunity to share your enthusiasm about books. Many of us became librarians because we love reading and books. Readers' advisory lets us share that love by helping teens find books they'd like to read (Vaillancourt 2000, 49).

Readers' advisory requires skills and knowledge: understanding the appeal of books, appreciating teens' reading experiences, staying familiar with collections, knowing what questions to ask and what to listen for in teens' answers, giving shelf talks, providing choices, and following a personal reading plan.

READING BOOKS WITH
TEEN READERS IN MIND

The foundation of providing readers' advisory service to teens is reading young adult fiction and nonfiction—as well as a smattering of children's and adults' books that appeal to younger and older teens, respectively (Vaillancourt 2000, 49). While young adult librarians can help teens find good books to read by familiarizing themselves with their collections and readers' advisory resources, there is no substitute for actually reading some of the books. Not only do you need to read, but also you need to understand reading, and all that teens get out of it. Through that understanding, you and teens can connect, reader to reader.

While reading and enjoying teen books, it is advisable to keep two things in mind: the appeal characteristics of books and the reading experiences of teens. In other words, what do teens like in books, and how do they feel and think about what they read?

Appeal Characteristics

Appeal characteristics are elements of a book that readers enjoy—and talk about. The term "appeal characteristics" means different things to different people, but young adult and adult readers' advisory experts agree that what readers enjoy in fiction is not so much the apparent "subject" of a book, but the elements of the book that the author chooses to emphasize. It's true that the subjects of some books make them easy— or difficult—to promote to teens, no matter what their appeal characteristics. For example:

Easy: Anything with vampires.
Difficult: 1950s historical fiction.

Appeal characteristics give readers those unquantifiable good (or bad) "feelings" about books they've read (Pearl 2002, xi). Because readers are more often looking for books for pleasure reading that have a certain "feel," they are usually not looking for books by subject (Saricks 2005, 40). For example, readers can be drawn to funny characters, whether they're in science fiction, adventure, romance, or weird tales of high school life.

As noted above, different readers' advisory experts focus on different elements of books that they describe as appeal characteristics. Diana Tixier Herald focuses on teens' interests in characters, strong plotlines, and cool or compelling covers (Herald 2003, 5). Joyce Saricks (2005, 40) describes books in terms of their pacing, characterization, story line, and frame. Nancy Pearl (2002, xi) highlights story, character, setting, and language.

Appeal characteristics operate on a deeper level than the apparent subject of a book. For example, the subject of both *The Voyage of the Continental* (Kirkpatrick 2002) and *Paradise: Based on a True Story of Survival* (Goodman 2002) is an ocean voyage to a new land. But the stories, characters, settings, and language differ tremendously. In *Voyage*, plucky Emeline gives readers a diary account of her ocean voyage in 1866, from New York to Seattle—an adventure/mystery driven by can-do girl power attitude. *Paradise*—a moody, tragic love story mired in sixteenth-century sectarian hatred—tells the somber story of Marguerite, a young woman abandoned on a deserted island with her lover and chaperone. These two ocean voyage books may not appeal to the same reader.

There are many more elements that teens enjoy (or don't enjoy) in fiction, such as genre, mood, sexuality, and length of book. It is also important to be aware of an array of plotlines and writing styles that may offend some teen readers and the parents of younger teens, regardless of appeal characteristics (Vaillancourt 2000, 50). High-awareness plotlines include those that highlight sexual relationships or criminal behavior, while writing styles are those whose effects are dependent upon incessant swearing, explicit sexual activity, or graphic violence.

Story

Young adult novels dominated by fast-moving plots have story appeal for many teens (Herald 2003, 5). Readers race to turn the pages because they have to know what happens next. Action, dialogue, and minimal description keep the story moving. Teen readers who go for story appeal books may read books featuring a variety of characters or settings, but it's the story that comes first. Novels driven by story often make good movies—and teens sometimes describe these books as being "like a movie."

Adventure, mystery, suspense, horror, and fantasy novels exemplify story appeal. The *Pendragon* fantasy series (MacHale 2002+) drops hero Bobby Pendragon into one parallel world, hurling him from one cliffhanging chapter to the next, before dumping him into another parallel world. The action is nonstop, the characters are colorful, and the settings are weird. And for those readers seeking more of an emotional bond with characters, there is the underlying poignancy of Bobby's exile from the home world in which he grew up.

Story appeal is not limited to fast-moving genre fiction. Sometimes a slow, deliberate pace can pull a reader inexorably through the pages (Saricks 2005, 45). The plots of many intense realistic young adult novels unfold slowly, surely, and with increasing speed as the truth emerges. In

Dead Girls Don't Write Letters (Giles 2003), Sunny's glamorous older sister, Jazz, dies in a fire. Months later, she writes to say she's coming home. A girl shows up, to their parents' joy, who may or may not be Jazz.

Characters

Young adult novels centered on the feelings and thoughts of their characters have character appeal. As teens discover who they are, strive to be accepted, build honest relationships, and master a variety of skills, they enjoy reading books whose characters are going through the same processes (Herald 2003, 5). They also like characters like the older teens they see around school, who seem to have it all: developed bodies, strong voices, cool clothes, fun social lives, and exciting futures. Older teen characters appeal to what marketing researcher Peter Zollo (2004, 50) refers to as teens' "age aspiration." Teens are learning how to be independent human beings, facing challenges, decisions, heartaches, and joys. They are interested in how older teens feel, think, talk, and act.

Books with character appeal often spend time inside their characters' hearts and heads, focusing more on the way in which the characters *experience* what happens, than on what actually happens. The first-person teen narrative was literally a new voice for teens when Holden Caulfield lit out from prep school in *Catcher in the Rye* (Salinger 1951). Teens loved that book—and still do. Young adult fiction as we know it arrived in the 1960s and 1970s, and teens also loved those books in which teens spoke for themselves. These days, they're also speaking through fiction written in the form of diaries, letters, poetry, e-mail, and instant messaging (IM).

Characters in young adult novels are mostly teens, with friends, parents, siblings, and perhaps a few significant adults mixed in. This reflects the reality of many teens' lives. Their primary relationships are still with their parents and siblings, but they are building new relationships with friends. With friends, teens are learning how to establish relationships of their choosing, and how to flourish—or at least function—in small groups. With friends, teens are learning that people may be different from them, but that it's still possible to like them. In fact, having friends stimulates teens to hone their own individual identities.

Teens' interest in friends is reflected by the popularity of such novels as *Sisterhood of the Traveling Pants* (Brashares 2001) and its two sequels. The lifelong bond among Lena, Tibby, Carmen, and Bridget is expressed as they mail their magical "traveling pants" from one girl to the next, for the jeans seem to arrive at the point when each girl needs their friendship the most. The character appeal of this book is that each girl speaks for herself, in rotating chapters, and that through friendship, the girls also have a supportive community.

Friendship can also spring up in unlikely places, and teens are intrigued by the attraction of opposites. Defensive Lucy, who lives in a group home, and snotty, wealthy Nate are thrown into detention and gradually get to know each other as individuals in *The Last Chance Texaco* (Hartinger 2004). Straight-A Antonia needs an extracurricular activity for college applications and signs up to be a peer counselor in *Define "Normal"* (Peters 2000). She becomes dismayed when her assigned counselee is Jazz, a punk rocker. Forced to spend time together, they see past their assumptions and become supportive friends.

Character appeal manifests in a variety of ways. Series fiction features ongoing characters who develop over time (Saricks 2005, 50–51), like Harry and his friends in the *Harry Potter* series (Rowling 1997+). Teen characters don't always have to be totally likeable to be fascinating, either. Like colorful villains in movies and TV, negative characters can hold readers' interest. Vicious, manipulative bullies like Rob in *Shattering Glass* (Giles 2002) can make for compelling reading: what horrible thing will he pull next? Conflicted characters torn between good and evil can be the most fascinating of all.

Setting

When a teen describes in great detail the place or time period in which a novel takes place, he is telling you that the appeal of the book is its setting. Also known as frame or background, the setting can be geographic (location), experiential (high school, the wilderness), or temporal (a time in history).

Sometimes the geographic setting is enjoyably familiar. Sometimes it is unfamiliar, and readers have the pleasure of exploring a new place. The minutely described worlds of fantasy and science fiction exemplify setting appeal for teens.

Sometimes the experiential setting is familiar, such as school. Many teens enjoy what I call the "cruel at school" theme of realistic fiction, exemplified by such books as *The Lottery* (Goobie 2002) and *Drowning Anna* (Mayfield 2002). Cruelty and abuse are themes in other young adult novels, but for many teens, it is the school setting that most strongly compels. School is where they spend so much time, and where their academic, athletic, or social success or failure has so many serious consequences.

Unfamiliar settings can also be appealing. Urban teens may enjoy the unfamiliar challenges posed by wilderness survival stories, while the high-gloss Manhattan settings make the *Gossip Girl* series (Ziegesar 2002+) a fun place to visit.

And while historical novels are not always the first choice of all teens, some teens enjoy their time-travel aspect, as well as gaining new perspectives on history (Herald 2003, 139). First-person and diary format novels pull teen readers into history through the first-person narrative of one character (Herald 2003, 140)—a narrative as personal as any by a character in a contemporary realistic teen novel.

Language

When a teen reader raves about the way a novel is written, she may be signaling a liking for what is defined as literary fiction, books in which the author's "voice" explicitly shapes the story. The writing reflects the author's mastery of language, and it enriches the entire book, whether the author's focus is on story, character, setting, or all three. Beautifully written young adult novels do so much more than lay out a story in serviceable prose. *Kit's Wilderness* (Almond 2000) weaves together life and death, past and present, with a narrative voice that echoes in the reader's mind long after the last page. Teens who enjoy this novel would probably also enjoy poetry and retold legends. The ironic, seen-it-all drawl of Daisy narrating *How I Live Now* (Rosoff 2004) tells a story of extremities, as Daisy pushes down emotions through sarcasm in a world shattered by war, occupation, desperate sexual love with her cousin, and heroism.

Another example of books with language appeal are humorous novels, which read like a good friend telling you a funny story, embellishing and exaggerating to make a point, not letting up until you're rolling on the floor laughing. In *Girl, 15, Charming but Insane* (Limb 2004), Jess wants to look good at a party, so she stuffs her bra with baggies full of minestrone soup in lieu of silicon implants. What happens next is funny, but it's the way Jess describes everything from party disasters to feeling inferior next to her beautiful best friend that weaves a humorous spirit through every sentence, making everything so hilarious.

Four-Appeal Books

While many books have one or two appeal characteristics, some books possess all four. Because these books appeal on so many levels, they are often universally popular, becoming big bestsellers, or they get passed around from one teen to the next until they fall apart. One of the best examples of a four-appeal book is the *Harry Potter* series (Rowling 1997+). It's a series that has it all: a fast-moving story; brightly drawn and compelling characters; a magical setting; and imaginative, original, and humorous language.

Reading Experiences

While reading young adult books, think also about the emotional and intellectual experiences they may engender in teens. Appeal characteristics are what keep teens turning the pages. Reading experiences are what happen inside their heads and hearts as they read. Through reading experiences, teens incorporate what exists on the page into their own lives. They can feel part of something larger than themselves, taking them beyond what they thought and felt about life before they started to read.

One way to understand reading experiences is to relate them to the seven stages of reading development, that is, what readers get out of reading. These stages were first identified by Margaret Early and G. Robert Carlson (Lesesne 2003, 28), and later by Kenneth L. Donelson and Alleen Pace Nilsen in their study of young adult literature (Donelson and Nilsen 1997). Once past the first two stages of reading development—understanding the attraction of words and stories, and learning the mechanics of reading—children, teens, and adults may advance through five subsequent stages of reading development. Just as their reading abilities exist on a variety of levels, teens enjoy a variety of reading experiences. One book gives them the thrill of a fast, fun story, while another allows them to plumb emotional and intellectual depths.

What follows is a brief explanation of teens' reading experiences, the reading stages they reflect, and how readers' advisory can help teens replicate those reading experiences.

"I Couldn't Put It Down!"

"All I want to do is read," a teen said in a fantasy/science fiction book discussion group. "Last night, my mom and dad had to come into my room and physically drag me out for dinner."

"I really like the Amelia Atwater-Rhodes books," said another teen. "Even though they're not a real 'series,' there's always one character from another book in each of them, so they create a world, and I can jump into any one of the books and know my way around."

Teens are discovering the bliss that comes when they plunge into a book and don't want to leave the world it creates. In fact, the "real world" recedes as they become lost in a book (Lesesne 2003, 126). Reading researchers refer to this third stage of reading development as "unconscious delight," that state of reading simply for the pleasure of escaping into another world. Teens who read with unconscious delight often stick with favorite series, genres, or authors (Donelsen and Nilsen 1997, 38), returning again and again to the place they found so enjoyable. The *New York Times* bestseller list confirms that many adults also stick with favorite series, genres, and authors (Lesesne 2003, 128).

When teens say that they want more of the same kind of book, young adult librarians can help them find more of those books—rather than try to guide them toward "better" books, as readers' advisory librarians took it upon themselves to do in past decades (Saricks 2005, 6). The girl who enjoys fantasy has hundreds of novels she can read. The girl who loves the world of Amelia Atwater-Rhodes has dozens of similar books she can read. And both genres continue into adult fiction.

"That Book Was Just Like My Life!"

"We read this book in class, and talked about how it's kind of like this school," three high school boys told me. We were talking about books after a booktalk performance, and they were holding copies of *Breaking Point* (Flinn 2002).

Not satisfied with fast plots and easy stereotypes, teens are discovering their enjoyment of complex plots and conflicted characters. These books are more like real life, and more like their own lives. Reading researchers refer to the fourth stage of reading development as "reading autobiographically." Teens are reading not to escape reality, but rather to find out about it. Teens devour stories of alienation, angst, friendship, conflict with parents, success or trauma at school—and books that put a humorous spin on those experiences. In these books, character is a major appeal characteristic. Teens also explore real lives, through biographies, autobiographies, and memoirs (Donelsen and Nilsen 1997, 42).

"It Would Be So Horrible If That Happened"

"That book was so sad. I would hate it if my best friend died."

"It was fun to see what it would be like to find out that you were a princess—a real princess, with a castle and throne and everything!"

As teens mature, they begin to appreciate and understand people living lives different from their own. What would it be like if your mother had cancer, beat it, and it came back? Read *Both Sides Now* (Pennebaker 2000). What would it be like to lose your best friend to a car accident or a random shooting? Read *Tears of a Tiger* (Draper 1994) or *Party Girl* (Ewing 1998). Reading researchers refer to the fifth stage of reading development as "reading for vicarious experience." Through reading realistic fiction or memoirs of suffering, teens can live through traumatic experiences at the safe distance of the printed page. Teens are aware of their lack of power in the world and empathize with those in tragic circumstances.

Vicarious experiences need not be horrible. They can also be challenging, upsetting, and fear-inducing, and yet be resolved in ways that are both hopeful and realistic, as when a loving adoption follows teen pregnancy in *Dancing Naked* (Hrdlitschka 2001). And it's lots of fun to laugh along with Mia's fish-out-of-water antics in the *Princess Diaries* series (Cabot 2000+).

"It Made Me Think about Stuff"

"I found out a lot by reading that book."

"I never thought about those things that way before."

When teens talk about books in these ways, they are describing reading experiences that taught them something or challenged their assumptions. Reading researchers refer to the sixth stage of reading development as "reading for philosophical speculation." Sometimes it is fantasy and science fiction that fosters philosophic speculation. Dystopias like those depicted in *The Giver* (Lowry 1993), the *Shadow Children* series (Haddix 1998+), and the *Fire-Us* trilogy (Armstrong and Butcher 2002–2003) force teen readers to examine their assumptions about society, including the technological innovations they have grown up consuming and expecting.

Sometimes realistic fiction fosters philosophic speculation, allowing teen readers to infer life lessons from the unfolding story. Jimmy figures out why the judge accepted old Duke's offer to take him and another young offender on as community service workers. The wise and funny commentary of the regulars at Duke's barbershop—on friendship, honor, treating women right, and more—constitutes a *Handbook for Boys* (Myers 2002). The regulars' discussion makes Jimmy—and readers—think about life in different ways.

As it does in the previous stage of reading development, nonfiction meets teens' curiosity directly, rather than symbolically. Popular nonfiction that meets teens' curiosity about themselves, each other, and the world includes books about UFOs, philosophy, dreams, personality, religions, urban legends, and mental health (Jones 2004, 123).

"I Loved the Way That Book Was Written"

Teens who rave about the way a book is written are telling you that they concur with reading researchers, who refer to the seventh stage of reading development as "reading for aesthetic experiences." Teens who read for aesthetic experiences will find them in young adult novels such as those given the Michael L. Printz Award, which is conferred upon books of outstanding literary merit. They also enjoy well-written adult fiction and nonfiction, as well as poetry, fairy tales, legends, and classics.

READERS' ADVISORY WARM-UPS
Ask Teens

Ask teens what books they're reading, and find out more details about what they liked and didn't like (Jones 2004, 82). If you haven't read the books they mention, ask what they're about. Read the books they talked about, plus more titles from the same theme, genre, or topic. When teens talk about what they don't like—such as too much description that slows down a plot—that's also useful information. Talking with teens about what they like to read is another way to promote reading. By paying attention to teens, you're showing them that you value them as people. By paying attention to their opinions about books, you're showing them that you value them as readers. Talking about reading reinforces the message that reading and books are our business.

Library Bestsellers

While it's helpful to know what books are flying off of actual or virtual bookstore shelves, nothing beats knowing what's popular with teens at your library. Find out what's hot by checking which teen books have circulated the most, and which have the most requests (Jones 2004, 82). Ask school media specialists what's hot with teens at their schools. School media specialists are in the enviable position of working on site at teens' workplace—schools—and of building relationships with avid readers. Talk with them. They can tell you a lot!

Readers' Advisory Resources

No matter how hard you try, you will not be able to read every young adult book ever written, nor will you be able to keep up with the flood tide of new books. If you do read a lot of books, it is difficult to remain well read in all genres and themes. By examining readers' advisory resources, you will better know how to connect cues from teens' descriptions of what they like to read, to books you can suggest. Some teens will forthrightly announce "I like (title), do you have anything like that?" Others may talk about the kinds of books they like to read. Listen for clues about the appeal characteristics embedded in their descriptions.

Acquaint yourself with the professional tools that can help you work with teen readers.

Teen Genreflecting (Herald 2003) covers themes in realistic fiction as well as such genres as adventure, mystery, suspense, fantasy, science fiction, paranormal, historical fiction, multicultural, and Christian fiction. A chapter on alternative formats describes such treatments as short stories, diaries, graphic novels, and novels in poems, while an appendix indexes fiction, by genre and theme, of possible interest to reluctant readers.

What Do Young Adults Read Next? (Spencer 1999), like others in the *What...?* series, takes books and then links them to more titles. Each title entry includes the book's subject, reading level, characters, setting, a summary, other books by the author, and other books a teen reader might like. There are two indexes of particular interest to young adult librarians, in addition to indexes about time or geographical setting, subject, character, and so on. The Age Index groups books by grade level, and the Page Count Index groups books by page count. "I have to read a book that's at least 200 pages, but I don't want anything longer than that," says a teen. No problem. Turn to the "151 to 200 Pages" section, and you'll find a long list of books. Appendix II lists print and electronic young adult resources that can be used for collection development, displays, booklists, readers' advisory, and booktalking.

Electronic databases, such as "What Do I Read Next, Online" and "NoveList" can also help you with readers' advisory. And don't forget the Internet—web sites for teen reading, such as those described in Chapter 7, can be found at many other libraries, not to mention commercial booksellers and individual teen sites. You can find more booklists by visiting Google, entering a book title, and adding the word "readalikes." Google will then list sites posting relevant "readalike" booklists.

Other resources include printed bookmarks and booklists, and the book sites you've collected on your teen web site.

READERS' ADVISORY CONVERSATIONS

Sometimes teens come up to the information desk and ask for help, sometimes they do not. Don't wait for them to come to you. Wander over to the teen space. If you see a teen standing at the book shelves, give him a minute or two to approach you for assistance. If he doesn't, walk over and ask, "Are you finding what you're looking for?" If he says, "Just looking," accept it and don't press. But depart with a friendly, "If you're looking for something in particular, just ask one of the library staff members walking around the library, or working at the information desk," smile, and walk away—slowly, in case he changes his mind. Teens are sensitive to what they perceive as pressure. Some teens think they need to please adults. Some teens think they need to ignore adults. Avoid forcing a choice either way. Be available, but don't hover.

If, however, he says, "I'm looking for a book to read," then you've got a readers' advisory conversation in the making. So, what do you say next?

Opening Questions

First of all, do not assume that teens only read fiction. And so the first question to ask is:

"Do you want a story, like a mystery or science fiction, or something true, like a true adventure or a biography?"

Having established fiction or nonfiction, a good way to start talking about books is to ask:

"Tell me about a book that you've really enjoyed" (Saricks 2005, 88). Note the emphasis on a teen simply telling a librarian about a book, rather than analyzing why he liked the book. By describing books, the teen telegraphs appeal characteristics (Jones 2004, 79).

If the teen doesn't come up with a specific title, ask:

"What kinds of books do you like to read?" If that doesn't work, ask:

"What kinds of movies and TV shows do you like?" The answer may give you some clues about the kinds of stories to suggest. Let's say the teen never missed an episode of the TV series "24." Even if you never missed an episode, ask the teen to tell you about the series. You want to hear what *he or she* liked about the series, not what *you* already know about it.

The teen might talk about such story elements as nonstop action, really bad villains, and how the fate of the world rested on the mental and physical stamina of the tough (if haunted) hero. If the teen likes fiction, suggest the *Alex Rider* series of teen spy novels by Anthony Horowitz. If nonfiction is the chosen genre, suggest books about real-life espionage, like *Hidden Secrets* (Owen 2002).

Let's say a teen says she really liked *Big Mouth and Ugly Girl* (Oates 2002).

"I liked it that the book went back and forth between the two characters, so they could each tell their side of the story. And I liked Ursula and Matt. I loved it when Ursula described herself as 'Warrior Woman.' It was funny, but a little sad, too, like when Matt's friends didn't answer his e-mail, like he'd just disappeared."

It sounds as though this reader likes books with well-developed characters, and the alternating-narrator style. In addition to character-centered realistic fiction, she may enjoy the dual narration of *Swallowing Stones* (McDonald 1997) or *Margaux with an X* (Koertge 2004).

Another good approach with teens is to ask them about books they don't like. Teens may be reluctant to commit to actually liking something, but they're not usually shy about telling you what they don't like. And by hearing comments like "Nothing happened" or "It was such a downer" or "This was so old-fashioned and syrupy sweet" or "The characters were total jerks," you'll be able to narrow the field and find out what kind of books to avoid.

More Questions

Keep drawing out appeal characteristics by asking more questions, such as the following:

- "Do you care if the main character is a boy or a girl?" Gender matters to some readers, more often to boys than to girls (Herald 2003, 5).

- "Do you like books where the characters are your age, or older, or younger?" Most teens prefer reading about characters who are slightly older than themselves (Jones 2004, 81). High school juniors and seniors may assume that teen fiction is only for younger teens. That's when you shelf talk compelling teen novels about older teens, such as *Catalyst* (Anderson 2002) and *Acceleration* (McNamee 2003).

- "What kinds of stories do you like?" List such genres as mystery, suspense, humor, romance, fantasy, retold fairy tales, science fiction, and historical fiction. Rattle off such realistic fiction themes as teens getting out of weird/strange/creepy situations, friendship, family problems, illness and death, and so forth.

- "Do you like books set in the here and now, or do you like books set in other times—the past or the future—or other places, like other locations, other countries, or other planets?"
- "Do you like getting into a fast-moving plot right away, or do you like description and a kind of unfolding plot—or do you like both?"
- "Do you like books set at school, or with zero about school?" School is teens' workplace, and is rife with intrigue, fun, self-discovery, and challenges.
- "What do you *not* like in a book?" You can learn a lot about a reader's preferences from their description, sometimes detailed and passionate, of what they don't like in a book.
- "If an author could write a book just for you, what would it be like?" (Lesesne 2003, 30). This is the ultimate readers' advisory question, in that it asks the reader to write the book he wants to read.

Just as there is no "typical" teen, there is no typical teen reader: the same readers' advisory questions will not necessarily be successful with all teens (31). But whatever particular story elements individual teens prefer, what most teens like are books whose characters are, like them, facing such challenges as fitting in, developing individuality, bonding with others, and discovering and developing their abilities (Herald 2003, 5).

Answers to Listen For—and What They Mean

As teens talk about books they read and enjoyed, listen for the key phrases that signal appeal characteristics, reading experiences, and genre and theme preferences.

- "It was so scary/dreamy/romantic..." Teens' response to the overall emotional mood and atmosphere of books is expressed in how the books make them feel. This reader might like suspense, romance, or historical fiction, which can be quite atmospheric.
- "The book was really exciting. It was nonstop action, going from one thing to the next. The characters had to go through all this stuff—mountains, snow, rivers—to save people." Sounds like this

teen reader enjoys adventure/survival fiction. Find out preferred settings, time periods, type of danger, and the like.

- "The descriptions were pretty, but that's all the book was: description. There was no plot." Further conversation can reveal that this reader doesn't dislike description of settings and characters per se—only if it weighs down or obliterates a plot.

- "I like books that are kind of scary but not gruesome. I mean, I like mysteries but more intense than like Nancy Drew or something. But not a lot of blood and stuff." Sounds like this teen reader would enjoy suspense, possibly psychological thrillers. Find out more about plot, character, setting, and atmosphere preferences.

- "Sometimes it seems like the only people who really get me are my friends. I like books with friends who help each other." Teen fiction abounds with books populated by friends, in plots and settings ranging from light-hearted to grim. Ask questions to find out what kinds of friends the reader likes: lifelong friends, new friends, unexpected friends.

- "I like intense books where the characters are in trouble, and have to figure things out." Realistic young adult fiction specializes in intense situations: relationships, sexual harassment, sudden disability, illness, depression, crime, racism, abuse, and more. Find out if there are particular challenges and issues that appeal to the teen reader.

Can You Recommend a Good Book?

When adult readers ask for a good book, chances are they're hankering for books with one or more of the following characteristics:

- a "good read," that is, a solid story well told, substantial in plot, subject, theme, and character which makes them laugh, cry, and teaches them something about history, an issue, or a subject; and/or

- a well-written book, or a book that's won a prize or recognition; and/or

- a book devoid of incessant swearing, explicit sexual activity, and graphic violence.

When teens ask for a good book, chances are they're looking for much the same thing. Notwithstanding high-profile promotions and reviews of edgy, gritty teen fiction and the manner in which teens are depicted in magazines, TV, movies, and hand-wringing news stories, there are teens who are postponing or shrugging off swearing, sexual activity, cruelty toward peers, alcohol, drugs, and all manner of high-risk behaviors. They cannot relate to fictional teen characters who hate themselves, their parents, and the world.

Many young adult novels of all genres and themes fit into the good book category. They may not win awards, they may not be selected for high-profile booklists, they may not garner starred reviews in professional journals, but they are being published, and teens are reading them. It is important for young adult librarians to read them, too.

Conversations with Parents, Caregivers, and Teachers

Sometimes a parent, caregiver, or teacher will be looking for books for a teen. If the teen is with the adult, communicate with the teen as much as possible (Jones 2004, 81). Pay attention to the teen, make eye contact, and manage the conversation so that the teen is obviously included (Herald 2003, 4), even if the adult is doing all the talking and the teen does not verbally participate. While you don't want to ignore the adult, don't forget that it's the teen who's going to read the books. If the adult asks about controversial content—swearing, sexual activity, or violence—be honest about the books, but place the content within the context of the story and characters.

Here are some common questions posed by adults, with suggestions for how to respond:

"My son doesn't like to read. Do you have anything he might like?" Perhaps his son doesn't like to read anything, or he just doesn't like fiction, or textbooks. Here is where the question, "Tell me about a movie or TV show that you've watched and enjoyed," really comes in handy. (If the teen is with the parent, address your questions to the teen.) If he enjoyed *Spider-Man* the movie, he might also enjoy *Spider-Man* the graphic novel, and such teen transformation novels as *Others See Us* (Sleator 1993), in which Jared falls into a toxic waste dump and emerges with the ability to hear other people's thoughts. Appendix III in *Teen Genreflecting* lists genre and realistic fiction for reluctant readers (Herald 2003, 203–207). On the Young Adult Library Services Association web site, the booklists page includes "Quick Picks" booklists, which are also good resources for teens who don't choose to read (Jones 2004, 81).

"My daughter is in fifth grade but reads at the eighth grade level. What can you recommend that she would enjoy reading but doesn't have content that is inappropriate for her age?" When parents say their child is reading at "eighth grade level," ask them to explain to you what that means for their child. Find out about other books (or types of stories) their child has read and enjoyed. Let the parent know that teen fiction is written for young people who are experiencing the social, emotional, and physical aspects of being a teen. This is where the Age Index in *What Do Young Adults Read Next?* (Spencer 1999) and the "MJS" (Middle, Junior, and Senior High School) codings in *Teen Genreflecting* come in handy. Children's and YA classics are another good resource: these are well-written novels featuring young people which were written for young people and adults.

"I need books on my school's Accelerated Reader list that my son or daughter will read. Can you tell me, from this list, what are good books?" Find out the required reading and point levels for the teen, and something about the kinds of stories—books, movies, TV—that the teen enjoys. Then skim down the list and tell the parent a bit about the books that tell those stories.

SHELF TALKS

Shelf talks, known as "hand selling" in the bookstore business, are short, lively descriptions of books. Some books can be shelf talked in three or four sentences. Others benefit from a longer description. Although it helps (a lot) to have read the book, you can usually pick up what you need from the back cover or inside flap: the basic story, setting, one or two characters' names, and the incident that puts the plot in motion.

Sometimes, the best way to find books for a teen is to go to the shelves while you're conversing, and just start pulling down books that look as though they might work. Tell the teen a little about each book. Don't get bogged down in plot details, just give a description that will give the teen a quick impression of the book. If the book touches on serious or controversial issues, mention them (Vaillancourt 2000, 50). These issues can include content—explicit sexual activity, graphic violence, disturbing characters such as demonic parents—and treatment, such as incessant swearing. Avoid gushy proclamations like "You'll just *love* this." You might have loved the book, but it doesn't mean it's right for that teen.

The exception to this rule is that readers' advisory rarity: a perfect match. I confess I did gush a bit when two high school girls came into the library looking for a copy of *Sloppy Firsts* (McCafferty 2001). One of them wanted her friend to read it. I loved that book too, and when I found it on a shelving cart we both gushed to her friend about what a great book it was, which was kind of fun. Just so the first girl would also walk out with something, I found *The Queen of Everything* (Caletti 2002) for her. A little more gushing ensued. It happens.

If you haven't read the books you're pulling off the shelves, say so (Herald 2003, 5). You might say something like, "I haven't read this, but (a) it's always on the shelving truck, so lots of teens are reading it; or (b) this author is really good at suspense."

Following are a couple of shelf talks:

- "Gavin and his sister Fleur like their new robot, the EGR3, known as 'Eager.' He's smart and friendly. Too bad Eager isn't gorgeous like the BDC4s. But the BDC4s are starting to act weird—even dangerous. Maybe Eager can help!" *Eager* (Fox 2004).
- "Sara and Rob post poems online and start e-mailing each other. Sara lives with her parents, loves high school, and brims with life. Rob has been sent to a wilderness school for 'troubled' teens—instead of jail. Can they be friends—or maybe something more?" *Rob&Sara.com* (Peterson and Ruckman 2004).

After shelf talking some books, ask the teen, "Are these the kinds of books that you are looking for?" (Vaillancourt 2000, 49). Based on your shelf talks, the teen may choose one or two of the books. Her choices will tell you more about the kinds of books she likes: with that additional information, perhaps you can find more books.

IT'S A BUFFET

You need to accept that you will not always be able to put the perfect book into a teen's hands that will change their lives forever. Readers' advisory is about guiding teens to a buffet, rather than taking their order and returning with one dish from a menu. In a reference interview, the teen and the librarian seek the answer to a question, or materials that will help with a topic. In a readers' advisory conversation, the teen and the librarian seek some books for the teen to read. Through the conversation, they establish the types of books the teen likes to read, and the librarian offers books that may satisfy those preferences. And give teens choices—don't recommend just one title—pull out a half dozen, and let the teen narrow the choices. This shows respect for the teen's judgment and also ensures a better reading match. After all, you're not the final expert of what any individual will enjoy reading.

What if the teen accepts your suggestions? Tell him you're glad he found some good books to read, and to please let you know what he thought of them the next time he comes to the library, so you can find some more books for him. Many teens like it when you show that you remember their reading interests (Vaillancourt 2000, 52). Keep the conversation about books going, by suggesting other titles, and by asking teens for recommendations, too.

What if the teen doesn't accept your suggestions? She or he needs to feel that it's okay to do that. It could be that you just didn't hit the nail on the head. It could be that the teen rejected the books because of the format—preferring paperback to hardcover—and the book covers, which may have depicted dorky-looking teens. Ask more questions, suggest more titles, reach for booklists or readers' advisory resources. But don't beat it into the ground. Stay welcoming, friendly, positive, and upbeat. Readers' advisory does not always work right away. What *does* work is leaving teens with the impression that you care, and that the library is a place where they can talk about what they like to read.

MAIL, E-MAIL, AND CHAT

Readers' advisory doesn't always happen face-to-face in the library, for a variety of reasons. To expand access to readers' advisory, libraries are offering patrons help through printed forms, web sites, e-mail, and live chat.

In many libraries, readers can ask for book recommendations by filling out printed or electronic readers' advisory forms. "Book Match" is available to teens through TeensPoint.org, the teen web site for the Central Rappahannock Regional Library in Fredericksburg, Virginia (http://www.teenspoint.org, accessed April 21, 2005). Teens click on "Reading Matters," then cruise down its menu and click on "Book Match." Teens can ask for a book they like (title, author), they can specify the type of book they like from a pull-down menu, and they can write in comments about what they like, what they don't want, and anything else. Responses are e-mailed in two to three working days, and may be posted on the Book Match page. The Archives of past Book Matches—a list of "If you liked (title/book type)..." read-alikes—serve as a readers' advisory for young adult librarians, too.

While many libraries' live chat services are geared toward home-work help, others encourage patrons to ask about good books. "Ask a Librarian—Live!" is a live chat service maintained by the St. Charles Public Library in St. Charles, Missouri (http://www.st-charles.lib.il.us/247ref/holdpage.htm, accessed February 4, 2006). Teens and other library patrons can chat online with librarians about books or other library questions.

YOUR READING PLAN

A reading plan forces you to boldly read where you have not read before. Reading a variety of genres, themes, and nonfiction topics, you'll be better able to relate to what teens are talking about when they describe books they've read and enjoyed. Creating a reading plan begins by keeping a reading log. There are many ways to keep track of the many young adult books that you have read. Some librarians keep a list of books as they read them, on paper or in an electronic file. They may include brief annotations, detailed plot summaries, or other notes. Some young adult librarians (like me) feel compelled to write a booktalk after reading every book they think they might booktalk one day, or if not, a book review.

You can organize your reading for readers' advisory, booktalking, or creating booklists by taking a young adult books self-assessment test. To take a test, you can pick up a resource like *Teen Genreflecting* (Herald 2003) and see how many titles you have read in its outline of genres and themes. If your library subscribes to the *NoveList* database, you can scroll down to "Read About Popular Titles and Topics," and click on "For Staff Only." From there, click on "ARRT Young Adult Fiction List: A Self-Evaluative Bibliography." You'll arrive at a young adult fiction self-assessment test designed by the Adult Reading Round Table (ARRT), an association of Chicago-area librarians dedicated to promoting readers' advisory services and skills.

Create your own personal readers' advisory resource by dropping your titles into *Genreflecting*'s genres and themes, or the categories delineated by the ARRT test. Now you can see what types of books you have read, and what types you have not read (Vaillancourt 2000, 51). Perhaps you're trying to keep up with new realistic teen fiction, and you have read most of what arrived last month. You skipped two new fantasy novels and that new lost-in-the-woods adventure novel because they didn't look that interesting to you. But you are not reading just for you. You are reading for the many different teens, with different reading interests, who come to the library looking for good books to read.

Let's say three new realistic teen novels just arrived, and you're trying to decide which one to read first. But face it: you have no idea what you'd say if a teen asked you for a book that was like the *A Living Nightmare* or one of its sequels in *The Saga of Darren Shan* series (Shan 2001+), because you haven't read any of those books. You don't usually read horror, and the only vampire books you like are the soulful, romantic ones. Skip one of the three new realistic fiction books, and read *A Living Nightmare* instead. Now you will have a frame of reference for a popular series that combines horror, humor, and adventure.

The same thing goes for any other genre. If you are drooling at the prospect of reading the four new fantasy novels that just arrived, set one aside for now and pick up a book from a theme or genre you don't know very well, or that new biography of a popular singer that teens listen to on MTV and read about in music magazines. Take the book less read.

Readers' advisory is a low-key, one-to-one conversation. Sometimes, however, you'll be promoting reading and books not just to one or two teens, but to entire classrooms or assemblies. So clear your throat, stand up straight, take a few deep breaths, and get ready to dazzle and delight the crowds—with booktalks!

REFERENCES AND SUGGESTED READINGS

Almond, David. 2000. *Kit's Wilderness*. New York: Delacorte Press.

Anderson, Laurie Halse. 2002. *Catalyst*. New York: Viking.

Armstrong, Jennifer, and Nancy Butcher. 2002–2003. *Fire-Us* trilogy. New York: HarperCollins.

Brashares, Ann. 2001. *Sisterhood of the Traveling Pants*. New York: Delacorte Press.

Cabot, Meg. 2000+. *Princess Diaries* series. New York: HarperAvon.

Caletti, Deb. 2002. *The Queen of Everything*. New York: Simon Pulse.

Donelson, Kenneth L., and Alleen Pace Nilsen. 1997. *Literature for Today's Young Adults*. New York: Longman.

Draper, Sharon M. 1994. *Tears of a Tiger*. New York: Atheneum.

Ewing, Lynne. 1998. *Party Girl*. New York: Alfred A. Knopf.

Flinn, Alex. 2002. *Breaking Point*. New York: HarperTempest.

Fox, Helen. 2004. *Eager*. New York: Wendy Lamb Books.

Giles, Gail. 2003. *Dead Girls Don't Write Letters*. Brookfield, CT: Roaring Brook Press.

———. 2002. *Shattering Glass*. Brookfield, CT: Roaring Brook Press.

Goobie, Beth. 2002. *The Lottery*. Victoria, BC; Custer, WA: Orca Books.

Goodman, Joan E. 2002. *Paradise: Based on a True Story of Survival*. Boston: Houghton Mifflin.

Haddix, Margaret Peterson. 1998+. *Shadow* Children series. New York: Simon and Schuster Books for Young Readers.

Hartinger, Brent. 2004. *The Last Chance Texaco*. New York: HarperTempest.

Herald, Diana Tixier. 2003. *Teen Genreflecting: A Guide to Reading Interests*. Westport, CT: Libraries Unlimited.

Horowitz, Anthony. 2001+. *Alex Rider* series. New York: Philomel Books.

Hrdlitschka, Shelley. 2001. *Dancing Naked*. Victoria, BC; Custer, WA: Orca Books.

Jones, Patrick, Michele Gorman, and Tricia Suellentrop. 2004. *Connecting Young Adults and Libraries: A How-To-Do-It Manual for Librarians*. New York: Neal-Schuman Publishers.

Kirkpatrick, Katherine. 2002. *The Voyage of the Continental*. New York: Holiday House.

Koertge, Ron. 2004. *Margaux with an X*. Cambridge, MA: Candlewick Press.

Lesesne, Terri. 2003. *Making the Match: The Right Book for the Right Reader at the Right Time, Grades 4–12*. Portland, ME: Stenhouse Publishers.

Limb, Sue. 2004. *Girl, 15, Charming but Insane*. New York: Delacorte Press.

Lowry, Lois. 1993. *The Giver*. Boston: Houghton Mifflin.

MacHale, D. J. 2002+. *Pendragon: Journal of an Adventure through Time and Space* series. New York: Aladdin Paperbacks.

Mayfield, Sue. 2002. *Drowning Anna*. New York: Hyperion.

McCafferty, Megan. 2001. *Sloppy Firsts*. New York: Crown Publishers.

McDonald, Joyce. 1997. *Swallowing Stones*. New York: Delacorte Press.

McNamee, Graham. 2003. *Acceleration*. New York: Wendy Lamb Books.

Myers, Walter Dean. 2002. *Handbook for Boys*. New York: HarperCollins.

Oates, Joyce Carol. 2002. *Big Mouth and Ugly Girl*. New York: HarperTempest.

Owen, David. 2002. *Hidden Secrets*. Toronto, ON: Firefly Books.

Pearl, Nancy. 2002. *Now Read This II: A Guide to Mainstream Fiction*. Greenwood Village, CO: Libraries Unlimited.

Pennebaker, Ruth. 2000. *Both Sides Now*. New York: Henry Holt.

Peters, Julie Ann. 2000. *Define "Normal."* Boston: Little, Brown.

Peterson, P. J., and Ivy Ruckman. 2004. *Rob&Sara.com*. New York: Delacorte Press.

Rosoff, Meg. 2004. *How I Live Now*. New York: Wendy Lamb Books.

Rowling, J. K. 1997+. *Harry Potter* series. New York: Scholastic Press.

Salinger, J. D. 1951. *The Catcher in the Rye*. Boston: Little, Brown.

Saricks, Joyce G. 2005. *Readers' Advisory Service in the Public Library*. 3rd ed. Chicago: ALA Editions.

Shan, Darren. 2001+. *The Saga of Darren Shan* series. Boston: Little, Brown.

Sleator, William. 1993. *Others See Us*. New York: Dutton Children's Books.

Spencer, Pam. 1999. *What Do Young Adults Read Next? A Reader's Guide to Fiction for Young Adults*. Westport, CT: Libraries Unlimited.

Spider-Man. 1997+. Various authors. New York: Marvel Comics.

Vaillancourt, Renee J. 2000. *Bare Bones Young Adult Services: Tips for Public Library Generalists*. Chicago: ALA Editions.

Ziegesar, Cecily von. 2002+. *Gossip Girl* series. Boston: Little, Brown.

Zollo, Peter. 2004. *Getting Wiser to Teens: More Insights into Marketing to Teenagers*. Ithaca, NY: New Strategist Publications.

9

BOOKTALKING

As a booktalker, you've probably experienced it. When you begin your first booktalk, teens are a bit skeptical, maybe a little restless. By the end of your third booktalk, they're quiet. By the end of your fifth booktalk, you could hear a pin drop. Everyone wants to hear what happens next. When you hear it, that collective "aah" at the end of a booktalk, of long-held breath let go, you know that the spell of Story is at work.

IT'S SHOWTIME!

As a readers' advisor, your job was to talk with teens about books they might want to read.

As a booktalker, your mission is nothing less than to set teen brains on fire for books. You'll be booktalking to all kinds of teen readers: resistant, reluctant, steady, and avid. You'll play to teens' established story interests by showcasing books with the same strong appeals as popular movies and TV. You'll expand teens' assumptions about books by highlighting titles that explore the big themes in their lives—family, friends, love, social issues, the future—in ways that are as intense as any rock song they know by heart. You'll pique teens' curiosity by booktalking titles about real-life topics, or books written in formats like graphic novels or poetry. And you'll have the opportunity to reach library users and nonusers alike, by promoting the public library as a place to meet friends, do homework, check e-mail, participate in events, and find magazines, CDs, DVDs, books, and more (Jones 2004, 170).

The biggest surprise for teens might be the nature of booktalking itself. Standing in a classroom or school library, you are not just some nice lady or nice guy describing a bunch of books. Instead, you are a performer delivering a tight, well-balanced program. You are an entertainer—but never a buffoon, and always in control of yourself, your material, and your performance (Mahood 2004, 163). What you are putting over is not simply the particular books, but reading itself, and all that it offers: excitement, wonder, heartbreak, hilarity, and insight.

For when you perform a booktalk, you are not presenting a review or evaluation of the book. You *are* the book. You are not telling your audience how to respond to a book by saying things like, "you'll really like this book," or "this is an exciting story." Instead, you are allowing the book to speak for itself through your performance.

Don't assume that you can't booktalk because

- you have no training in theater;
- it's hard for you to memorize text; or
- you're shy.

You can do it, because

- you can learn booktalk performance styles—by watching DVDs or videos or listening to recordings of storytellers, booktalkers, stand-up comics, and stage-trained actors and singers;
- if you can remember the characters' names and the gist of your booktalk, you'll do fine; and
- it can be a lot easier to disappear into a booktalking persona than it is to "talk" about books as "yourself."

WRITING BOOKTALKS

To prepare for readers' advisory, you read with another reader in mind. To prepare for booktalking, you read with another reader in mind, and a listener, too. Because that is how teens will first encounter the book, as listeners. As you're reading, be alert for that moment or moments when your interest in the book quickens. It could be the clever idea, the "what if..." that drives the plot. It could be a scene. It could be a character, two characters in dialogue, or a setting you know you can paint with words. Whatever it is, it is the heart of the book.

Write from the Heart

It's best to write—and rewrite—your booktalks before you perform them. Sometimes as you're reading, the booktalker part of your brain recognizes and pounces on the heart of the book, and the booktalk practically writes itself.

At other times, even though you love the book and you know you can sell it to teens, you just can't see how to write the booktalk. Let your mind wander. Try to remember what it was that kept you reading, and build your booktalk around it.

Still nothing? Maybe you need to break out of linear thinking with a writing technique called clustering (Rico 1983, 35). Write a word or phrase on a sheet of paper, draw a circle around it, and then let your mind wander through the book, free-associating. As words and phrases pop up, write them down quickly, expanding outward from the center circle. Circle them, and link associated ideas together. When a new chain of ideas pops up, link it to the center, and look around for cross-links. Random at first, associations will suddenly form into patterns, then coalesce into a focus for your booktalk. The focus—the heart—might be the word or phrase with which you began your clustering. Then again, it might not. For more on clustering and other right-brain writing techniques, see *Writing the Natural Way* (Rico 1983).

As you're writing a booktalk, read it aloud, if only in front of your tablet or computer screen. You are writing for the ear, not the eye, so how does it sound? Does it present the heart of the book in a natural-sounding way? Does it flow? Keep revising—and stay open to the possibility that when you perform the booktalk, you will find out what works with an audience, and can incorporate those discoveries into the booktalk.

Linking Books to Life

At the beginning of any presentation—music, political speech, class, booktalks—audiences ask themselves, "What's in it for me? Why should I listen to this?" Give teens reasons to listen to your booktalks by linking books to their lives. Just a half-sentence will do the job. But avoid beginning every booktalk with a link, which can become repetitious.

Link the book to . . .

- *teens*, by comparing what happens in the book to what is happening (or not) in their lives. For example, just about every teen can relate to problems with school. "Cody is flunking out of high school, something I know will never happen to anyone in this room," is how I begin my booktalk of *Vampire High* (Rees 2003).
- *current events*, by referring to a recent news story or an ongoing issue or concern. "Heck always wanted to ride in a cop car, just to see what it was like. Once they put him inside, though, he was nervous," begins my booktalk for *Heck Superhero* (Leavitt 2004).
- *pop culture*, by dropping in a reference to a current movie, TV show, or popular music celebrity or album. Stay current. Back in the 1990s, it was okay to refer to science-fiction-in-real-life novels as "X-Filesy." Pop culture moves on. "Getting voted out of some house by a bunch of insanely competitive people is nothing compared to what happens to Maya," begins my booktalk for *The Girls* (Koss 2000).

Booktalk Models

Booktalkers model their booktalks on a variety of presentation styles and entertainment forms, including storytelling, stand-up comedy, songs, movie and TV trailers, book-jacket blurbs, and news stories.

In short booktalks, the focus is usually on a description of just one thing: a plot set-up, a brief scene, a character, or a setting and the mood it evokes. When written and performed well, a short booktalk gives teens a tangy taste of a book. If not, a short booktalk can be over before teens have had a chance to get a grip on the book. Performance tip: after delivering a short booktalk, pause for a few seconds to let it sink in. Give teens a little time to fix the book in their memories before you begin the next booktalk.

In longer booktalks, you have the opportunity to present more than one aspect of the book. When written and performed well, longer booktalks allow teens to bond with the characters, pulling them into the story. If not, longer booktalks will lose teens' attention as their minds wander away from the point you don't ever seem to make. Performance tip: while delivering a long booktalk, pause for a few seconds at least once, to let what you've just said sink in. The tiny pause also interrupts the solid stream of sound coming out of your mouth. Then pick it up again, with a snap of energy.

Booktalks are a combination of "show" and "tell." Sometimes you are showing: enacting short scenes from a book, quoting dialogue. Sometimes you are telling: filling in background on characters, explaining plotline. The interaction between show and tell keeps a booktalk lively because you are switching between two interdependent modes of communication. An all-show booktalk, without any explanation to give context, can make no sense. An all-tell booktalk, consisting solely of your recapitulation of the book, can be boring. Keep teen brains moving by mixing communication modes. Here are a few booktalk models.

Get Right into a Scene

"It's a beautiful, moonlit night . . ." begins my booktalk for *Son of the Mob* (Korman 2002), establishing Vince's problem with a scene. "On a date with Angela, Vince pops the trunk of his car to get a blanket so they can sit on the beach. The blanket is there, only it's wrapped around a (live) body. End of date." Then I fill in the background on the problem Vince can't talk about: his father is the local mob boss. Now Vince meets Kendra, and we switch into a short scene that concludes with Kendra's eyes lighting up as she tells Vince about her FBI dad, who is dedicated to putting guess who in prison. This booktalk follows a "show, tell, and show" outline.

Meet the Characters

"This is a book about a girl named Meg, and a guy named . . . Belch," begins my booktalk for *The Wish List* (Colfer 2000). A slight emphasis on "Belch" gets a laugh, and puts all of us in a good mood. I sketch in background, establishing Meg as a good person with problems who is talked into doing something she knows is wrong, and Belch as a creep without a conscience. Then I switch into the scene where Meg and Belch rob the old man's house, Belch sics the dog on him, Belch and Meg run out with the gun, it goes off and blows up an oil drum, ". . . and the next thing Meg knows, she and Belch are hurtling down a long . . . dark . . . tunnel. Up ahead are two bright lights. One is blue, one is red. The blue light is the entrance to the tunnel up to heaven. The red light . . . well, you can guess where that leads." The booktalk concludes with a brief explanation of Meg accepting St. Peter's deal. This booktalk follows a "tell, show, and show" outline.

Say It with Music

A song can tell a story, portray a character, illuminate a mood, or bedazzle with wordplay. A song has a beginning, middle, and end that leaves the listener wanting to hear more. Sounds like a booktalk, doesn't it? Everybody enjoys different types of music. To illustrate what you can learn from songs, I'll share some thoughts about opera. Years of listening to opera have influenced how I use my voice, create drama, and structure and pace my booktalks.

Like booktalking, an operatic aria is performed by one person using one instrument, the human voice. Opera singers don't just sing notes. They sing stories, coloring their voices to express meaning and emotion through sound.

Giuseppi Verdi and other composers worked hard to wring drama out of every moment on stage through music, words, action, and stage effects. They wanted their audiences to feel intense emotion. And they never forgot what people really paid to see: singers who could reveal those intense emotions through their masterful performance of arias. Human beings and their travails and triumphs connect with audiences. Through arias, composers concentrated the drama of an opera into minutes.

The pacing of arias is driven by the characters singing them and the situations in which they find themselves. A stormy beginning, a meditative middle, and an even stormier ending pace many arias, following a "show, tell, and show" outline. The pace of the singer's delivery is swift, it's slow, it picks up again, it dies away, it concludes with a crash. When delivering a booktalk, sometimes you speak swiftly, sometimes slowly. You're loud, you're quiet. You speak hesitantly, you speak confidently. You vary the pace in order to reflect the unfolding drama of the booktalk, just as the music and pacing of an aria reflect its unfolding drama.

Reading Aloud

Begin your booktalk by reading aloud from the book, looking up at your audience every half-sentence or so. Close the book while you appear to continue to recite from it word for word, and then segue into your booktalk. By reading aloud, and then letting the spirit of the book take over, you are reenacting the enchantment of reading. The story may begin on the page, but it reaches its fullest meaning in the imagination. Well-written or striking opening pages work best with this model, which follows a "show, tell" outline.

PREPARING BOOKTALK PROGRAMS
Something for Everyone

Booktalking is not about what you like to read. Sure, you need to have read the books, and it really, really helps if you love them (or at least like them), but you are not booktalking so you can hear yourself talk about books *you* love. You are booktalking so teens can hear about books that *they* might love.

Include boy-appeal books, girl-appeal books, books that will appeal to both genders, and books that will appeal to all sexual preferences. Include books featuring stories and characters from diverse cultural and ethnic backgrounds, so that teens can see themselves, their friends, and teens they see at their school or in movies, TV, music, and the news. Look for books that address universal teen themes and concerns, experienced by a variety of characters. No matter what their outward appearance, role, or clique identification—jock, brainiac, class clown, substance abuser, troubled teen, prom queen, and so forth—teens are experiencing loss, joy, excitement, fear, hope, and more, as they learn to be themselves.

Teens are looking ahead, so choose fiction that features characters who are their age or a year or two older, and nonfiction exploring issues relevant to those ages. For middle school teens, focus on books addressing middle school or high school freshmen concerns. Younger teens in sixth grade will also enjoy some children's books featuring sixth- and seventh-grade characters, as well as young adult fiction featuring middle school characters. For high school teens, focus on books addressing high school and after-graduation issues, featuring high school or young-20s characters. Because high school teens are already reading adult books, include adult fiction and nonfiction. And bring a variety of books accessible to a variety of reading abilities: fast reads, longer books, magazine-format nonfiction, and magazines.

Fiction and Graphic Novels

As you saw in Chapter 8, teens enjoy all kinds of books. Include a variety of popular fiction genres and realistic fiction themes, in print and graphic novel formats. Chapter 3 outlines fiction categories.

Nonfiction

Teens are into their own lives, and may be more interested in books about "real stuff" than the vicarious experiences found in fiction. Bring stories of real teens and young 20s, as well as books about doing and making things, from climbing mountains to making couch potato food. Chapter 3 outlines categories of nonfiction.

Poetry

Some teens say they hate poetry ... but they listen to rock, rap, and hip-hop and can quote songs. Some teens say they love poetry ... especially the poems that they and their friends write. Good choices are collections of poetry by teens or poems on teen-appeal topics, or books about poetry writing or performance. A growing number of teen novels are written in poetry form, and can be booktalked by reading aloud a poem ("show"), filling in some background ("tell"), and then reading aloud another poem ("show").

Classics and Adult Books

High school English and Social Studies teachers may ask you to booktalk some classics, usually from their school's classics list. I always ask if I can mix in some additional classics. If it's been a while since you read the classics on the school list, or any classics, look up their entries in *Masterplots* (Magill 1996). Each entry includes a plot summary, major characters, settings, and interpretations. Next, get a copy of the book, look at the first page, and leaf through the book. Anything coming back to you?

Think about how you can link classics to teen lives, by tying them to current events, trends, problems, ideas, or interests affecting teens (Mahood 2004, 179). For example, *The Plague* (Camus [1947] 1991) can be tied to AIDS and other disasters. Then again, you can show teens that classics can be fun, fast reads, with a book like *Michael Strogoff* (Verne [1876] 1997), a fast-moving adventure about a courier for the Russian Tsar which, like action-adventure bestsellers today, hit the movies.

To find teen-appeal adult books, ask high school teens what they're reading. Scan the book reviews in *Booklist* that flag adult fiction and nonfiction of interest to teens. *School Library Journal* also reviews adult books with teen appeal. A fun way to booktalk adult books is to bring in some "readalikes," that is, books by authors with appeals similar to books by best-selling authors. Readers who snapped up *Confessions of a Shopaholic* (Kinsella 2001) and other books by the author might also enjoy chick lit by Claire Naylor, Jennifer Weiner, and Wendy Holden. Stephen King fans might also enjoy horror fiction by Clive Barker, Dean Koontz, and Anne Rice.

Program Models

When people begin to watch TV or a movie, read a book, listen to a song, eat a meal, or exercise, they anticipate a beginning, a middle, and an end. Many entertainment forms are based on the classic structure of a story: stage setting, rising action, complication, climax, and resolution. Meals also follow a structure, of moving the palate from light but spicy foods to increasingly substantial dishes to palate-cleansing desserts. In exercise and sport, the athlete warms up, performs, and cools down.

Program models offer ways to structure booktalk programs that correspond to entertainment and life experiences that teens already know and enjoy. Program models are not the same as program themes. Program themes gather books around a genre or theme. Program models organize booktalks into logical sequences, transforming random collections of booktalks into presentations with shape and purpose.

Here are a couple of examples of program models.

All's Well That Ends Well

This program model follows the five-act structure of plays, movies, and TV dramas, which are often based on the structure of a story. Each "act" prepares the viewer for the next act, moving through a dramatic progression toward a conclusion. The idea is to find books that carry the dramatic requirements of each act in the "play" (Anderson and Mahood 2001, 107).

- *Act I* grabs teens' attention with books about ordinary teens who are suddenly plunged into extraordinary situations, in action/adventure or fantasy books like *The Wish List* (Colfer 2000) or *A Crack in the Line* (Lawrence 2004).

- *Act II* is your opportunity to build on your quick bonding with your audience. Now that they're listening to you, they're ready to be pulled in deeper, with books that address more serious or emotional issues, such as *On the Run* (Coleman 2004) or *Double Dutch* (Draper 2002).

- *Act III* lightens the mood. Both you and your audience have been dealing with some heavy stuff, so it's time for a change of pace. Give your audience a breather with books that are humorous in treatment, but with a serious underlying theme, such as *Cheating Lessons* (Cappo 2002) or *Handbook for Boys* (Myers 2002).

- *Act IV* is when you bring out the intense stories about teens undergoing emotional, psychological, social, or physical challenges or trauma. Realistic teen fiction abounds in such books as *Kissing the Rain* (Brooks 2004) and *The Lottery* (Goobie 2002).
- During *Act V*, you and your audience can relax. The drama is over, the trauma is soothed, and all's well that ends well in such sunny-side-up books as *Twists and Turns* (McDonald 2003) or *Girl, 15, Charming but Insane* (Limb 2004).

What's for Dinner?

Just as the same old thing at dinnertime gets stale after a while—cruel-at-school novels *again?*—booktalkers can serve up a program as balanced as a good meal, moving from course to course in a familiar sequence.

- *Appetizers* wake up taste buds. Wake up teen brains with tweaked tales like *Things Not Seen* (Clements 2002) or *Heir Apparent* (Vande Velde 2002).
- *Salads* continue opening up palates. Open up teen brains with mixed-up, multi-textured books like mysteries, fantasies, and school stories, such as *Head Games* (Fredericks 2004) or *Stravaganza: City of Masks* (Hoffman 2002).
- *Main course* books come next, when gastric juices are flowing and brain synapses are firing. Your audience is now ready to digest books about meaty issues, such as *Geography Club* (Hartinger 2003) or *Players* (Sweeney 2000).
- *Comfort food* sounds like a good idea at this point. All those flavors, all those textures . . . how about something that's easy to digest, like a baked potato, a historical novel, or a retold tale? Take a look at *Pagan's Crusade* (Jinks 2003) or *Jenna Starborn* (Shinn 2002).
- *Dessert* caps a good meal, and comedy caps a good booktalk program, with books like *I Was a Non-Blonde Cheerleader* (Scott 2005) or *Flavor of the Week* (Shaw 2003).

More Program Models

Once you start looking for program models, you'll see them all over the place. Find books that correspond to classes at school, from homeroom to math to sports. Focus on emotions, and you'll find books that express joy, anger, fear, love, and more. Begin a booktalk program with books that shine with the bright colors of summer, darken the mood with autumnal tales, go deeper into winter, and spring back up to meet the returning sun. Stay open to experiences that encompass structure and growth.

CONNECTING WITH SCHOOLS
It's Their World, We Just Booktalk in It

Inside the public library, teens are free to walk up to displays, pick up booklists, look at books, and check them out. During a private readers' advisory conversation, they can talk about their reading interests, and how they feel about controversial aspects of books like swearing, sexuality, violence, and racial and ethnic conflict. You can individualize your recommendations, and teens are free to pick and choose from them. They can check out books written for teens, children, or adults.

Walk into a school, and all of that is changed—you're in a new world. Now teens have no choice. They are going to have to listen to you whether they want to or not. Yes, you're promoting the public library, talking about books and other library materials and services. But you're doing it on class time. You are, in effect, part of the curriculum. Serving *in loco parentis*, schools are required to carry a level of responsibility for youth from which public libraries are excused. School libraries support the curriculum, and operate with less latitude than public libraries when choosing extracurricular books such as teen fiction (Langemack 2003, 134).

All of this means that different books are appropriate for different venues, and different audiences. Because students are required to listen to your booktalks, it's best to stick with books free from incessant swearing, graphic sexual activity, alcohol and drug abuse, violence, and racial, ethnic, and sexual slurs. When teens hear about or see books with controversial content or language in the public library, they can pick them up, or they can walk away. Sitting in a classroom or school library, they cannot walk away: they have to sit and listen. Teens relate to intensity; booktalking books that are intense, hard-edged, and touched by edgy behavior promotes reading as an intense experience. It's a great way to promote the resources of the public library. At the same time, it's desirable that the content and language of the book you booktalk be free from *incessant* swearing, graphic sexual activity, violence, and racial, ethnic, and sexual slurs. Before you booktalk books with these characteristics, talk with the school media specialist and the teachers in whose classrooms you'll be a guest (Jones 2004, 172). They may welcome edgy books. They may not. And while you're talking, ask her or him what teens are reading and enjoying. Booktalk those kinds of books, and a few more from the edges. But don't go off the deep end. You might not get invited back.

Getting Into Schools

Contact the school media specialist and explain that you would like to promote reading, books, and the public library. You'll be booktalking, and telling teens about library resources, services, events, and volunteer opportunities. Ask about visiting English, Social Studies, Reading, Developmentally Delayed, and Honors classes. Find out if there are particular types of books the school would like teens to hear about, such as all types of genre fiction; realistic fiction that relates to nonfiction books about teen issues; classics; popular science or other nonfiction titles; books about crafts or other hobbies; or historical fiction that highlights particular times and places. (For those of you who work in schools, these curriculum connections will come naturally!) In the spring, ask about visiting summer school classes. I offer schools a presentation time range of 25–45 minutes so that I can fit in with what teachers have to accomplish during their class period. Include the dates you are available, and your e-mail address and phone number. If you haven't heard back in a week, contact them again. E-mail has made it much easier to contact school media specialists and teachers, who are teaching classes most of the day and can't talk on the phone. E-mail also makes it easier for schools to send you a schedule of the classes you'll be visiting, and for you to send them a copy of your handout.

Young adult librarians work in libraries and library systems of different sizes. Some librarians work with schools in one town, city, or county, and it is possible to foster ongoing relationships with schools by speaking for 10 minutes at faculty meetings, dropping in at schools, or chatting with school media specialists and teachers when they stop by your library. Other young adult librarians in large library systems serving multiple municipalities work with branch staff members to contact local schools. Sometimes librarians can visit schools in teams of two, which allows teens to enjoy two booktalking styles.

GETTING THERE

The afternoon before a school visit, I fill up my book box with the following: a file folder of my booktalks; books; magazines; a book on CD and a book on cassette; a DVD and a video; 100 copies of my handout;

library card applications and library brochures; booklists and bookmarks; and book easels. My double-sided handout includes basic information about the library, news about upcoming teen events, an annotated booklist, my contact information, and the library's web site, address, phone number, and hours. In the morning, I add my food box, a small insulated camping box packed with two blocks of blue ice, a water bottle, orange slices for breaks, and lunch.

Psyching Up

I get psyched for booktalking through a combination of preparation, self-confidence, and music. Some booktalkers prepare by memorizing their booktalks word for word. Other booktalkers (like me) find it difficult to memorize. Instead, I do four things:

- One, I read each booktalk over and over and *over*, pounding it into my head. I think about other parts of the book that are not in my booktalk. If I forget part of a booktalk during a performance, I know the book well enough to pull out some detail that I can use to keep talking (Anderson and Mahood 2001, 107).

- Two, I focus on the names of the characters, and repeat them during the booktalk. Characters' names anchor the booktalk in your audiences' minds, giving them a reason to keep listening.

- Three, I memorize a few key phrases that serve as signposts along the road of the booktalk. The content of the booktalk may vary from performance to performance, but if I hit those signposts, I can get to the end of the booktalk.

- And four, I improvise. After you've heard your booktalks more than a few times, they can get boring. So I change a line of dialogue or a line of description of a scene.

Self-confidence comes from knowing that if you prepare well, if you take this booktalking thing really seriously and not as a last-minute deal where you stand up and talk a little about a bunch of books, you will be able to present a tight, compelling show about books. Self-confidence builds with experience, as you present booktalks. While it's advisable to learn from your mistakes and to look for ways to improve your booktalking, it's equally wise to learn from your successes, those times when you saw teens' faces light up with interest.

And music? Driving to schools, I listen to my favorite music. Sometimes I'm in the car for a long time to get to a school—one, two, almost three hours. I listen to what I know will put me in a good mood, what will calm me, and the closer to my destination, I listen to what will get me excited, exalted, and ecstatic. By the time I arrive at the school, I'm flying.

Checking In and Setting Up

I stop by the school office to sign in, pick up a visitor's badge, and chat—introducing myself, talking about the library, just being friendly.

Arriving at the classroom or library, I set up my book easels. I stack my books in the order I plan to booktalk them. I stack more books nearby so I can substitute them in if necessary. Sometimes I'll have less time to booktalk than I had planned, sometimes more, and sometimes I just don't feel like doing a book. I also stay sensitive to who is in the audience. For example, I may have a wonderful story about an overweight boy or girl, but if I spot an extremely overweight teen in the audience, I may set the booktalk aside. I consult with the school media specialist or teacher to find out if he or she thinks it would be okay to include the book.

Before class starts, I read through my booktalks. I also read them between classes, even though after the second show of the day I've pretty much got them down. This is to keep feeding details into my head, so I can keep coming up with new vocal inflections. I do not fasten notes or note cards to the backs of the books. While booktalking, my eyes are looking at one place, and one place only: *into the eyes of teens*.

During setup, teens will drift into the classroom or library.

"Are you a substitute? What's this?" they might ask, pointing to your materials. Explain, in a friendly and welcoming fashion. There may be teens who stop to chat. But during the precious few minutes between classes, teens are usually much more interested in their friends, classmates, and homework than some lady or guy they may or may not recognize from the public library. That's okay. We're all just going about our business. Just because you're an adult doesn't mean that you're "in charge" of the space.

BOOKTALK PERFORMANCE

"We Have a Guest from the Library Today..."

However you are introduced by the school media specialist or teacher, add a few words that will give your audience more of an idea of who you are and what you do (Langemack 2003, 142). Teens listen to their teachers all day long. Now they're going to listen to you. What you say completes the transition from their teacher to you. Be jolly and upbeat—but not clownish.

"Hi, and thanks again (nod to teacher) for giving class time so that I could come in and talk about some books, and your public library. As your librarian/teacher said, my name's Kristine Mahood. I'm the District Young Adult Librarian for Timberland Regional Library, and it's my job to work for teens: recommending books and other materials, planning teen services and events, and visiting schools. I go all over the five counties in the library district. Last week I was out on the coast in Ilwaco, next week I'll be down south in Onalaska, and today I'm here in Olympia. I've brought some books to talk about, but before I get into that, I just want to make sure you know about all the things you can get from your public library...."

Booktalk Style

Every booktalker's personality comes out in performance. Some book-talkers emphasize the performance aspects of booktalking. Others prefer to sound like a friend casually talking about some great books that they just read. Some booktalkers blend the two styles. Whatever you do, stay true to the spirit of the book, and to yourself. Be fun—but not a fool. Be intense—but not dreary. Be yourself—amped up a little.

Your Body

Booktalking is physical work. The more strength and stamina you can bring to it, the better. You don't have to be able to run a marathon, bench-press 200 pounds, or twist yourself into a pretzel to be a great booktalker. However, aerobics (walking, running, swimming, etc.) will build your heart and lungs; strength training (free weights or weight machines) makes it easier to carry books; and flexibility (stretching, yoga, Pilates) tones and soothes your muscles. Eating well helps, too. A good breakfast with a little protein will see you through until lunch. During the night, your body can dehydrate. I've learned to drink a lot of water before my first booktalk program. I keep drinking between programs. If it's been four or five hours since breakfast, I eat a few orange sections to tide me over until the lunch break.

During your booktalk program, stand up straight. While you don't need to stand dead still, try to avoid pacing back and forth across the front of the room like a caged tiger, or rocking back and forth on your toes and heels like an inflated clown. Moving around while booktalking means your audience will watch your movements instead of listening to what you are saying (Langemack 2003, 69).

While recovering from a foot injury, I asked schools to provide me with a high stool to perch on. At first I thought, "Oh no, I won't be able to stand commandingly, or move around and look active and athletic and hip!" I scooted up onto the high stool, sat up very straight, held up my first book, and started booktalking. I found out that by sitting high up enough to be visible, I could still look into every teen's eyes. All of my energy went into my voice, my face, and a few gestures, which are what most directly communicates to audiences (Langemack 2003, 69). And just as many teens came up to look at the books as if I'd been standing.

Your Voice

Not all spaces are the same size. Two dozen teens in a classroom can hear you just fine. Now try speaking to eighty teens in the school library. Your classroom voice will be absorbed by the larger space. Consider using a microphone. I love mics. They free you from having to shove all of your energy into vocal projection, which can flatten your voice into a high-pitched, strident monotone. Librarians can benefit from vocal training at a community college or other institution. But this is not always an option. Maybe no training is available. Maybe you don't choose to spend your time and money on vocal training. So use a mic when you need to, and you'll be free to put your vocal energy where it belongs, into delivering booktalks that amuse, caress, frighten, and move your audience.

As you grow into booktalking, you'll want to keep improving your performance. You'll want to bring more dimensions of the books to life through your delivery. For a humorous book, deliver your booktalk fast and funny, letting jokes and funny comments tumble out one after the other. For an intense book, slow down your delivery as you draw your audience into the hushed heart of darkness. Caught up in the spirit of the book, you'll sweep your audience along with you. One way to keep improving is to listen carefully to stage-trained actors reading books on CD or audiocassette. Stage-trained actors know how to act with their voices. So also do singers, classical and popular, whose focus stays on the songs rather than on themselves. Their voices move with the music, and they sing the words with the attention and respect that impart meaning. As a beginning booktalker, I used to superimpose the same hyper-dramatic style on every booktalk. Then I let years of opera listening, and the many styles and moods of arias, percolate through and influence my booktalk writing and performing. I also discovered Ella Fitzgerald's recordings of American standards in her "songbook" collections. These gems of storytelling, pacing, and delivery are collaborations among composers, arrangers, and a singer. From music, I learned to shape my speaking style to the rhythm and flow of the words I'd written. I'm still listening and learning.

Props

Props add yet another dimension to booktalks. They make books come alive, they underscore dramatic points in booktalks, and they make teens laugh. What's not to like? However, it's a good idea to avoid bringing in so many props that your audience focuses on and remembers the props, and not the books. We've all seen TV advertisements that were so clever that we forgot the name of the product. So keep it simple.

Here's an example. Concluding my booktalk of *The House Next Door* (Cusick 2002), I describe Emma waking up in the "haunted" house next door to her own, smiling from her dream about Daniel, the handsome young man who died there one hundred years ago. In the dream, Daniel showed Emma the ring he wanted his true love, another Emma, to wear.

"...so she's brushing her hair out of her eyes," I say, brushing my hair away from my left temple, "...and she sees..." pausing to stare at my wedding ring, "...the ring." I hold the back of my hand up beside my head, fingers pointed up, so that the audience can see my ring. "The ring that Daniel gave her...in her dream."

Chatting During and After the Show

Communication between teens and the booktalker takes many forms. Communication can be unspoken, through eyes and smiles. Looking into teens' eyes, you are saying, thank you for listening, and please keep listening, because there is more. That girl who stares unblinkingly at you, hanging on every word, is communicating with you. That boy who listens with a slight smile is communicating with you.

And sure, you'll experience your share of teens making wisecracks, or talking to themselves or one another during your booktalks. I usually let one remark go by. The next one, I look at the teacher, stop, and then look at the teen or teens.

"It's better for everybody if you don't talk while I'm speaking, thanks!" I'll say, with a nod and a smile, and another glance at the teacher. This usually works. It's also fun to do this in a hoarse stage whisper. What you don't want is to start a dialogue, or to spend a lot of time on interruptions.

A fun dialogue, however, can ensue at the conclusion of a booktalk.

"What happens next?" a teen will ask.

"I can't tell you that."

"What? Why not?"

"That would be a direct violation of the Librarian Code."

Groans, laughter . . . Have some fun!

I like to leave five-plus minutes at the end of each program so I can say, "I've told you about some good books, now I need you to tell me about good books. What do you recommend? What do you think people should read?" Create an open, playful mood by being friendly, cajoling, and a bit whimsical. First one teen will mention a book, followed by another teen, then a third says that the book was so cool, and a fourth disagrees, and pretty soon the air is sparkling with book titles. You have just changed the focus of your program from what *you* have to say about books to what *they* have to say about books, creating the conditions for teen-to-teen book promotions. And by stirring up a book-excited atmosphere, once the presentation is over and you're packing up, you make it more possible for teens to come up to you afterward to chat some more about books.

FOLLOW-UP

Returning to your library, create a display of books that you book-talked, with a poster exclaiming, "Hey! I heard about those books at school!" Include copies of your handout. Give a copy of your handout to librarians at the information desk, to refer to in case teens ask them about the books. Type up a list of the books that teens recommended at the conclusion of your programs, add copies of the list to the display, and send a copy, with a note, to the school media specialist. Some libraries also create a page on their teen web site that lists books that were booktalked in schools.

It's also a nice idea to give your library's youth materials selector a copy of the handout, and a copy of the list of books that teens recommended. Think of the teen-created list as a local best-seller list!

The YALSA Professional Development Center: Booktalking web site, located at http://www.ala.org/ala/yalsa/profdev/booktalking.htm (accessed April 25, 2005), is a good resource for books, articles, web sites, and advice about booktalking to teens. A good resource for advice about booktalking to adults—and teens—is *The Booktalker's Bible: How to Talk about the Books You Love to Any Audience* (Langemack 2003). More resources are listed in the Appendix of this book.

CONNECTING WITH OTHER ORGANIZATIONS

Once you've booktalked in middle and high schools, consider reaching out to other venues. Literacy groups, parent groups, and other organizations are usually looking for guest speakers. Many parents and adults know what the public library offers young children and school-age children, but may not be as aware of the books, other materials, other resources, services, programs, and volunteer opportunities that public libraries offer to teens.

You've set teen brains on fire in the classroom, and sparks are flying. Teens are talking about books! Now it's time to create more opportunities for teens to rave about books and reading, by planning some book-centered activities and events.

REFERENCES AND SUGGESTED READINGS

Anderson, Sheila B., and Kristine Mahood. 2001. "The Inner Game of Booktalking." *Voice of Youth Advocates* 24 (2): 107–110.

Bromann, Jennifer. 2001. *Booktalking that Works*. 2001. New York: Neal-Schuman Publishers.

Brooks, Kevin. 2004. *Kissing the Rain*. New York: Scholastic.

Camus, Albert. [1947] 1991. *The Plague*. Trans. Stuart Gilbert. Reprint. New York: Vintage Books.

Cappo, Elaine Willard. 2002. *Cheating Lessons*. New York: Atheneum Books for Young Readers.

Coleman, Michael. 2004. *On the Run*. New York: Dutton Children's Books.

Colfer, Eoin. 2000. *The Wish List*. New York: Hyperion Books for Children.

Cusick, Richie Tankersley. 2002. *The House Next Door*. New York: Simon Pulse.

Draper, Sharon M. 2002. *Double Dutch*. New York: Atheneum Books for Young Readers.

Fredericks, Mariah. 2004. *Head Games*. New York: Atheneum Books for Young Readers.

Goobie, Beth. 2002. *The Lottery*. Victoria, BC: Orca Books Publishers.

Hartinger, Brent. 2003. *Geography Club*. New York: HarperTempest.

Hoffman, Mary. 2002. *Stravaganza: City of Masks*. New York: Bloomsbury.

Jinks, Catherine. 2003. *Pagan's Crusade*. Cambridge, MA: Candlewick Press.

Jones, Patrick, Michele Gorman, and Tricia Suellentrop. 2004. *Connecting Young Adults and Libraries: A How-To-Do-It Manual for Librarians*. New York: Neal-Schuman Publishers.

Kinsella, Sophie. 2001. *Confessions of a Shopaholic*. New York: Delta Trade Paperbacks.

Korman, Gordon. 2002. *Son of the Mob*. New York: Hyperion Books for Children.

Koss, Amy Goldman. 2000. *The Girls*. New York: Dial Books for Young Readers.

Langemack, Chapple. 2003. *The Booktalker's Bible: How to Talk about the Books You Love to Any Audience*. Westport, CT: Libraries Unlimited.

Lawrence, Iain. 2004. *A Crack in the Line*. New York: Greenwillow Books.

Leavitt, Martine. 2004. *Heck Superhero*. Asheville, NC: Front Street.

Limb, Sue. 2004. *Girl, 15, Charming but Insane*. New York: Delacorte Press.

Magill, Frank, ed. 1996. *Masterplots: 1,801 Plot Stories and Critical Evaluations of the World's Finest Literature*. Pasadena, CA: Salem Press.

Mahood, Kristine. 2004. "Off the Page and Onto the Stage: Booktalking to Older Teens." *Serving Older Teens*. Westport, CT: Libraries Unlimited.

McDonald, Janet. 2003. *Twists and Turns*. New York: Frances Foster Books.

Myers, Walter Dean. 2002. *Handbook for Boys*. New York: HarperCollins.

Rees, Douglas. 2003. *Vampire High*. New York: Delacorte Press.

Rico, Gabrielle. 1983. *Writing the Natural Way: Using Right-Brain Techniques to Release Your Expressive Powers*. Los Angeles: J. P. Tarcher.

Scott, Kieran. 2005. *I Was a Non-Blonde Cheerleader*. New York: G. P. Putnam's Sons.

Shaw, Tucker. 2003. *Flavor of the Week*. New York: Hyperion.

Shinn, Sharon. 2002. *Jenna Starborn*. New York: Ace Books.

Sweeney, Joyce. 2002. *Players*. Delray Beach, FL: Winslow Press.

Vande Velde, Vivian. 2002. *Heir Apparent*. San Diego, CA: Harcourt.

Verne, Jules. [1876] 1997. *Michael Strogoff*. Reprint. Simon & Schuster Children's Books.

10

IT'S HAPPENING AT THE LIBRARY: BOOK-CENTERED ACTIVITIES AND EVENTS

You're sitting with teens at a round table, drinking hot chocolate. One girl is talking about a book she just read. "I *loved* that book!" exclaims another girl. A boy talks about a book. "Maybe you'd like this other book," says another boy, and he suggests a title. You talk about books, teens talk about books, and you all dash down the titles. . . .

You walk into the teen space, and smile at the bulletin board plastered with postcard-size book reviews by teens. . . .

Dim lights . . . cool jazz . . . and teens up front at the mic, reading their poems—or favorite poems by other poets . . .

"Where do you get your ideas?" a teen asks an author, and he explains. Teens ask more questions, write down answers, laugh at the author's jokes, and afterward tell you that they've always wanted to write, and now they're definitely going to start. . . .

Pinch yourself. Are you dreaming? No, you're awake, and this is real! Teens are not only reading, they're talking about books, writing reviews, and reading their poetry out loud. They're creating bookmarks and journals, and writing books. They're meeting authors.

Book-centered activities and events expand the solitary joy of reading into the social sphere. You've worked hard to build and display collections, and to promote reading and books through print promotions, a teen web page, readers' advisory, and booktalking. Teens have been finding books, reading them, and asking about more books. It's been fun. And now it's time to have even more fun, with activities and events. In Chapter 2, you saw that the character of teens' consumer behavior is more about meeting psychological and social needs—developing and expressing individuality, and connecting with others—than it is about meeting basic survival needs. Teens are discovering their own interests, tastes, and enthusiasms, and they're discovering how much fun it is to share them with others. Connecting with other teens through music, electronic communication, fashion, and sports, teens are on the lookout for fun activities and events. They like to do things, to make things, to talk, to laugh, and to eat. They enjoy socializing with friends, and they're interested in meeting new people. Book-centered activities and events offer teens more opportunities for connecting with others.

So what are "activities" and what are "events?" Activities are book-centered programs that are ongoing, with multiple points of access: in person, in print, and online. Examples include book reviews, surveys or polls, contests, book discussion groups, and seasonal reading programs. Events are book-centered programs that happen at one time on one day, necessitating in-person participation. Examples include book craft workshops, open mic nights, writing workshops, and author visits.

The purpose of book-centered activities and events is to create the conditions that make it possible for teens to contribute content to the library, or to make something for themselves. A book review contributes content. Learning how to write a journal helps teens to make something for themselves. This chapter will focus on planning and publicizing programs, with examples of specific activities and events ranging from bookmark contests to book discussion groups—concluding with a turnaround success story.

PLANNING ACTIVITIES AND EVENTS

The goal of preschool storytime is to support young children at the pre-reading stage, as they listen to stories, and as they participate by chanting rhymes or singing songs. Their enjoyment in seeing picture books, hearing stories, and participating in rhymes and songs builds positive associations about books. Later, the goal of book-centered programs for school-age children is to reinforce their reading, turning an educational skill into a powerful tool for entertainment and knowledge.

The goal of book-centered activities and events for teens is also to support teens at their reading stages, and to continue fostering positive associations about books. While young children do participate in story-times, their focus is on the librarian. School-age children participate in book-centered events, with the guidance of the librarian, and may contribute content, in such programs as book discussion groups. The participation of teens is more various and complex. Like school-age children, teens contribute content to book discussion groups. But they also contribute content to such programs as focus groups, activity boards, and poetry open mics, where they read their own poems as well as favorites written by other poets. When planning a book-centered activity or event, look for ways to foster teen engagement, participation, teen-to-teen promotions, and contribution.

Talk with Teens and Staff Members

Tell teens that you're planning activities and events, and you need to run some ideas past them: What sounds like fun? What sounds boring? You want their reactions and their ideas. Talk with teens during casual conversations, reference and readers' advisory conversations, school visits, at teen programs, and in focus groups. Ask follow-up questions to maximize teen input. Simply asking, "What about a book discussion group?" sounds vague and unfocussed. Follow up by saying that the group can be open to all kinds of books, or that it can focus on a particular theme or genre, such as realistic teen fiction or fantasy. The format can be open to whatever teens are reading, or it can focus on books chosen in advance to read and discuss. Talk with library staff members. Everyone in the library serves teens, and many staff members are parents of teens. Get their input on teen-appeal activities and events.

Talk with teens and staff members also about good days and times for library events: weekday afternoons, evenings, or weekends. Notice days and times when teens are *not* in the library. Maybe teens flood the library on Monday, Tuesday, and Wednesday afternoons, and then their numbers begin to decline on Thursday and Friday, and hardly any teens come in on the weekend. You may live in a community where teens find it difficult to get to the library after school, and so entire families, or groups of teens, visit on Saturdays. Early evenings might be a time when teens are in the library. Or not. Find out scheduled school dates for such events as breaks, conference weeks, big athletic events, dances, and major tests, whether state-mandated or finals.

Like adults, teens who participate in a scheduled event have either come to the library specifically for the event, or they happened to be in the library and noticed that something interesting was going on. Unlike young children, teens are usually the ones deciding whether or not they will participate in an event. Even if they want to come to an event, they may not have transportation. Stay aware of the times that teens seem to be most able to be in your library.

Resources

The resources listed at the end of this chapter describe such book-centered activities and events as book discussion groups, bookmaking workshops, contests, poetry coffeehouses, annual reading promotions, and book-buying trips. For more information on book and card crafts, consult art, craft, design, and bookmaking books and web sites. For more information on manga and graphic novel drawing techniques, consult drawing workbooks and web sites. Resources on facilitating adult book discussion groups can help with teen book discussion group planning and facilitation.

Such journals as the *ALAN Review*, *School Library Journal*, *Teacher Librarian*, *Voice of Youth Advocates*, and *Young Adult Library Services* include articles about book-centered activities and events, such as book discussion groups, poetry contests, and read-a-thons. Electronic resources include such mailing lists as PUBYAC, YA-YAAC, and YALSA-BK, where young adult librarians describe and analyze activities and events for teens. And speaking of the Internet, a great way to find activities and events is to hit the road—the virtual road, that is, and look at library web sites. That's how I discovered the teen book discussion groups described later in this chapter.

People resources include teens, library staff members, and people in the community. Teen volunteers and teen advisory board members may want to facilitate book discussion groups, or they may be able to teach book-related crafts such as bookbinding, book decoration, or scrapbooking. Maybe they know somebody in art class at school who draws superheroes or manga, and who could teach a class to teens. Maybe they know some teen writers who'd like to meet other teens who write.

Library staff members may have skills and enthusiasms they can share, such as calligraphy, bookmaking, or drawing. If they'd rather not teach a workshop by themselves, offer to be their assistant or helper. Involving more staff members in teen activities and events is a nice way to expand available programming for teens—and to give more staff members additional arenas for interacting with teens.

Community resources include poets, writers, artists, bookstore people, and academics, who can serve as contest judges, discussion facilitators, writing event emcees, and workshop teachers.

Funding and Partners

Find out what you can pay for out of your programming budget, such as workshop teachers, and what you can purchase using your library's supply budget, such as art supplies. If you have a Friends of the Library group, it may be able to help you pay for refreshments and prizes, and to hire authors. Author visits can be expensive, and are often presented in partnership with schools. Typically, the author visits schools during the day, and presents a program for the general public at the public library in the evening.

PUBLICITY
Talk with Teens and Staff Members

One of the best ways to publicize activities and events is to talk with teens and to put a brochure, flier, or bookmark into their hands. Ask teens if what's happening would interest them and their friends, and why? If not, why not? Get library staff members involved and enthusiastic by talking up the activity or event, and placing posters at public service desks. Keep a copy of the library's events brochure near all telephones so that staff members can easily answer questions.

Print Promotions, Mailing Lists, and Web Alerts

Use color palettes, fonts, language, graphics, and page layouts, as discussed in Chapter 6, to create posters and fliers. Plaster the library with posters, and bring posters to schools and teen-appeal places like coffeehouses, music stores, and clothing stores. Bookmarks listing book group meeting dates, or the dates of a series of book-centered events, can be inserted into books on display, or given to teens as they check out materials.

Ongoing publicity about book-centered activities and events is a good way to establish and maintain connections in the community. Send e-mails to school media specialists about activities and events, suggesting they forward those messages to English teachers and other school personnel who may be interested in book-centered activities and events. Contact counselors and sports coaches about a presentation by an author who writes self-help or motivational books for teens. Contact art teachers about book craft events, and theater teachers about open mic events. Attach fliers to e-mail, and schools will be able to put print materials into students' hands.

Send e-mail about activities and events to local home school groups. Home school families are often looking for group activities and events for teens—whether their teens are still being homeschooled or not. Ask other groups and agencies, such as recreation departments and community youth services, if they'd like a brief monthly e-mail notice of activities and events for teens. Send publicity to newspapers, radio stations, and other local media.

Publicize activities and events on the teen web site with thumbnails of your posters. The colors of posters catch teens' attention, but text on posters may be hard to read. Caption posters with the date and time of the event, adding a "click *here*" live link for more information.

A week before the event, fax a short announcement to the schools and ask that the schools consider including it in their regular announcements on one or two specified days. Print the announcement double-space so that it's easy to read.

Book Displays

As discussed in Chapter 5, activities and events make excellent themes for scheduled displays. Publicize a teen poetry night with a book display of poems by teens, young adult fiction in poetry form, and books on writing and performing poetry. Promote author visits with a display of their books, and books about related topics. For example, promote an author of adventure fiction by displaying the author's books, plus nonfiction books on hiking, rock climbing, rafting, and the like. Promote an author of realistic fiction by including nonfiction books on teen issues, such as family problems, alcohol and drug abuse, and school and other social pressures.

Everybody Had a Great Time!

From the posters, the book discussion group sounded okay, but . . . did anybody show up? That manga-writing workshop sounded kind of cool, but . . . was it any good? Show teens proof that activities and events are worth their participation. Reporting on activities and events tells teens that what happened at an event was not an isolated, one-time thing; rather, the event was part of ongoing library services for teens.

Report back about a book group meeting by typing up a list of the books teens talked about, with a sentence or two about each book. Include a sentence about the food—definitely an important feature. Conclude with a line giving the dates and times of upcoming meetings, in an eye-catching display font. Make some photocopies and leave them in the teen space, stacked in front of a poster reading "Teens Pick Good Books." Add copies of the books teens talked about: now it's a display. Post the list on the teen web site, and include it in your teen newsletter. Give a copy to the information desk in case teens come looking for the books that were discussed.

Some libraries report back with photographs, posted in the teen space or on the teen web site. As with any other photographic depictions of youth under 18 that the library will use in its materials, you will need to obtain signed parental permission to post photographs.

BOOK ACTIVITIES

Teens are not always in control of their schedules or transportation. As noted in the introduction to this chapter, ongoing book-centered activities give teens the opportunity to participate in library programs on their own time.

Book Reviews

Whether submitted on paper or online, writing book reviews gives teens the opportunity to express their opinion about books—and hone critical thinking and writing skills. Reading teen book reviews gives teens the opportunity to find out about books they might want to read from a respected source: other teens. Most libraries ask reviewers for the book's title, author, a brief summary, and the reviewer's first name, age, and library (if part of a multi-library system). Many libraries also ask reviewers to rate books on a one- to five-star scale. Lubbock Public Library's Teen Scene book review form adds a pull-down menu of possible answers to the question, "What did you think of the book?" Answers are, "Loved it," "Hated It," or "It was OK" (http://www.lubbocklibrary.com/teen/book%20review%20form.htm, accessed March 4, 2005). The SmartGirl book review form poses eleven questions, such as "How does the title relate to the story line?" (http://www.smartgirl.org/reviews/books/

review_survey.html, accessed February 4, 2006). The Q&A format transforms the review into an interview with the teen reviewer. To help teens to write, use prompts such as the following: "This book was . . . (list adjectives, check all that apply)," "You want to read this book because . . ." and "I liked this book because . . ."

Book reviews by teens can be used to promote books—and to give attention to teens who read. Create a poster display of book reviews by cutting neon paper into quarters, typing up reviews, mounting them on the neon paper, and scattering them around the bulletin board. Insert reviews into poster holders, find the reviewed books, and create a display, with a poster telling teens how they can contribute reviews.

Add teen book reviews to print promotions and the teen web site. Start a bookmark with a one-sentence teen book review. Insert a boxed teen book review into a brochure listing teen programs, or into a general brochure about library services. Add teen book reviews to the teen newsletter. Create a "Reviews by Teens" page on the teen web site, and link to it from your library's readers' advisory site so that adults can see it, too. Make sure everybody knows that teens are reading, enjoying, and talking about books.

Book reviews can also be incorporated into other library activities. For example, short book review forms are sometimes used as tickets in prize drawings for summer reading or other programs. Several of the libraries in the King County Library System in Washington state offer an activity called "Read 3, Get 1 Free." For every three books they read and review, participating teens aged 12–18 may select a free paperback (Koelling 2004, 274). This program is supported by grant funding and local Friends of the Library groups.

Quizzes, Surveys, and Polls

Quizzes, surveys, and polls are standard features of teen magazines and web sites, asking teens their opinions on everything from celebrities to social issues. You can encourage teens to participate in state or national book polls—and you can create your own.

State library associations and other organizations honor children's and young adults' books with annual awards; some awards are based on children's or young adults' opinions. Contact the organization for posters, ballots, and voting procedures. To find award information, check with your state library association. The web site "Awards for Children's and YA Books by State (and U.S. Awards)" lists youth choice, adult choice, and national awards, at http://www.cynthialeitich.com/lit_resources/awards/state awards.html (accessed February 4, 2006). Create displays using the books on the ballot, together with copies of the ballot and an annotated bibliography of titles (which you may need to write yourself). Promote the award by including nominated books in booktalk presentations in schools. Once the awards have been given, post the information in the teen space, the teen newsletter, and on the teen web site. Show teens that what they think about books is important. "Teens' Top Ten" is an online poll activated during Teen Read Week, the annual teen reading promotion sponsored by the Young Adult Library Services Association (YALSA). Teen involvement in the design of this project has steadily increased since its inception in 1999 (Tuccillo 2004, 23). YALSA chooses five public and school teen book groups every year, asking them to evaluate teen books published during the previous November–October, and to assemble a ballot for voting by all teens. YALSA posts the ballot on the Teens' Top Ten web site, tabulates votes cast during Teen Read Week, and announces the ten winners.

As with state book awards, you can display nominated books, and print and distribute ballot lists from the Teens' Top Ten web site, located at http://www.ala.org/ala/yalsa/teenreading/teenstopten/teenstopten.htm (accessed February 4, 2006). The site also lists the year's teen book groups. Looking at the groups' web sites, you might get some ideas for your own book groups, discussed later in this chapter.

You can also create your own print and online surveys, polls, and quizzes. A survey form can ask teens to name a favorite book, with a sentence or two telling why they like it. A poll or quiz can list five or ten titles, themes, genres, or nonfiction topics, asking teens to rank them in order of preference. As results come in, post them in print in the teen space and online on the teen web site.

Contests

Bookmark contests promote teen creativity, teen reading, and books. Schools and libraries often sponsor bookmark contests in conjunction with National Library Week, summer reading programs, Teen Read Week, or other promotions. The Denver Public Library in Denver, Colorado, invites teens to design bookmarks promoting the summer teen reading program. Middle and high school art teachers are encouraged to promote the contest to their students, and to consider offering them extra credit for participating (http://teens.denverlibrary.org/involved/view_links.html, accessed February 4, 2006).

Writing contests promote reading and books by encouraging teens to create their own books, and are open to poetry, short stories, essays, and comic strips (Edwards 2002, 38). The creativity of teen entrants is endorsed by displaying their work, whether by posting entries on bulletin boards, including them in notebooks on display, or posting them on the teen web site. Winning entries can be recognized at an awards event, as are the winners in the annual "Take Flight and Write" contest sponsored by Burlington Public Library in Burlington, Ontario (http://www.bpl.on.ca/bplteens/time.htm, accessed February 4, 2006). Teens can be invited to read their work at coffeehouse events (41) or bookstore events, and their work can be published in library-produced chapbooks (43) or on bookmarks.

Book-related prizes for bookmark and writing contests can include anything from books to bookstore gift cards, blank journals, gel pens, art supplies, and poetry magnet sets.

Annual Reading Promotions

Annual reading promotions such as National Poetry Month in April, summer reading in the summer, and Teen Read Week in October are great opportunities for book-centered activities and events. Poetry-writing workshops, contests, and open mic events are naturals for April, and you might want to highlight some novels-in-poems at a book group meeting. Promote books related to the summer reading theme at book group meetings, and find ways to relate the theme to such events as book crafts and writing workshops.

The Teen Read Week site is located at http://www.ala.org/ala/yalsa/teenreading/trw/teenreadweek.htm (accessed April 9, 2005), and features ideas for displays, booklists, activities, events, and publicity. Each year's promotions are built around a theme.

"Get Real! @ Your Library," the theme for Teen Read Week 2005, put the spotlight on nonfiction. "Best Real-Life Books Ever!" was an activity that invited teens in Timberland Regional Library to fill out surveys all through October naming the best real-life book they'd ever read. Paper copies were available at all libraries and online at the library's web site, http://www.trlib.org, by clicking on the Teen Read Week logo. I also asked teens about real-life books during school visits, library events, and conversations, and titles appeared on the teen web site and a bookmark. This is an activity that easily adopts to any reading promotion theme. The theme for 2004 was "It's Alive! @ Your Library," focusing on horror fiction and the unexplained; teens were encouraged to name the "Creepiest, Scariest Books

Ever!" Previous years' themes have been "Slammin' @ Your Library" (poetry, 2003), "Get Graphic @ Your Library" (comics, graphic novels, and manga, 2002), "Make Reading a Hobbit @ Your Library" (fantasy fiction, 2001), "Take Time to Read" (2000), and "Read for the Fun of It" (1999).

BOOK DISCUSSION GROUPS

Book groups create the conditions for teens to talk about books they like (or hate), find out what other teens think, and build on many teens' love of socializing with friends and meeting new people. Being with other teens who are excited and articulate about books validates teens who read. Books, journal articles, and web sites are devoted to this topic, and space does not permit covering all the issues and possibilities, but what follows is some basic information.

In a contemporary teen pop culture that values physical appearance, clothing, sports prowess, music, fast cars, and the like, it's important for someone to make time and a place for teens who read, and who like to talk about books. That someone is you, the time is now, and the place is your library.

"If you talk to other random teens, they're like, 'You read?' " notes a high school junior named Alison, who appreciates the opportunity to meet with other teens who don't think it's weird to read (Pierce 2003, 56). James, age 16, another member of the Arlington County Public Library's Teen Advisory, depends on book group members' recommendations to find good books. And not only do book groups give teens a place to talk about books with fellow readers, but also they show teens that adults are making time for them, listening to them, and valuing their opinions and expertise. They can see that adults value their contributions. You benefit, too, from this opportunity to sit down and talk with teens, getting to know them a little better, learning about teen-appeal books, and sharing your own enthusiasm for books.

Formats

Some book discussion groups are open to all types of books, and others focus on specific titles, themes, genres, or topics. Most groups are open to teens only. Parent-teen groups (including mother/daughter, father/son, and variations of this sort) bring parents and teens together, usually to discuss a particular book that group members have agreed to read in advance. Some teen book groups write reviews. Some meet online. Teens are meeting to talk about all kinds of books:

- Separate teen book groups meet to talk about realistic fiction, fantasy, books made into movies, and more, sponsored by the Ocean County Library, New Jersey, http://oceancounty.lib.nj.us/Teens/Tevents.htm (accessed March 4, 2005).
- Teens talk about graphic novels, sponsored by the Los Angeles Public Library, California, http://www.lapl.org/teenscape/library/ts_events.html (accessed March 4, 2005).
- Teens talk about classics, sponsored by the Carroll County Public Library, Maryland, http://teens.carr.org/ (accessed March 4, 2005).
- Teen book groups of girls 12–16 meet with an adult, teen book groups of boys 11–16 meet with an adult, and girls 10–12 with an adult, sponsored by the Kings Park Teen Book Discussion Groups, Fairfax County Public Library, Virginia, http://www.co.fairfax.va.us/library/branches/kp/kpteens.htm (accessed December 28, 2004).

Structure

Some teen book discussion groups, like adult book groups, are structured to discuss one or two books at each meeting. The group often decides what they will read. Because everyone has read the same book, it can be easy to get lively discussions going.

Another structure is for the group to discuss books of a particular theme, genre, or nonfiction topic. For example, one month teens will talk about realistic fiction, the next month they'll discuss adventure fiction, next they'll share self-help nonfiction, and so on. This way, all teens don't have to read the same book and everybody gets to hear about a lot of books.

Finally, there's the relatively unstructured book group in which teens talk about whatever they've recently read or would recommend, regardless of genre, theme, or topic. This can be a fun free-for-all that expands into more general topics, such as what teens like in books and what they don't like, the merits of school-assigned books, movies versus the books they're based on, and much more.

Starting a Book Group

Talk with teens and find out what they think about starting a book group in the library. Talk with school media specialists and English teachers. Decide on a day, time, format, and structure. Ask interested teens to tell their friends. Print posters and bookmarks with all the meeting dates on them. E-mail reminders about meetings to school media specialists, asking them to forward the message to English teachers. Remember to mention the refreshments in all forms of communication!

Facilitating Discussion

After setting up refreshments and stacking a half-dozen books to talk about if conversation lags, welcome everyone at the table. An easy way to start is to have everyone introduce themselves with their name, and one quick fact about themselves. The fact could be their school, their favorite type of book, the best movie they saw recently, or something else. Now that the group is ready to talk about books, you might want to review a few suggestions for discussion that book groups have found useful:

- Please listen with an open mind to what is said, rather than to who says it.
- Please do not interrupt when someone else is speaking.
- Please comment to the group as a whole, rather than only to someone seated next to you, or a friend, or the librarian.
- Avoid summarizing the entire book: this is not a book report. Also, avoid getting sidetracked into long-winded personal anecdotes.

If you are the first person to talk about a book, model reviewing by giving a brief shelf talk, as described in Chapter 8, only with a bit more detail. Be ready for some questions about the book.

As in readers' advisory conversations, both you and the teens may find that follow-up questions, like those delineated in Chapter 8, will help the reader describe the book and its appeal to readers. As noted above, reading is a very individual activity. Different teens like different types of books. Even if they love the same book, it may be for different reasons.

Activities

Although teens who read are generally ready to talk about books they like, the conversation may stall. And sometimes an hour seems like a long time to be talking nonstop about books. Plan for those slow times with some activities, such as:

- *Quizzes.* Short quizzes about books, movies, and TV are fun. We did a quiz about classic science fiction and fantasy at a meeting of TTAFSF (Teens Talk About Fantasy and Science Fiction): the fun part was hooting over ridiculous answers to multiple-choice questions.

- *Reader Advisory Resources.* Teens who like to read are always looking for good books. *What Fantastic Fiction Do I Read Next?* (Barron 1998) was a hit at another TTAFSF meeting, because I showed teens how to find more books like the last one they liked so much. They hadn't known that such resources exist. Good online resources include readers' advisory sites, *NoveList,* and Google.

- *Teen Picks Booklists.* As teens talk about books, write down titles and authors. Review the list with teens at the meeting, and tell them that you'll be creating booklists of teen picks. Print them up as bookmarks or post them on the book page of the teen web page. Be sure to identify the book discussion group as the source of the booklist.

- *State Book Awards.* Fill out ballots for your state's young adult book award(s).

- *Teen Book Reviews.* Write book reviews for posting on the teen space bulletin board, the book page of the teen web page, or the teen newsletter.

- *Guest Librarian.* Periodically invite another library staff member to a book group meeting. A guest librarian brings an additional range of reading experience and perspective to the discussion, and can help out with readers' advisory.

- *Book Buying.* There are a number of ways for teens to participate in book buying for the library. Ask teens about their favorite series, and fill out order slips for volumes your library doesn't own. Bring copies of book reviews or pre-publication catalogs for teens to look over, and select titles. Some libraries organize book-buying trips to local bookstores (Honnold 2003, 157–161).

Online Book Discussion Groups and Blogs

Like book reviews, online book discussion groups and blogs are book-centered activities that teens can participate in at any time. One way to set up an online book discussion group is to join the Teen Book Club at DearReader.com (http://www.dearreader.com, accessed February 5, 2006) (Jones 2004, 284). Each weekday, the site e-mails members a short section of a book, which librarians can forward to participating teens. Teens can comment about the book on book club forums.

You can also set up book blogs at such sites as Blogger (http://www.blogger.com, accessed April 21, 2005). You and the teens can use the blog to post comments on books they're reading. You can also insert reminders about book-centered activities and events at the library and in the community.

PRESENTING EVENTS

Set up a display of books related to the topic and call the audience's attention them before the event begins, sharing one or two books—quickly (Nichols 2002, 101). The audience will accept a few introductory words about the library, upcoming programs, and books. Afterward, however, some of the audience may want to talk one-on-one with the speaker.

When teens come to an activity or an event, ask them how they found out about it. Maybe they were in the library anyway and heard the announcement over the public address system, or saw some teens heading for the teen space or the library meeting room. Perhaps they saw a poster in the library. Or they heard an announcement that morning at school, or their teacher or school media specialist said something last week about it, or a parent saw a notice in the paper and mentioned it to them. Or they heard about it from a library staff member as they were checking out books.

Before teens leave an event, thank them for coming, be open to talking about the event if they choose to, and give them a quick preview of upcoming events.

BOOK EVENTS
Book Crafts

Many teens like to make things. Examples of book crafts include bookmaking (Edwards 2002, 8–10) and chapbook binding (43). Scrapbooking is popular with both teens and adults, and has inspired books, magazines, web sites, and sections in craft stores. For all of these craft programs, look for facilitators in school and college art departments, art supply stores, and craft supply stores.

Writing Events

Writing events offer more opportunities to promote reading and books, transforming teens from readers into writers. Writing is a solitary activity, and so these events meet teen needs to be reassured that they are not alone in their interests, and to find others who like to write, too. Examples of writing events include workshops for poetry, journal-writing, short stories, and graphic novels. As with any other type of library event, you can develop and present writing workshops yourself, or find presenters in your area with the necessary expertise.

"Throwdown Poems and Stories" is a workshop I created that asks teens to pick up a pinchful of laminated words and drop them on a page. Straightening the words into several lines, no attempt is made to change their random, unplanned order into something that makes more sense. Instead, the method is to read the words over and over, letting new ideas bubble up spontaneously, so that the writer uses the thrown down words as a starting-off place for writing, overcoming the tendency to freeze up in the face of a blank page and other forms of writer's block. Teens are often surprised by the poems and stories they create from unpredictable word combinations.

"That poem was in your head," I tell them. "You just didn't know it!"

Books on display at this workshop include poetry collections, poetry-writing books, and young adult novels in poem form.

"Journal Writing for Teens" is a journal-writing workshop I created. I begin by asking teens about their journal-writing experiences—writing steadily, tried to write but gave up, never started—and share some of my own as well. Once we see that our experiences vary, but our purpose is shared, I explain basic writing methods, special techniques, and quirky writing prompts. We stop to write two or three times. I booktalk a selection of the books on display, which include real-life diaries, journal-writing books, personal essay– and memoir-writing books, and teen novels written in diary form.

Today's teens are reading comics, graphic novels, and manga, and some are creating their own books. As described in Chapter 3, these books blend the graphic conventions of comics with the themes and genres of young adult fiction. Comics continue to follow their superhero antecedents, while graphic novels often present stories, memoirs, or histories in a variety of visual styles and texts. Manga are graphic novels written in Japanese or Korean and translated into English, some of them based on Japanese anime (cartoons), which offer story lines ranging from contemporary life and romance to wild fantasy and science fiction. Teens who doodle, cartoon, or draw may also be interested in participating in workshops. Contact your local comics and graphic novels shop to find out about artists in your area who may be interested in presenting graphic novel–drawing or -writing workshops.

Poetry Events

Poetry is about passion; poetry is about gritty realities; poetry is about dreams. What better venue for teens? Poetry open mics can be presented as the culminating event for a series of poetry-writing workshops or a contest, as an observance of National Poetry Month, or simply because they are a good opportunity for teens who write to enjoy the spotlight.

At "Teen Poetry Jam," we played cool old jazz on the CD player, served up hot chocolate and cookies, and watched as the strains of music and fumes of chocolate curled out the door and lured teens inside the meeting room. To start the event, we announced that we wanted to hear from as many poets as possible, so we encouraged each poet to read one poem, and then we'd go to the next poet.

No one wanted to go first.

"Okay, while you're getting ready to read, I'll start off with a poem," I said, and reached for one of the books I'd brought just in case teens were a bit shy, reading a short, funny poem. The ice was broken, and teens started jumping up to read. A high school boy read a poem he'd written about lost love. A high school girl read a poem she'd written about fear. A high school girl declaimed some Shakespeare, then recruited two more girls to be backup witches as she enacted the "double, double, toil and trouble" scene from "Macbeth." A younger teen boy wanted to read, and found a poem in one of the books on display.

"How do I tell when it's over?" he innocently asked. I hung back, betting that another teen would come up and show him how to find the end of the poem, and one of the teen girls did. And so, besides participating and contributing content, teens also felt free to help facilitate the event.

AUTHOR VISITS

When teens hear authors speak about their work, books become real. By seeing a real person who writes books, teens can see that the books they like didn't arrive solely by inspiration. While inspiration plays a part, it becomes clear that writing a book is work: writing, revising, reconceptualizing, rewriting. Teens can also come away with an appreciation of the world of books (Follos 2004, 11), and the culture of reading. You can listen to music on CD, but there's nothing like going to a concert for the total experience.

Planning the Visit

To plan an author visit, allow six to twelve months' lead time. Many authors have their own web site; some offer details about booking visits. Some authors prefer to be contacted directly, while others prefer that a publicist at their publisher be contacted. Fees can range from $250 to $2,500 and up, so if you think you'll need a partner to help with finances, such as a middle or high school, contact the school and secure its cooperation before contacting the author and beginning negotiations. Author visits to schools and public libraries generally comprise a day of presentations at one or more schools, and an evening program at the public library. Find out what days will work for the school or schools, and what days will work for the library, before contacting the author. Decide who will be driving and escorting the author.

Now you're ready to contact the author or publicist. Check the author's or publisher's web site for the tour schedule. If the author is going to be near your area, perhaps he or she would be available for a visit. Send an e-mail or letter to the author or publicist, inviting the author to visit your library. Give a range of possible dates, ask the fee, and ask what the fee covers: travel, accommodation, meals, mileage, and the presentation itself. Find out the nature of the presentation. Will it be a lecture with some readings from the author's books, followed by questions from the audience? Does the author also offer a writing workshop or writing critique session for teens who write?

Most authors are happy to sell and sign their books after their presentation: find out if the author brings his or her own copies to sell, or if you will need to make an arrangement with a local bookstore to bring in books and a bookstore employee.

Once the author is interested, ask how many presentations he or she will do per day, the size and age of audiences, and any room configuration or equipment needs. If you'd like to videotape the presentation, find out if this is okay with the author. Clarify transportation: will the author be driving herself from place to place, or will you or another library or school employee be driving? If the latter, agree when and where to pick her up. Once all the details have been ironed out, send the author or publicist a letter of understanding, reiterating such information as date, times, speaking venues, type of presentation, and fee. Ask the author how he or she would like to be introduced. Include a map, driving directions, and contact names and phone numbers, whether the author is doing the driving or not. If the author will be visiting schools, include the day's itinerary: the author's arrival at the airport or first speaking venue, other venues, breaks and meals, overnight accommodation, and back to the airport. Notify the local newspaper, giving information about the author, dates of the visit, books published, and itinerary.

Promote the author's visit in your library by making a display of his or her books. Talk about the books in teen book group meetings, and invite teens to attend the event—and to help out as ushers. Display the author's books as the "Book of the Day" on public service desks prior to the visit. Talk about the author and his or her books with staff members, booktalk titles at staff meetings, and encourage staff members to read a book by the author.

At the Event

A week or two before the event, e-mail the author, just to check in and to answer any questions that may have arisen since the last time you communicated. At the event, arrange chairs for the audience, a podium or table for the author with a pitcher and a glass of water, and tables to the side of the room: one for a display of author's books from the library, another for refreshments, and a third table for selling and signing books. Test the audiovisual equipment, such as microphone, projector, computer, and network connections, if needed.

Begin the event by thanking the author for coming, welcoming the audience, and telling the audience what is about to happen. Your opening comments could introduce the author, what he or she will talk about, and refer to a question-and-answer period. Invite the audience to stay for refreshments, and to talk with the author. Let the audience know that copies of the author's books are available for purchase and signing. When you outline the sequence of activities in this way, everybody—the audience, and the author—knows what to expect, and can relax. Introduce the author, then step back as he or she moves into the spotlight.

After the Event

After the event, send thank you letters to the author, publisher, and funding partners. If the local newspaper covered the event, it's a nice idea to include photocopies of the article in your letter to the author. Send a report about the event to the head librarian, who may wish to include it in her monthly or quarterly report to library administration. Make a poster featuring the newspaper article, with a sidebar about the library's role in the author visit.

"Author Visits at Your Library—How To," a web site sponsored by the Michigan Center for the Book, was very helpful in the writing of this section. The site is located at http://www.michigan.gov/hal/0,1607,% 207-160-17449_36788_38908---,00.html (accessed February 4, 2006).

SOMETIMES IT FLOPS—AND SOMETIMES IT FLIES!

There are no guarantees that teens will participate in library events, even if you provide food (Jones 2004, 220). Carefully researched and prepared events may garner an audience of zero, for reasons that are beyond your control: nice weather in the middle of a rainy winter, a sudden change in the school schedule, and the like. You may scrape along with two, three, or five teens at events, and wonder why aren't more teens coming. Look closely at what you are doing. Are these activities and events that teens you know might like? Have you publicized them in every possible way? Are teens simply not able to come to the library due to transportation challenges?

Keep talking with teens. Tell them you want their unvarnished opinions about programming, publicity, and accessibility. And keep trying, no matter what. Event-planning is an art and a complex skill. And so if at first you don't succeed . . .

One year, three of us decided to participate in a January national reading promotion for teens, and planned an hour of booktalks in the teen space. We brought in lots of refreshments. We brought in lots of books. Three or four teens were studying in the teen space and about a half-dozen were chatting in the conversation area just outside the teen space. Great, we thought: the food will bring them in, and we can share some books!

Then we made the announcement over the public address system about the event. As we were returning to the teen space, teens were stuffing textbooks into their backpacks, vaulting out of chairs, and heading for the front door. In fact, they couldn't get out of the library fast enough!

Traipsing into the deserted teen space, we each took a cookie and sat down to talk about what had gone wrong. We'd put up the national reading promotion publicity, we'd notified the schools, the food was good, but teens were racing for the exits. We agreed that one thing we had not done enough of was to talk about the event in advance with individual teens. Instead, we had relied on institutional publicity. We hadn't made enough personal connections.

Fast forward to December. Throughout the year, we talked with teens. We offered activities, scheduled events, and started to attract teens to the library's teen space during the spring, through the summer, and during and after Teen Read Week. One afternoon in mid-December, just before winter break, I made the public service announcement for "Hot Books for Cold Days," a booktalk and book discussion event. Rolling a booktruck piled with books, cookies, and hot chocolate toward the teen space, I had no idea if anyone would be there.

To my astonishment, eight teens were sitting in the teen space. They were waiting for me. They all smiled. They jumped up to help set up the food.

"Hi!" they said. "What did you bring?" Six more teens appeared. They pounced on the cookies, they pounced on the books, and we were off: talking about books, laughing, recommending books we loved, giving the thumbs-down to books we despised, pulling books off the shelves to share, and basking in the glow of *all* of our brains on fire—for reading and for books.

That's what this book has been all about: creating the conditions that strike sparks, fan flames, set teen brains on fire, and awaken a passion for print. By bringing together such topics as reading theory and practice, commercial pop culture, space and design principles and elements, print and online promotions, readers' advisory, booktalking, and programming, I hope I have shown you how much knowledge, understanding, inspiration, and fun we can bring to promoting reading and books to teens.

REFERENCES AND SUGGESTED READINGS

Edwards, Kirsten. 2002. *Teen Library Events: A Month-by-Month Guide*. Westport, CT: Greenwood Press.

Follos, Alison. 2004. "Making an Author's Visit Your Best 'Good Time.'" *Teacher Librarian*. (June): 8–11.

Honnold, RoseMary. 2003. *101+ Teen Programs that Work*. New York: Neal-Schuman Publishers.

Jones, Patrick, Michele Gorman, and Tricia Suellentrop. 2004. *Connecting Young Adults and Libraries: A How-To-Do-It Manual for Librarians*. New York: Neal-Schuman Publishers.

Koelling, Holly. 2004. "Read 3, Get 1 Free." *Voice of Youth Advocates*. (October): 274.

Michigan Center for the Book. "Author Visits at Your Library—How To." Located at http://www.michigan.gov/hal/0,1607,%207-160-17449_36788_38908---, 00.html (accessed February 4, 2006).

Nichols, Mary Anne. 2002. *Merchandising Library Materials to Young Adults.* Greenwood Village, CO: Libraries Unlimited.

Pierce, Jennifer Burke. 2003. "Talking Books with Teens." *American Libraries.* (September): 56–57.

Tuccillo, Diane. 2004. "Teens Meeting the Challenge: Young Adults Gain a Voice Deciding What's Hot to Read." *ALAN Review.* (Winter): 23–26.

Young Adult Library Services Association. http://www.ala.org/yalsa (accessed April 21, 2005).

Appendix I

YOUNG ADULT FICTION, GRAPHIC NOVELS, CLASSICS, AND NONFICTION

Alias series. 2002+. New York: Bantam Books.

Almond, David. 2000. *Kit's Wilderness*. New York: Delacorte Press.

Anderson, Laurie Halse. 2000. *Fever 1793*. New York: Simon & Schuster Books for Young Readers.

Anderson, M. T. 2002. *Feed*. Cambridge, MA: Candlewick Press.

Asai, Carrie. 2003+. *Samurai Girl* series. New York: Simon Pulse.

Atwood, Margaret. 1988. *Cat's Eye*. New York: Doubleday.

Auch, Mary Jane. 2002. *Ashes of Roses*. New York: Henry Holt.

Avon True Romance series. 2002+. New York: Avon Books.

Baldwin, James. [1953] 1963. *Go Tell It on the Mountain*. Reprint. New York: Dial Press.

Barrett, Tracy. 2000. *Anna of Byzantium*. New York: Delacorte Press.

Bechard, Margaret. 2002. *Hanging on to Max*. Brookfield, CN: Roaring Brook Press.

Bendis, Brian Michael. 2001+. *Ultimate Spider-Man* series. New York: Marvel Comics.

Black, Jonah. 2001+. *The Black Book: Diary of a Teenage Stud* series. New York: Avon Books.

Blacker, Terence. 2002. *Angel Factory*. New York: Simon & Schuster Books for Young Readers.

Brashares, Ann. 2001. *Sisterhood of the Traveling Pants*. New York: Delacorte Press.

Brennan, Michael. 2000+. *Electric Girl* series. San Francisco: AiT/PlanetLar.

Brisick, Jamie. 2004. *Have Board, Will Travel: The Definitive History of Surf, Skate, and Snow*. New York: HarperEntertainment.

Bronte, Charlotte. [1847] 1942. *Jane Eyre*. New York: Dodd, Mead.

Cabot, Meg. 2002. *All-American Girl*. New York: HarperCollins.

Caletti, Deb. 2002. *The Queen of Everything*. New York: Simon Pulse.

Camus, Albert. [1947] 1991. *The Plague*. Trans. Stuart Gilbert. New York: Knopf.

Cappo, Nan Willard. 2002. *Cheating Lessons*. New York: Atheneum Books for Young Readers.

Carolson, Melody. 2000+. *Diary of a Teenage Girl* series. Sisters, OR: Multnomah Publishers.

Carvell, Marlene. 2002. *Who Will Tell My Brother?* New York: Hyperion.

Cather, Willa. [1918] 1996. *My Antonia*. New York: Alfred A. Knopf.

———. [1915] 1943. *The Song of the Lark*. Boston: Houghton Mifflin.

Choron, Sandra, and Harry Choron. 2002. *Book of Lists for Teens*. Boston: Houghton Mifflin.

Chotjewitz, David. 2004. *Daniel Half Human and the Good Nazi*. Trans. Doris Orgel. New York: Atheneum Books for Young Readers.

Clamp. 2002+. *Rayearth* series. Los Angeles: Tokyopop.

Clark, Catherine. 2000. *Truth or Dairy*. New York: HarperTempest.

Clements, Andrew. 2002. *Things Not Seen*. New York: Philomel Books.

Clowes, Daniel. 1997. *Ghost World*. Seattle, WA: Fantagraphics Books.

Cofer, Judith Ortiz. 2004. *Call Me Maria*. New York: Orchard Books.

Coleman, Evelyn. 2001. *Born in Sin*. New York: Atheneum Books for Young Readers.

Colton, Larry. 2000. *Counting Coup: A True Story of Basketball and Honor on the Little Big Horn*. New York: Warner Books.

Cooney, Caroline B. 2001. *For All Time*. New York: Delacorte Press.

Cotner, June. 2002. *Teen Sunshine Reflections: Words for the Heart and Soul*. New York: HarperTrophy.

Cox, Terry. 2000. *You Can Write Song Lyrics*. Cincinnati, OH: Writer's Digest Books.

Crowe, Chris. 2002. *Mississippi Trial, 1955*. New York: P. Fogelman Books.

Crutcher, Chris. 2001. *Whale Talk*. New York: Greenwillow Books.

Davidson, Dana. 2004. *Jason and Kyra*. New York: Hyperion/Jump at the Sun.

Dear America series. 1996+. New York: Scholastic.

Desai Hidier, Tanuja. 2002. *Born Confused*. New York: Scholastic.

Dessen, Sarah. 2002. *This Lullaby*. New York: Viking.

———. 2000. *Dreamland*. New York: Viking.

Deuker, Carl. 2003. *High Heat*. Boston: Houghton Mifflin.

———. 2000. *Night Hoops*. Boston: Houghton Mifflin.

Dickinson, Peter. 2001. *The Ropemaker*. New York: Delacorte Press.

Donnelly, Jennifer. 2003. *Northern Light*. San Diego, CA: Harcourt.

Dostoyevsky, Fyodor. [1866] 1993. *Crime and Punishment*. Trans. Richard Pevear and Larissa Volokhonsky. Reprint. New York: Bantam Books.

Dokey, Cameron. 2004. *How Not to Spend Your Senior Year*. New York: Simon Pulse.

Draper, Sharon M. 2002. *Double Dutch*. New York: Atheneum Books for Young Readers.

Dreiser, Theodore. [1925] 2000. *An American Tragedy*. New York: New American Library.

Dugan, Ellen. 2003. *Elements of Witchcraft: Natural Magick for Teens*. St. Paul, MN: Llewllyn.

Easton, Kelly. 2001. *Life History of a Star*. New York: M. K. McElderry Books.

Eliot, George. [1859] 1980. *Adam Bede*. New York: Penguin USA.

Espeland, Pamela. 2003. *Life Lists for Teens: Tips, Steps, Hints, and How-Tos for Growing Up, Getting Along, Learning, and Having Fun*. Minneapolis, MN: Free Spirit.

Fama, Elizabeth. 2002. *Overboard*. Chicago: Cricket Books.

Farmer, Nancy. 2004. *The Sea of Trolls*. New York: Atheneum Books for Young Readers.

Farrell, Juliana, and Beth Mayall. 2001. *Middle School, the Real Deal: From Cafeteria Food to Combination Locks*. New York: HarperCollins.

Farrell, Mary Cronk. 2004. *Fire in the Hole!* New York: Clarion Books.

Ferris, Jean. 2001. *Of Sound Mind*. New York: Farrar, Straus & Giroux.

———. 2000. *Eight Seconds*. San Diego, CA: Harcourt.

Flaubert, Gustav. [1856] 1957. *Madame Bovary*. Trans. Francis Steegmuller. Reprint. New York: Random House.

Flinn, Alex. 2002. *Breaking Point*. New York: HarperTempest.

———. 2001. *Breathing Underwater*. New York: HarperCollins.

Ford, Michael Thomas. 2000. *Paths of Faith: Conversations about Religion and Spirituality*. New York: Simon & Schuster Books for Young Readers.

Forde, Catherine. 2004. *Fat Boy Swim*. New York: Delacorte Press.

Fornay, Alfred. 2002. *Born Beautiful: The African-American Teenager's Complete Beauty Guide*. New York: John Wiley and Sons.

Fox, Annie. 2000. *Can You Relate? Real-World Advice for Teens on Guys, Girls, Growing Up, and Getting Along*. Minneapolis, MN: Free Spirit.

Fraustino, Lisa Rowe. 2002. *Soul Searching: Thirteen Stories about Faith and Belief*. New York: Simon & Schuster Books for Young Readers.

Fry, Ron. 2003. *101 Smart Questions to Ask on Your Interview*. Franklin Lakes, NJ: Career Press.

Gaiman, Neil. 2002. *Coraline*. New York: HarperCollins.

Gallo, Donald, ed. 2004. *First Crossing: Stories about Teen Immigrants*. Cambridge, MA: Candlewick Press.

———, ed. 2001. *On the Fringe*. Cambridge, MA: Candlewick Press.

Geras, Adele. 2001. *Troy*. San Diego, CA: Harcourt.

Giles, Gail. 2003. *Dead Girls Don't Write Letters*. Brookfield, CT: Roaring Brook Press.

————. 2002. *Shattering Glass*. Brookfield, CT: Roaring Brook Press.

Glenn, Mel. 2000. *Split Image*. New York: HarperCollins.

Goethe, Johann Wolfgang von. [1774, 1787] 1993. *The Sorrows of Young Werther and Novella*. Trans. Elizabeth Mayer and Louise Bogan; poems translated by W. H. Auden. Reprint. New York: Modern Library.

Goodman, Alison. 2003. *Singing the Dogstar Blues*. New York: Viking.

Graydon, Shari. 2004. *In Your Face: The Culture of Beauty and You*. Toronto, ON: Annick Press.

Greene, Rebecca. 2001. *Teenager's Guide to School Outside the Box*. Minneapolis, MN: Free Spirit.

Guinness Book of World Records. 1963+. New York: Bantam Books.

Haddix, Margaret Peterson. 2005. *Among the Enemy*. New York: Simon & Schuster Books for Young Readers.

————. 2000. *Turnabout*. New York: Simon & Schuster Books for Young Readers.

Harrar, George. 2003. *Not as Crazy as I Seem*. Boston: Houghton Mifflin.

Hart, Christopher. 2001. *Manga Mania: How to Draw Japanese Comics*. New York: Watson-Guptill.

Hartinger, Brent. 2003. *Geography Club*. New York: HarperTempest.

Hautman, Pete. 2003. *Sweetblood*. New York: Simon & Schuster Books for Young Readers.

Haven, Kendall F. 2001. *That's Weird! Awesome Science Mysteries*. Golden, CO: Fulcrum Resources.

Healy, Mark. 2000. *Spiritualized: A Look Inside the Teenage Soul*. New York: Alloy Books.

Heneghan, James. 2000. *The Grave*. New York: Farrar, Straus & Giroux.

Horowitz, Anthony. 2001+. *Alex Rider* series. New York: Philomel Books.

Hrdlitschka, Shelley. 2001. *Dancing Naked*. Victoria, BC; Custer, WA: Orca Books.

Huegel, Kelly. 2003. *GLBTQ: The Survival Guide for Queer and Questioning Teens*. Minneapolis, MN: Free Spirit.

Hughes, Dean. 2001. *Soldier Boys*. New York: Atheneum Books for Young Readers.

Jemas, Bill. 2002. *Origin: The True Story of Wolverine*. New York: Marvel Comics.

Jenkins, A. M. 2001. *Damage*. New York: HarperCollins.

Jinks, Catherine. 2003. *Pagan's Crusade*. Cambridge, MA: Candlewick Press.

Johnson, Angela. 2003. *The First Part Last*. New York: Simon & Schuster Books for Young Readers.

Jordan, Sherryl. 2002. *Hunting of the Last Dragon*. New York: HarperCollins.

Joyce, James. [1915] 1976. *A Portrait of the Artist as a Young Man*. Reprint. New York: Penquin Books.

Jukes, Mavis. 2002. *The Guy Book: An Owner's Manual for Teens: Safety, Maintenance, and Operating Instructions for Teens*. New York: Crown Publishers.

Kaehler, Kathy. 2001. *Teenage Fitness: Get Fit, Look Good, and Feel Great!* New York: Cliff Street Books.

Kafka, Franz. [1915] 1981. *The Metamorphosis*. Trans. and ed. Stanley Comgold. Reprint. New York: Bantam Books.

Kamio, Yuko. 2003+. *Boys Over Flowers* series. San Francisco: Viz.

Katz, Jon. 2001. *Geeks: How Two Lost Boys Rode the Internet Out of Idaho*. New York: Villard Books.

King, Stephen. 2000. *On Writing: A Memoir of the Craft*. New York: Scribner.

Klass, David. 2001. *You Don't Know Me*. New York: Farrar, Straus & Giroux.

Knowles, Beyonce. 2002. *Soul Survivors: The Official Autobiography of Destiny's Child*. New York: Regan Books/HarperCollins.

Koja, Kathe. 2003. *Buddha Boy*. New York: Frances Foster Books.

Konigsburg, E. L. 2000. *Silent to the Bone*. New York: Atheneum Books for Young Readers.

Korman, Gordon. 2002. *Son of the Mob*. New York: Hyperion Books for Children.

Lavender, William. 2002. *Just Jane: A Daughter of England Caught in the Struggle of the American Revolution*. San Diego, CA: Harcourt.

Lawrence, D. H. [1915] 1961. *The Rainbow*. New York: Viking.

Lawrence, Iain. 2005. *The Convicts*. New York: Delacorte Press.

Lee, Stan. 1984. *How to Draw Comics the Marvel Way*. New York: Simon & Schuster.

Lekich, John. 2002. *Reel Adventures: The Savvy Teen's Guide to Great Movies*. New York: Annick Press.

Lester, Julius. 2000. *Pharaoh's Daughter: A Novel of Ancient Egypt*. San Diego, CA: Silver Whistle/Harcourt Brace.

———. 2001. *When Dad Killed Mom*. San Diego, CA: Silver Whistle/Harcourt Brace.

Levithan, David. 2003. *Boy Meets Boy*. New York: Alfred A. Knopf.

Levitt, Susan. 2003. *Teen Feng Shui: Design Your Space, Design Your Life*. Rochester, NY: Bindu Books.

Light, Richard J. 2001. *Making the Most of College: Students Speak Their Minds*. Cambridge, MA: Harvard University Press.

Logue, Mary. 2002. *Dancing with an Alien*. New York: HarperTempest.

London, Jack. [1913] 2001. *John Barleycorn*. New York: Modern Library.

MacHale, D. J. 2002+. *Pendragon: Journal of an Adventure through Time and Space* series. New York: Aladdin Paperbacks.

MacPhail, Catherine. 2005. *Underworld*. New York: Bloomsbury.

Mann, Thomas. [1924] 1995. *The Magic Mountain*. Trans. John E. Woods. Reprint. New York: Alfred A. Knopf.

Mannarino, Melanie. 2000. *Boyfriend Clinic: The Final Word on Flirting, Dating, Guys, and Love (Seventeen)*. New York: HarperCollins.

Manzoni, Alessandro. [1827] 1984. *The Betrothed*. Trans. Bruce Penman. Reprint. Penguin USA.

Markandaya, Kamala. 1954. *Nectar in a Sieve*. New York: J. Day Co.

Marriner, Michael, Nathan Gebhard with Joanne Gordon. 2003. *Roadtrip Nation: Find Your Path in Life*. New York: Ballantine Books.

Maugham, Somerset. [1915] 1991. *Of Human Bondage.* New York: Bantam Books.

Mazer, Norma Fox. 2001. *Girlhearts.* New York: William Morrow.

McBay, Bruce, and James Heneghan. 2003. *Waiting for Sarah.* Victoria, BC: Orca Books.

McCafferty, Megan. 2003. *Second Helpings.* New York: Three Rivers Press.

———. 2001. *Sloppy Firsts.* New York: Crown.

McCaughrean, Geraldine. 2002. *The Kite Rider.* New York: HarperCollins.

McCormick, Patricia. 2000. *Cut.* Asheville, NC: Front Street.

McDonald, Janet. 2002. *Chill Wind.* New York: Farrar, Straus & Giroux.

McDonald, Joyce. 2001. *Shades of Simon Gray.* New York: Delacorte Press.

———. 2000. *Shadow People.* New York: Delacorte Press.

McWilliams, Kelly. 2004. *Doormat: A Novel.* New York: Delacorte Press.

Medley, Linda. 2000. *Castle Waiting: The Lucky Road.* Columbus, OH: Cartoon Books.

Metz, Melinda. 2001+. *Fingerprints* series. New York: Avon Books.

Meyer, Carolyn. 2001. *Beware, Princess Elizabeth.* San Diego, CA: Harcourt Brace.

Meyer, Stephanie, and John Meyer. 2000. *Teen Ink: Our Voices, Our Visions.* Deerfield Beach, FL: Health Communications.

Mishima, Yukio. [1956] 1959. *Temple of the Golden Pavilion.* Trans. Ivan Morris. Reprint. New York: Alfred A. Knopf.

Moore, Peter. 2002. *Blind Sighted.* New York: Viking.

Moriarty, Jaclyn. 2001. *Feeling Sorry for Celia.* New York: St. Martin's Press.

Murray, Jaye. 2003. *Bottled Up.* New York: Dial Books.

My Name Is America series. 1998+. New York: Scholastic.

Myers, Walter Dean. 2002. *Handbook for Boys.* New York: HarperCollins.

Myracle, Lauren. 2003. *Kissing Kate.* New York: Dutton Children's Books.

Nam, Vickie. 2001. *YELL-OH Girls ! Emerging Voices Explore Culture, Identity, and Growing Up Asian American.* New York: Quill.

Namioka, Lensey. 2002. *An Ocean Apart, a World Away: A Novel.* New York: Delacorte Press.

Nix, Garth. 2003. *Abhorsen.* New York: Eos.

Ohkami, Mineko. 2002+. *Dragon Knights* series. Los Angeles: Tokyopop.

Oppel, Kenneth. 2004. *Airborn.* New York: HarperCollins.

Osa, Nancy. 2003. *Cuba 15.* New York: Delacorte Press.

Otomo, Katsuhiro. 2000–2002. *Akira* series. Milwaukie, OR: Dark Horse Comics.

Paolini, Christopher. 2003. *Eragon.* New York: Alfred A. Knopf.

Pennebaker, Ruth. 2000. *Both Sides Now.* New York: Henry Holt.

Perry, Susan K. 2000. *Catch the Spirit: Teen Volunteers Tell How They Made a Difference.* New York: Franklin Watts.

Peters, Julie Ann. 2003. *Keeping You a Secret.* New York: Little, Brown.

Philbrick, Rodman. 2000. *The Last Book in the Universe.* New York: Blue Sky Press.

Pierce, Meredith Ann. 2001. *Treasure at the Heart of the Tanglewood.* New York: Penguin Putnam.

Pierce, Tamora. 2000+. *Circle Opens* series. New York: Scholastic.

Plum-Ucci, Carol. 2000. *The Body of Christopher Creed*. San Diego, CA: Harcourt.

Potash, Marlin S. 2001. *Am I Weird or Is This Normal? Advice and Info to Get Teens in the Know*. New York: Fireside.

Powell, Randy. 2001. *Run If You Dare*. New York: Farrar, Straus & Giroux.

Rabb, M. E. 2004. *Missing Persons* series. New York: Penguin Putnam.

Rees, Douglas. 2003. *Vampire High*. New York: Delacorte Press.

Reeves, Philip. 2003. *Mortal Engines*. New York: HarperCollins.

Rinaldi, Ann. 2004. *Sarah's Ground*. New York: Simon & Schuster Books for Young Readers.

Rolvaag, O. E. [1927] 1999. *Giants in the Earth: Saga of the Prairie*. New York: Perennial.

Rowling, J. K. 2005. *Harry Potter and the Half-Blood Prince*. New York: Scholastic.

Rozakis, Laurie. 2002. *Super Study Skills: The Ultimate Guide to Tests and Studying*. New York: Scholastic Reference.

Russo, Marisabina. 2002. *House of Sports*. New York: Greenwillow Books.

Saint-Exupéry, Antoine de. [1943]. *The Little Prince*. New York: Harcourt Brace.

Sakai, Stan. 2002+. *Usagi Yojimbo: Grasscutter II* series. Milwaukie, OR: Dark Horse Comics.

Sanchez, Alex. 2004. *Rainbow High*. New York: Simon & Schuster.

Satrapi, Majane. 2003. *Persepolis: The Story of a Childhood*. New York: Pantheon.

Schlosser, Eric. 2001. *Fast Food Nation: The Dark Side of the All-American Meal*. Boston: Houghton Mifflin.

Seino, Shizuru. 2004+. *Girl Got Game* series. Los Angeles: Tokyopop.

Shan, Darren. 2001+. *Cirque du Freak* series. Boston: Little, Brown.

Shanley, Ellen L., and Colleen A. Thompson. 2001. *Fueling the Teen Machine*. Palo Alto, CA: Bull Publishing Company.

Shaw, Tucker. 2003. *Flavor of the Week*. New York: Hyperion.

———. 2001. *Who Do You Think You Are? 12 Methods for Analyzing the True You*. New York: Alloy Books.

Shusterman, Neal. 2003. *Full Tilt*. New York: Simon & Schuster Books for Young Readers.

Sleator, William. 2004. *The Boy Who Couldn't Die*. New York: Amulet Books.

———. 2002. *Parasite Pig*. New York: Dutton Children's Books.

Solzhenitsen, Alexander. [1962] 1993. *One Day in the Life of Ivan Denisovitch*. Trans. Ralph Parker. Reprint. New York: Signet Classic.

Soryo, Fuyumi. 2003+. *Mars* series. Los Angeles: Tokyopop.

Spark, Muriel. [1961] 1962. *The Prime of Miss Jean Brodie*. Philadelphia: Lippincott.

Spinelli, Jerry. 2000. *Stargirl*. New York: Alfred A. Knopf.

Stavans, Ilan. 2001. *Wachale! Poetry and Prose about Growing Up Latino in America*. Chicago: Cricket Books.

Stendhal. [1830] 2002. *The Red and the Black*. Trans. Roger Gard. Reprint. New York: Penguin USA.

Stewart, Mark. 2002. *One Wild Ride: The Life of Skateboarding Superstar Tony Hawk.* Brookfield, CT: Millbrook Press.

Strasser, Todd. 2000. *Give a Boy a Gun.* New York: Simon & Schuster Books for Young Readers.

Sweeney, Joyce. 2000. *Players.* Delray Beach, FL: Winslow Press.

———. 2004. *Takedown.* New York: Delacorte Press.

Takahashi, Rumiko. 2000+. *Inu-Yasha: A Feudal Fairy Tale* series. San Francisco: Viz.

Takaya, Natsuki. 2004+. *Fruits Basket* series. Los Angeles: Tokyopop.

Tashjian, Janet. 2003. *Fault Line.* New York: Henry Holt.

Taylor, Mildred D. 2001. *The Land.* New York: Phyllis Fogelman Books.

Thompson, Craig. 2003. *Blankets: An Illustrated Novel.* Marietta, GA: Top Shelf.

Thoms, Annie. 2002. *With Their Eyes: September 11th: The View from a High School at Ground Zero.* New York: HarperTempest.

Tiernan, Cate. 2001+. *Sweep* series. New York: Puffin Books.

Toriyama, Akira. 2000+. *Dragon Ball* series. San Francisco: Viz.

Traig, Jennifer. 2002. *Crafty Girl: Slumber Parties.* San Francisco: Chronicle Books.

Truly, Traci. 2000. *Teen Rights: A Legal Guide for Teens and the Adults in Their Lives.* Naperville, IL: Sphinx Pub.

Tsao, Hsueh-Chin. [18th century] 1997. *The Story of the Stone (aka The Dream of the Red Chamber).* 1–5 vols. Trans. David Hawkes et al. Reprint. New York: Viking.

Tsuda, Masami. 1999+. *Kare Kano: His and Her Circumstances* series. Los Angeles: Tokyopop.

Turgenev, Ivan. [1861] 1998. *Fathers and Sons.* Trans. Richard Freeborn. Reprint. New York: Oxford University Press.

Undset, Sigrid. [1922] 1955. *Kristin Lavransdatter.* Trans. C. Archer and J. S. Scott. Reprint. New York: Alfred A. Knopf.

Van Draanen, Wendelin. 2002. *Sammy Keyes and the Search for Snake Eyes.* New York: Alfred A. Knopf.

Vaughan, Brian K. 2004. *Mystique: Drop Dead Gorgeous.* New York: Marvel Comics.

Vibe magazine. 2001. *Hip Hop Divas.* New York: Three Rivers Press.

Vinnizi, Ned. 2002. *Teen Angst? Naaah—A Quasi-Autobiography.* Minneapolis, MN: Free Spirit.

Von Ziegesar, Cecily. 2002+. *Gossip Girl* series. Boston: Little, Brown.

Wallens, Scott. 2002. *Sevens* series. New York: Puffin.

Walsch, Neale Donald. 2002. *Conversations with God for Teens.* New York: Scholastic.

Weaver, Will. 2001. *Memory Boy.* New York: HarperCollins.

Werlin, Nancy. 2004. *Double Helix.* New York: Dial Books.

———. 2000. *Locked Inside.* New York: Delacorte Press.

Wharton, Edith. [1905] 1997. *The House of Mirth.* New York: Bantam Classic.

Williams, Terrie. 2002. *Stay Strong: Simple Life Lessons for Teens.* New York: Scholastic.

Wilson, Jacqueline. 2002+. *Girls in Love* series. New York: Delacorte Press.

Winick, Judd. 2000. *Pedro and Me: Friendship, Loss, and What I Learned*. New York: Henry Holt.

Wolf, Stacey. 2001. *Get Psychic! Discover Your Hidden Powers*. New York: Warner Books.

Woodson, Jacqueline. 2004. *Behind You*. New York: G. P. Putnam's Sons.

Wright, Richard. [1940] 1993. *Native Son*. New York: HarperPerennial.

Wulffson, Don. 2000. *Soldier X*. New York: Viking.

Appendix II

RESOURCES FOR COLLECTION DEVELOPMENT, DISPLAYS, PRINT PROMOTIONS, READERS' ADVISORY, AND BOOKTALKING

Whatever their focus, these resources feature booklists that can be used for collection development, displays, print promotions, readers' advisory, and booktalking.

Anderson, Sheila B., ed. 2003. *Serving Older Teens*. Westport, CT: Libraries Unlimited.

Barron, Neil. 1998. *What Fantastic Fiction Do I Read Next?* Detroit, MI: Gale Research.

Beers, Kylene, and Teri S. Lesesne, eds. 2001. *Books for You: An Annotated Booklist for Senior High*. Urbana, IL: National Council of Teachers of English.

Bromann, Jennifer. 2001. *Booktalking That Works*. New York: Neal-Schuman Publishers.

Carman, L. Kay, ed. 2004. *Reaching Out to Religious Youth: A Guide to Services, Programs, and Collections*. Westport, CT: Libraries Unlimited.

Carpan, Carolyn. 2004. *Rocked by Romance: A Guide to Teen Romance Fiction*. Westport, CT: Libraries Unlimited.

Carter, Betty B., Sally Estes, and Linda Waddle. 2000. *Best Books for Young Adults*. Chicago: ALA Editions.

Herald, Diana Tixier. 2003. *Teen Genreflecting: A Guide to Reading Interests*. Westport, CT: Libraries Unlimited.

Jones, Patrick, Michele Gorman, and Tricia Suellentrop. 2004. *Connecting Young Adults and Libraries: A How-To-Do-It Manual for Librarians*. New York: Neal-Schuman Publishers.

Jones, Patrick, Patricia Taylor, and Kirsten Edwards. 2003. *A Core Collection for Young Adults*. New York: Neal-Schuman Publishers.

Langemack, Chapple. 2003. *The Booktalker's Bible: How to Talk about the Books You Love to Any Audience*. Westport, CT: Libraries Unlimited.

Lesesne, Teri S. 2003. *Making the Match: The Right Book for the Right Reader at the Right Time, Grades 4–12*. Portland, ME: Stenhouse Publishers.

LiBretto, Ellen V., and Catherine Barr. 2002. *High/Low Handbook: Best Books and Web Sites for Reluctant Teen Readers*. Westport, CT: Libraries Unlimited.

Lynn, Ruth Nadelman. 2005. *Fantasy Literature for Children and Young Adults: A Comprehensive Guide*. 5th ed. Westport, CT: Libraries Unlimited.

Nichols, Mary Anne. 2002. *Merchandising Library Materials to Young Adults*. Greenwood Village, CO: Libraries Unlimited.

Schall, Lucy. 2001. *Booktalks Plus: Motivating Teens to Read*. Englewood, CO: Libraries Unlimited.

Sullivan, Michael. 2003. *Connecting Boys with Books: What Libraries Can Do*. Chicago: American Library Association.

Young Adult Library Services Association. Located at http://www.ala.org/yalsa/ (accessed April 25, 2005).

INDEX

About the Author

KRISTINE MAHOOD is the District Young Adult Librarian for Timberland Regional Library, comprising twenty-seven libraries in five counties in southwestern Washington state. She spends her days talking with teens and library staff; promoting reading and books; performing booktalks; creating booklists, web pages, and programs; and presenting training in teen and readers' advisory services. Previously she served as the Readers' Services and Young Adult Librarian for Rowan Public Library in Salisbury, North Carolina, and as a Librarian for Palo Alto City Library in her hometown, Palo Alto, California. She wrote "Off the Page and Onto the Stage—Booktalking for Older Teens" for *Serving Older Teens* (Anderson 2004) and co-authored "The Inner Game of Booktalking," published in the June 2001 issue of *Voice of Youth Advocates*. Conference presentations include "I'm Looking for a Book to Read. Can You Help Me?" (Washington Association of Library Employees, 2005), "Teens in the Life of the Library" (Oregon/Washington Library Association, 2002), "Be a Performing Body, Not a Talking Head: Blueprints for Booktalk Programs" (American Association of School Librarians, 2001), "Booktalking Psyche-Up Tricks and Program Models" (Public Library Association, 2000), and "Get Real: Booktalking Nonfiction to Teens" (Washington Library Media Association, 2000).